THE STORY OF

Barbie™

By
Kitturah B. Westenhouser

COLLECTOR BOOKS
A Division of Schroeder Publishing Co., Inc.

Searching For A Publisher?

We are always looking for knowledgeable people considered to be experts within their fields. If you feel that there is a real need for a book on your collectible subject and have a large comprehensive collection, contact us.

COLLECTOR BOOKS
P.O. Box 3009
Paducah, Kentucky 42002-3009

Barbie® is a registered trademark of Mattel, Inc.

Photography by Geoffrey A. Westenhouser.

Cover Design: Beth Summers
Book Design: Beth Ray

Additional copies of this book may be ordered from:

COLLECTOR BOOKS
P.O. Box 3009
Paducah, Kentucky 42002-3009

@$19.95. Add $2.00 for postage and handling.

Copyright: Kitturah B. Westenhouser, 1994

Printed by IMAGE GRAPHICS, INC., Paducah, Kentucky

Table of Contents

Dedication

To my ever devoted husband, Geoff, children Emily, Nicolle, and Michael, special friend Marl Davidson and all the former and present Mattel employees who have devoted their working lives to the Barbie Project.

About the Author

As a writing enthusiast, Kitturah B. Westenhouser spent her early years working as a reporter for the *Columbus Evening Republican*, Columbus, Indiana, and the *Lancaster Eagle-Gazette*, Lancaster, Ohio. She has contributed to such publications as *Dolls, Doll Reader, International Doll World, International Doll World Price Guide, Collectors Showcase, Insider Collector, Collectors Edition, Barbie Bazaar, Hearthstone,* and *Christian Standard.*

As a Barbie collector, she has spent twelve years collecting Barbie dolls plus their family and friends.

She is married to Geoffrey A. Westenhouser, who serves as her photographer. The Westenhousers have three children and reside in Ohio.

As an active church worker, she has taught Sunday School and Children's Churchtime classes for the past twenty years.

Acknowledgments

Gratitude should go to a multitude of people because without their knowledge this book could not have been pieced together: to Marl Davidson, who finds any Barbie item a collector's heart desires; Lisa McKendall, for her help in Mattel's office and her staff including Denise Hamma; Barry Sturgill, for photography; Geoffrey A. Westenhouser, for photography and editing; F. Glen Offield, who knows prototypes; Ruth Handler, for her memories; Gordon Shireman, for his insights; Carol Spencer, for being a wealth of information; Alva Christensen, for her encouragement; Ralph Dunn, former Mattel chemical engineer; Wanda Clearwater, former Mattel chemical engineer; Jackie Leighton, former Mattel fashion and toy designer; Jean Ann Burger, former Barbie hairstylist; Joe Blitman, for answering endless questions; Udo Leidner of the Museum der Beutschen Spielzeugindustrie, Neustadt, Germany; Seymour Adler, Clifford Jacobs, and Frank Nakamura, retired Mattel executives; Bill Robb, former Mattel inventor; Dick May, former Mattel inventor; Mellie Phillips, Barbie hairstylist; Hiroe Okubo-Wolf, face painter; Aldo Favilli, Mattel sculptor; Dieter Jeschke, Barbie doll collector; Sherry Simonek and her staff, Mattel Alumni Association; Steve Lewis, retired research and development department manager; Bob Mackie, fashion designer; U.C.L.A. Archives Research Department; Richard Whittick, Cotswold; Shelba Riggenbach, for the loan of her Dream House; Irene Davis, photography; Joseph A. and Marie Toth, photography; and Henrietta Pfeifer, curator of the Mid Ohio Historical Museum, Canal Winchester, Ohio, who started this whole thing twelve years ago when she sold me my first vintage Barbie doll. Also thanks to her for allowing us to photograph some of her dolls.

Introduction

Few toy manufacturers can boast of the longevity of any product like Mattel's Barbie doll. Still a top selling item after thirty plus years, the doll has a history which encompasses an army of talented people who were called on to contribute to the project. Originating as an idea by Ruth Handler, then co-owner of Mattel with her husband Elliot, Barbie required engineers, chemists, machinists, hair specialists, graphic artists, fashion designers, metal workers, and face painters. One need led to another and added people to the ever growing number of Mattel employees hard at work on the doll.

With this book I have attempted to cover the many innovations of Barbie and the history behind the doll. Each year brought a new and improved product to catch the attention of children everywhere. With so many years of the doll, collectors now need a guide to assist them in determining where the doll fits in the schedule of production. Also needed, is a chapter on the cleaning to place these rare finds back in their original condition. The dates used in this publication are the dates the doll was sold in most cases, not the patent date.

Work on this project required piecing together an oral history of the doll and the many innovations pertaining to her. Several years ago, Mattel had an official Barbie doll historian in Norma Milldrum Green at their offices in Hawthorne, California. Inclement weather caused three feet of muddy water to flood her basement office, damaging both the files and her collection of prototype dolls which she held as examples of each year's production. Many days of cleaning by Mrs. Green were required to set her office right again. Unfortunately, both the files and the dolls were not salvageable and had to be discarded. Because of this there were many misrepresentations of Barbie's history, spawned by speculative collectors and even former Mattel employees. One such person gave an apparent first-hand account of the Bild Lilli being dipped in wax, from which molds were then made and Bild Lilli became Barbie. Careful examination of the Mattel records dispelled this myth for the employee was not hired until after 1962 and was not associated with the beginning of the project. As time passes, necessity dictates that those that did the work be heard.

At the anniversary of her thirtieth year, Barbie was declared an art form as well as a child's toy. This kindled even more interest from the ever-growing army of collectors who search flea markets, doll sales, and doll shops for the lady of their dreams — Barbie doll. Mattel is drawing ever closer to their fortieth year of manufacturing this doll and continue even today to change and improve the 11½" mannequin which has more clothes and accessories than any woman on earth. Each year requires a new wardrobe change. Thirty-five fashion designers and staff in El Segundo, California, labor long hours to produce the needed garments for a small but demanding client. Barbie was made to be shared and with this publication we share the enthusiasm of "Barbiemania" with everyone.

Kitturah B. Westenhouser

Chapter 1

Humble Beginnings

Two 1959 first wave Barbie dolls model rare early outfits called Easter Parade and Gay Parisienne. Roman Holiday Separates are modeled by a blonde second wave Barbie doll from 1959.

Barbie creators Elliot and Ruth Handler pose with a blonde bubblecut doll circa 1961. Note the similarity between "mother" Ruth's hair style and that of Barbie doll. Photo by Allan Grant. Photo courtesy of Ruth Handler.

Insignificant events change lives and many people credit their success to the summation of these minor experiences. In our vast land of limitless opportunities few stories can compare to the tale of two young newlyweds forging their careers and in turn altering the lives of all who worked with them or enjoyed the fruits of their labor.

In 1938, newly arrived in Los Angeles, Elliot and Ruth Handler found themselves living in a small, cramped, furnished apartment. Not happy with their new surroundings, they rented a newer and more attractive unfurnished apartment. Along with this honeymoon suite was a garage which Elliot wasted no time in turning into a workshop for his many projects. As an Industrial Design major, Elliot was working with lucite. Landlords will be landlords, and he asked the Handlers to stop in the workshop or move. Not to be deterred, the Handlers rented a former chinese laundry at $50.00 for six months and moved.

As the story goes, Ruth took a day off work as a secretary at Paramount Studios and stuffed a suitcase with Elliot's gift item designs and went to an elegant store on Wilshire Boulevard called Zacho's. The owner of the store, Mr. Zacho, was impressed with the items and asked to come visit the Handler's plant. Ruth was not anxious for Mr. Zacho to see the humble environment in which Elliot produced his crafts but he insisted. Coming to the Handler's rented workshop, after carefully examining the finely detailed workmanship and precision, Mr. Zacho that day gave Elliot a large order for his store.

Elliot moved on from gift items to costume jewelry. The work load became so heavy the Handlers hired their first employee, Harold Mattson, a creative engineer who was also an expert machinist. As business grew working capital was needed and they took on partners and then more partners. As the old saying goes, "too many cooks spoil the soup," and here too this saying was true. Mattson decided to leave the business and go on his own. Ruth was a housewife and mother to the Handler's two small children. Being someone who had worked most of her life, she was becoming restless. She offered to help Mattson market whatever he made from his garage workshop. With the expertise of Ruth Handler, it was not long until Mattson had his first sale.

Elliot too became dissatisfied with the costume jewelry business and moved into his own garage to work on wooden products. In his workshop, he designed and crafted wooden picture frames. These wooden picture frames soon fell by the wayside as the two old friends, Harold Mattson and Elliot Handler again joined forces. They formed a business in 1945 called Mattel. The "Matt" was for Mattson and "El" for Elliot. It was from the bits and pieces of wood amidst the sawdust that frugal Elliot recognized and announced to Ruth, that the hard woods would make excellent dollhouse furniture. Mrs. Handler says from this statement, "that was the beginning of Mattel." Harold Mattson did not stay with the project and left Elliot and Ruth once again. Business grew as doll furniture was followed by an array of toys for the children's market. New employees were added to the company as they became needed. The early toys were musical. They made jack-in-the-boxes, toy pianos, guitars, ukuleles, makeup sets, and later went into the gun making business with Winchesters and small cap pistols. At this stage of the Mattel business no dolls were being produced. Mrs. Handler always wanted to try making dolls but was unable to gain enthusiasm from her designers. They were comfortable with the success of the products being made as the company advanced into the fifties.

The inspirational spark was as she tells, her young daughter, Barbara, and her friends as they played with paper dolls. Mrs. Handler remembers watching the girls sitting on Saturday afternoons playing with the girl and boy dolls and their piles of cut out clothes. They played adult or teenage make-believe with the paper dolls. Their imagination placed them in roles of college students, cheerleaders, schoolgirls, and even adults with careers. They had conversations, even pretending to be grown up. Mainly, she says, "they talked and mimicked what they had heard their parents say." Everytime she took Barbara shopping in the dime stores she headed straight for the paper doll counter. She always chose teenage or adult type paper dolls. She liked to play grownup. By the way they played, girls were expressing their dreams for the future. Mrs. Handler was sensitive to an important need of children to express their dreams. It was a way of experimenting with the future from a safe distance. Pretend and make-believe are an important part of growing up, it aids in the psychological development of all children. A marketing void existed and Ruth was determined to fill that niche with a durable three-dimensional product.

"It was time for us," Mrs. Handler says, "to get

Elliot Handler poses with children showing Mattel-made toys in 1961. Photo courtesy of the Department of Special Collections, University Research Library, UCLA.

7

into the doll business." She kept telling her all-male design staff about this adult-bodied doll that she wanted to have made to sell. Ralph Dunn, retired chemical engineer with Mattel says, "she came back time and again with this doll idea."

The doll she wanted should have a narrow waist, long tapered legs, and high heeled feet. She would have detailed facial features, painted finger nails and toes. This dream doll was the idea which later became the Barbie doll. Unfortunately, Mrs. Handler was facing one of the major obstacles that befalls every corporation in its lifetime. The menace that has stymied the growth of many visionaries, the age old statement by the nay sayers, " we have never done that before."

Unable to get any of her design people to become interested, she says they kept telling her, "the doll would cost too much to make." "Even harder to produce," they said, "it would have to sell for too much money." Periodically, she persisted in coming back to them with her same wish to make such a doll.

The summer of 1956, the Handler family went on a combined business trip and vacation to Europe. Mrs. Handler recalls walking with her daughter down a picturesque street in Lucerne, Switzerland. Along with the shops and markets she saw a toy store. In the window was a display of a doll in a Swiss Snowsuit costume sitting in a wood and rope swing, reminiscent of the swings that hung from many a tree in the yards of middle America. At this time Barbara was approximately thirteen years old. She no longer played with dolls but did have a collection sitting on a shelf in her room. The doll was very mature and continental in appearance. The same doll in different costumes was also merchandised in the store. Barbara wanted one of the dolls but had difficulty deciding which of the dolls she wanted her mother to purchase. In the course of trying to decide which doll she liked best, Mrs. Handler asked the sales clerk if

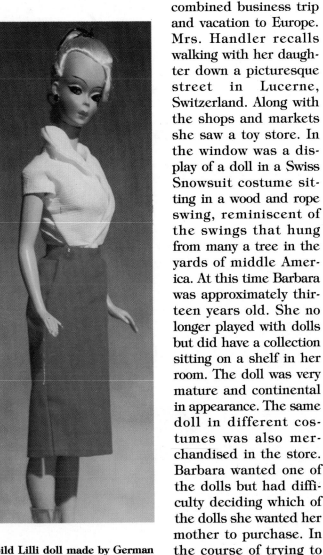

Bild Lilli doll made by German toymakers O.M. Hausser. Doll courtesy of the Mid Ohio Historical Museum.

this doll and the costumes could be purchased separately. She said the salesgirl looked at her like she was a crazy American, "You buy it the way it is," Mrs. Handler recalls the saleswoman saying. Another marketing idea was taking shape, merchandising interchangeable outfits for a uniform size doll — variations on a common theme.

In Vienna, Austria, they again saw this same type toy store with the same dolls but this time they were attired in more glamorous costumes. Barbara saw the Austrian dolls and voiced an interest in one. She liked the detailing of the Austrian costuming better than the Swiss. Both the Swiss and Austrian doll bodies were the same, they were only costumed differently. At this point Mrs. Handler knew she must take home more of these dolls to show to her design department. Two more dolls were purchased in Vienna. This adult-bodied doll was just what she had been trying to tell her people the world needed. Sometime later Mrs. Handler learned this adult- bodied doll was none other than the Bild Lilli doll. Based on a cartoon which began on June 24, 1952, by Reinhard Beuthien, this character called Lilli was a German sensation.

The O.M. Hausser Co., of Neustadt, Germany was the manufacturer of this doll. Founded in 1904 by Otto and Max Hausser, the O.M. Hausser Co., was a well established toy manufacturer in Germany. Although it began in Ludwigsburg, by 1936 two Hausser sons, Kurt and Rolf, had moved the family operation to Neustadt. Neustadt was nestled in the area of Bavaria known for its tradition of toy and doll makers.

Because of the charm of the cartoon, toy manufacturers in Germany were asked to submit proposals for a new doll. O.M. Hausser received the contract on a proposal submitted by their designer, Max Weißbrodt. He came to be known as the designer of Bild Lilli, the doll. Final work, however, was done by M.E. Maar, who also made the clothing.

Sold both as a blonde and brunette, she had painted nails and a bow mouth. Instead of separate shoes, she came with high heeled shoes molded on the body. Although she had a ponytail, there were no bangs, just a single stray curl fell over her forehead. She wore tiny black earrings. Bild Lilli's arms, legs, and head were strung to the body with a flexible string. Not sold in a box, she was packaged in a clear plastic cylinder. O.M. Hausser's name appeared nowhere on either the doll or the cylinder. As was customary for toys from this company, they did not mark their products with their own name, their craftsmanship was their identifiable trademark. Unlike Barbie, Lilli was not as slender and had larger legs. Normally a twelve inch doll, she was also sold in a seven inch size. The mouth on Lilli was not like Mattel's Barbie. The German counterpart had poutier lips reminiscent of the porcelain and bisque dolls of the European designers. Barbie came with more natural lips. Because of the difference in body build, it is doubtful Bild Lilli could fit into many Barbie doll clothes. The bend at the wrist of the Lilli doll would also create difficulties changing clothing on the mannequin.

Although the Lilli doll had a character face, she was built like an adult female and it was this idea Mrs. Handler had been trying to get across to her designers for so long. Mrs. Handler took the Lilli dolls home and Barbara kept one. Along with the Lilli, Ruth Handler took to work with her were the ideas she had gleaned from markets in Europe. It was show and tell day in the design department at Mattel. This was the style body she was looking for and with the right face and body, one could be marketed in American stores. The all-male design staff agreed a cheaper production could be achieved if they could find a company in

Japan to make the parts. Bild Lilli was sent upstairs to the Mattel sculpting staff. Not having sculpted a doll previously, made this a challenge to their artistic talents. Seymour Adler, research and development director in the 1950's for Mattel says he hired an additional sculptor to attempt to design a face for Barbie doll.

As a cost saving measure, in 1957 Mattel made a never-before attempted effort to have toys manufactured in the Orient. One problem that was first in the mind of Elliot Handler was no one could speak or write Japanese at Mattel. To arrange the necessary negotiations required command of the language. Elliot called a friend at Carson Advertising Agency and asked if he knew anyone who could fulfill this need. He did, and

Production of the first Barbie Dolls was in Japan. Arrangements were made by Elliot Handler, Frank Nakamura, Mattel's Japanese language translator, Seymour Adler, Vice President of Mattel, and Yono Matsumoto Khaugyo, a Japanese garment manufacturer. Photo circa 1959 courtesy of Frank Nakamura.

A dinner party held in Japan by Kokusai Boeki Kaisha Ltd. for Mattel executives included Frank Nakamura, Seymour Adler, and Sumiyo Mamaski of Pony Doll who manufactured those first Barbie dolls in 1959 for Kokusai Boeki Kaisha Ltd. Photo is circa 1966 courtesy of Frank Nakamura.

Mattel Executives negotiated the best possible method for manufacturing these first dolls with Japanese artists. Pictured here in Japan are from left to right Frank Nakamura, Seymour Adler, Mr. Suzuki, Barbie's first sculptor—an electroplated mold maker, Elliot Handler, and Miss Sato. Photo is circa 1960 courtesy of Frank Nakamura.

Frank Nakamura went to the Mattel office to meet Elliot Handler. Elliot hired him immediately. A long career with Mattel lay ahead for this Japanese-American. Even today, though he retired in 1980 his friendship with the Handlers continues.

Nakamura tells of the adventure of arranging the Oriental production of toys done by himself, Elliot Handler, the late Jack Ryan and Mattel's Chief of Productions, Seymour Adler. Many weeks of living and working in Japan were required to arrange all the details. First to be produced was wooden doll furniture which was designed by Elliot and Nakamura at night in the Imperial Hotel. During the daytime they negotiated with Japanese vendors about production possibilities. Arrangements for this furniture production were made with Taihei Mokko Ltd., Toyama, Japan. Still a translator, Naka-

mura says, "Taihei means calm or tranquil Pacific and Mokko is woodworks." This furniture was designed for an 11½" doll but Nakamura says, "it was a big mistake making doll furniture without the doll." The problem would prove to be a difficulty for only a short time, however.

One Saturday in 1957, while preparing to leave for Japan, the late Jack Ryan and Seymour Adler were in Mr. Handler's office receiving last minute instructions. A copy of the Bild Lilli doll sat on Handler's desk. He gathered up the doll and handed it to Jack Ryan saying, "Jack, see if you can get this made in Japan." Both men left the country with the German doll. Ryan was concerned with manufacturing toy cars he had designed, leaving Adler with the job of locating a company who would make the Barbie doll. Ryan was unsuccessful in the Japanese production of his

Manufacturing in Japan required many trips to the Orient for Mattel executives to inspect the work. Pictured here in Japan are Jim Steiner, Mattel staff, Richard Saffir, Mattel's Foreign Manufacturing Executive, and Tomio Tanabe of Kokusai Boeki Kaisha Ltd. Mr. Tonabe visited the United States in 1957 to check for Kokusai if Mattel was a business worth producing dolls. He returned home with a positive response. Photo circa 1968 courtesy of Frank Nakamura.

Kuni Kato of the Kokusai Boeki Kaisha Ltd. pictured here was responsible for work on the early Barbie dolls. Photo circa 1968 courtesy of Frank Nakamura.

Kokusai Boeki Kasisha staff spent long hours on the Barbie doll project. Pictured here are Kui Kato of Kokusai and an engineer Mr. Uchimura who labored on the project. Photo is circa 1969 courtesy of Frank Nakamura.

Mr. Oshiga served as plant manager of the Kyowa Kagaku doll assembly plant which assembled all doll parts. Photo circa early 1960's courtesy of Frank Nakamura.

10

toy cars, because in that island nation, zinc was an imported product. It would be extremely costly to produce in Japan. Not to be deterred, Mattel went to Hong Kong and Ryan's toy cars were manufactured for Mattel and called Hot Wheels.

First visiting the Ministry of Trade, Adler was directed to Kokusai Boeki Kaisha Ltd. who only had experience in making vinyl. This was a trading company which controlled the manufacturing of the doll. They were taken to see a man who served as a subcontractor, Pony Ltd., named Yamasaki, who with his wife had a rotocast method of molding vinyl. Ryan and Adler returned to the United States and six months passed with no word from Kokusai.

While traveling back from a government trade mission in Canada, Tomio Tanabe from Kokusai, stopped in Hawthorne, California, and visited the Mattel facility. He was directed to Seymour Adler who assured him Mattel was a company anxious to do business with them.

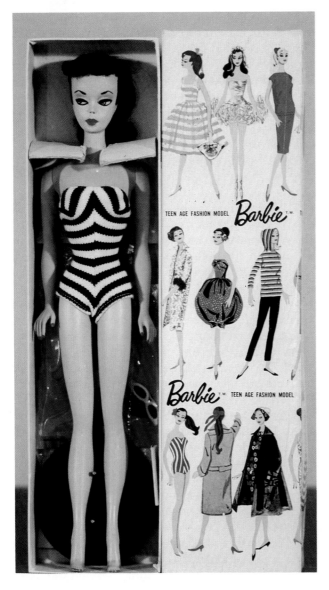

A first wave Barbie doll manufactured for Mattel by Pony Ltd. in Japan.

As Nakamura tells, "Seymour Adler and I went in November, 1957 to Japan to set up the manufacturing facilities for the dolls and the costumes." He says things progressed very slowly. No one had made a doll of this type before and this made it, "a learn as you go experience." Ground work for the technique of making the doll was laid. At this point, only one doll was produced and as Nakamura tells it, it was a triumph. Nakamura removed the doll parts from the mold and put the doll together at the Yamasaki plant. Mrs. Yamasaki was the Barbie doll hair rooter in those first years.

Stands for the new dolls also had to be produced and the company who first made wooden doll furniture for Mattel was enlisted to compression mold a two prong stand. These stands were only used for the dolls produced during the "first wave" as Mattel refers to these dolls. They went to a wire rack stand next. Later still another stand designed to hold the doll under the arms was made. When asked why the two prong stand was discontinued, Nakamura says the tolerance needed to drill holes in the doll legs was too tight. The doll was found to not stand in many cases and every step had to be 100 percent inspected. It all became a costly operation making it necessary to redesign the doll stand.

This one doll returned to Hawthorne, California, with Adler and Nakamura. Along with the doll were questions about pricing. This required another trip to Japan by Adler to try to work out pricing for the doll and to make further arrangements for the manufacturing process. From 1957 until 1964 Seymour Adler was in charge of the Barbie doll production. During that time, production was expanded to Hong Kong and Korea.

With this as their first doll, new trails were blazed. Each hurdle had to be approached and planned for accordingly. Mrs. Handler's farsightedness helped clear each obstacle as they came. Mat-

A view of the assembly line in Japan at the Kyowa Kagaku doll plant where legs and arms were attached to the torso in one operation. The Japanese ladies then cleaned the doll. Photo circa early 1960's courtesy of Frank Nakamura.

tel had never before produced dolls and they did not have anyone to make clothing or design hair styles. Mrs. Handler had to immediately recruit new talent to the company.

Elliot Handler called Chouinard Art School in Los Angeles, California, to ask if they knew of anyone who had a talent for designing and making doll clothes. The staff at Chouinard offered Charlotte Johnson, a freelance women's clothing designer, who also taught classes at the school. They felt she would be perfect for the new doll project. This was in 1956 and much work needed to be done before Barbie doll was a completed product. Contact was made with Charlotte, and Mrs. Handler, unable to show her a Barbie, took one of the European Bild Lilli dolls to her home. Later, as the early Barbies were completed, Mrs. Johnson worked with the real subject. Although over thirty years have passed, the

The packaging line where dolls are made ready for market. Japanese ladies who worked this line were from nearby neighborhoods and were mostly middle age or older employed parttime for the Kyowa Kagaku doll assembly plant. Photo circa early 1960's courtesy of Frank Nakamura.

The assembly line where Japanese ladies placed the finished heads on the dolls and then put on Barbie doll's bathing suit. Note the doll bodies in bins in front of each of the ladies in the line. Photo circa early 1960's courtesy of Frank Nakamura.

original Bild Lilli which Mrs. Handler gave Charlotte still is displayed in Mattel's design department as a reminder of years past.

Mrs. Handler, in her first meeting with Charlotte, told her what style clothing she needed designed. She wanted a bridal gown, tennis dress, ballerina outfit, and something for the football game. She described what type of play pattern she had in mind for this doll. Unlike other dolls competitive toy companies had designed, Ruth Handler was creating a doll with a long future. She had the uses for this doll mapped out in her mind. The idea of the doll with clothes sold separately was rooted from her experience in Switzerland. Toy stores had never seen this concept before. New ideas and innovations were not foreign to the Handlers. They were the first to create a toy piano with raised keys that could really be played. This precept of constant recreation and innovation was to become a hallmark for Mattel designs.

Mrs. Johnson began immediately to design the style clothes requested by Mrs. Handler. Finding the small prints in fabric was a major challenge. Doing this to Ruth Handler's specifications required using the best fabrics and materials. She wanted the clothes to look just like those that little girls saw on adult women and teenage girls. Mrs. Handler says it got very exciting as she would go back and forth to Charlotte's home two or three evenings a week. Seeing the progress added and built to the long sought dream of a doll that would have an adult body and an array of clothes. Charlotte needed a woman to help with sewing all those tiny clothes and it was soon evident that this would be a full time job. Mattel hired her from Chouinard and she became Barbie dolls' personal clothing designer with her own office at Mattel. Charlotte was still having difficulty getting prints small enough for doll clothes. She traveled to Japan and met with fabric producers telling them exactly what she wanted for the project. Mrs. Handler says, "she really had to go over there and fight the good fight." Charlotte lived and worked with the Japanese company for two years teaching them how to root hair and paint facial features on the doll. Not only did Charlotte have clothing design talents but she was a true artist able to share her expertise with the Kokusai staff.

Sculpting the first doll was filled with difficulty. The hands were designed and redesigned with Charlotte Johnson showing the sculptor how to position the hands with her own. They needed to be made so clothing could easily be put on and off the doll. Finger placement was essential to insure little hands would not have difficulty dressing this toy. A slender face was accomplished with the use of Charlotte as the model. "The dolls' facial contour was fashioned like that of Charlotte Johnson," says Carol Spencer. Nakamura tells that the plaster mold was unsuccessful because of shrinkage. The plaster dried to five percent smaller and was not acceptable. Finally a zinc alloy mold was made by Kohei Suzuki. Suzuki was a metallurgist and was successful in fashioning the arms, legs, and head of zinc with no shrinkage. The torso used the shell cast method by another designer. At a later time Suzuki was again called upon to mold a zinc likeness, the Ken doll, a new design, for production.

Dick May, an inventor at Mattel from 1962 until 1972, says for many years old rejected torso molds for the first Barbie doll were in his desk drawer at his office in Hawthorne, California. Some torso molds contained ribs and nipples. Made of copperplated material, they were covered with an epoxy. The mold used for the marketed doll did not have such detailing. These ribbed and nippled versions were rejected because they were not in the character that the Handlers wanted to create for Barbie doll.

Charlotte Johnson insisted the body sculpting each time be the same dimensions according to May. With each new innovation a new mold needed to be made and she wanted those first fashions to fit on each newly designed doll over the years. It was her strict adherence to this that kept Barbie doll uniform over many years. Ms. Johnson insisted that new innovations could be attained with the body and still the size and dimensions could remain uniform.

In later years other sculptures of the doll were successfully made by Joyce Christopher and Joyce Clark for Mattel.

Right: An outside view of the Kyowa Kagaku doll assembly plant which was a subsidiary of Kokusai Koeki Kaisha Ltd. where dolls were packaged. Photo circa early 1960's courtesy of Frank Nakamura.

Bottom Right: Another outside veiw of the Kyowa Kagaku plant where Barbie dolls were packaged for the American market. Photo circa early 1960's courtesy of Frank Nakamura.

Some Mattel employees still insisted that this type doll with clothes and painted nails would not sell in the United States. They felt the doll would cost too much. They did not feel the American public was willing to buy such a grownup toy.

Jack Ryan did analysis research for Mattel in those early years. As a trained engineer and industrial designer, Ryan did research on how many costumes would be needed and at what price points the costumes should be sold. He did marketing studies, working out the price of dolls and costumes. The findings were that the project was indeed viable and the staff expanded into marketing.

New hurdles faced Mattel after the doll was finally in hand. Marketing any product is a challenge which requires an approach to bring the product to public attention. Cliff Jacobs was Mattel's first sales and marketing manager beginning in 1952. He served the company for twenty-four years. Jacobs was in charge of bringing Barbie doll to public awareness.

It took three years for the first Barbie doll to appear at the 1959 International American Toy Fair in New York City. At this toy fair, along with the doll, the Handlers introduced twenty-two outfits. Barbie was well received from the beginning by the buying public. The European trip translated into several marketing ideas for the Handlers:

1. A durable three dimensional image of Barbara's paper dolls was indeed a "doable" project.

2. Just as paper dolls had interchangeable outfits, there must be several different outfits for the doll and they must not require the purchase of a doll each time a new outfit is sought.

3. Pay attention to detail — it is the small things like a purse, shoes, or jewelry that enhance the likelihood of capturing and holding children's imaginations.

Barbie doll was introduced to the trade community in February, 1959 at the American International Toy Fair in New York City. Although they met the toy fair deadline, there were some last minute problems to be solved. Ruth Handler remembers that the boxes for those first dolls did not arrive from the manufacturer. Sample boxes, still on hand in the office, were immediately called into service to hold these new dolls. Some even, as Mrs. Handler states, required hand gluing.

Jacobs says the doll was met with mixed reaction at the toy fair. "Some liked it and other did not," he says. "At that particular time, dolls Barbie's size and smaller did not sell well. Trade in general felt there was not a need for another little doll. They were extremely cautious." But as Mattel found out, half did decide to try this new doll and ordered a supply for their toy shelves.

Mattel, a first for a toy company, had been on television since 1955 with advertisements during the Mickey Mouse Club. Jacobs reveals the company had

made plans to show the Barbie doll during these ads. This would put the new doll before the consumer and would bring children into the toy stores.

Using the philosophy, "the doll sells the clothes and the clothes sell the doll," they had to present the various costumes so that children could make a choice from among them. "The problem," says Jacobs, "at the retail counter the costumes and doll were so new, how to let children see how costumes looked on the doll." Mattel came up with yet another first with displays at the retail counter. Mattel was always aware of a conscious need to present the product at the store counters. "Retailers have neither the time nor skill to demonstrate the products at store level," tells Jacobs. With the store display system, customers would know what use the product would serve.

With Jacobs as his sales and merchandising manager, Herbert J. Holland, used a Viewmaster to allow children to insert a disc and see pictures of each outfit on the doll. To have the doll photographed for this disc, Jacobs took dolls and cos-

Two of the pink boxed Barbies sold to stores to be used as displays. These dolls came dressed in outfits which were sold separately by Mattel. Photo courtesy of Marl Davidson.

tumes to a Hollywood photographer. Individual pictures were taken of the doll as a way for children to see the costumes. With the disc, Mattel offered the retail stores an assortment of dolls, costumes, and one of these Viewmasters on a chain so customers would not carry off the viewer. Dolls, outfits, and the display were all shipped in one carton to stores. Retailers set up the counter with the dolls in boxes, a display for the costumes, and the Viewmaster. Mothers and children could look at the various costumes and select the one they wanted, then pick the packaged costume. Barbie was available in stores in May, 1959, children were attracted to them immediately. Jacobs says they found the Viewmaster was not really necessary. Stores had difficulty keeping dolls and costumes in stock.

Diorama displays in the form of a luxurious turntable enclosed in lucite were constructed for stores. Here again was another first for a toy company. These were offered for sale to retail stores to assist in selling the product. The lucite case held as many as sixteen dressed mannequins. Collectors have in recent years found beautiful pink rather than white boxed dressed dolls. Cliff Jacobs says, "these pink boxed dolls were sold to retail stores as Barbie display models." Marked on the end of the box is "Display Doll" with the name of the costume the doll is wearing. Retailers often sold these dolls in their pink boxes after they were no longer needed for displays. Alas, they are still out there on the secondary market.

Yet another way to present the doll to retail stores was with a colorful catalog which pictured the dolls and outfits available. Also listed in the book was the amount of dolls per box which were twelve per carton. Costumes were packaged twelve to a carton also. By 1965 counter displays and header cards were also available for retail stores.

Cliff Jacobs designed for himself a sample case which was on wheels for easier mobility. It unfolded to reveal twenty-eight dressed Barbie dolls. He used this sample case to present this new Mattel Barbie to "trade people."

It is this innovative flair, like that demonstrated by Mr. Jacobs, which Mattel sought out. Artisans who were highly trained and had a vision and talent far superior to others were drawn to the Mattel Corporation. A nationwide talent search in the early 60's brought to the company personnel with unique abilities. Persons were given a test and each interviewee completed an entrepreneurial profile. With this profile Mattel was able to judge the imagination and ability to create. Like a hospital of specialists with a common goal, these engineers, stylists, designers, painters, and assorted other craftsmen and women were working on one project. If Barbie appears perfect, it is only because of the personnel at Mattel, who strove to make her this way. "Where other toy companies would use doll parts with only

approximately the correct size, Mattel engineered their doll to have exactly the properly proportioned parts," says chemical engineer Ralph Dunn. The key word was "perfection" for this company. In the words of their advertising slogan from the past, "if it's Mattel, you know it's swell."

Mattel proved that they could go where no toy company had gone before when in 1965 they launched a new sales promotion. Investing $12,000,000 in their new "Total Go" toy promotion, Mattel blanketed all three television networks with product advertising. Appearing on ABC, CBS, and NBC Mattel planned wall-to-wall daytime and nighttime television commercials. Also advertisements appeared in *Life* and *Jack and Jill Magazine* as well as the Sunday Comics distributed in newspapers. All the thrust was not to just children. In many cases, Mattel also stressed their marketing technique toward parents. This same year, the company began making in-store sales ads which included window banners, ad mats, and even display suggestions. Total Go promotion came in four big thrusts with May and June 1965 being named "Agent Zero M TM Total Go," July and August, 1965 was the "Barbie Look TM Total Go," September through mid October, 1965 was "Boys and Girls Together Total Go," and finally mid October through November was "Total Go For All The Exciting New Make 'N Play Toys For 1965." The result was a marketing explosion.

A gauge of the success of Mattel's marketing of the Barbie doll is reflected in the numbers enrolled in the Barbie Fan Club in 1965. The fan club membership exceeded 600,000 which made it second in membership only to the Girl Scouts of America. A 1988 figure records a Barbie doll fan club membership at 650,000.

Through humble beginnings, the dream was fulfilled by a few dedicated and driven individuals who took those dreams and turned them into substance. It is ironic that the goal they sought to bring into existence would be the conveyance by which the dreams of many more could be reached – the joy of sparking a child's imagination. This was the true litmus test of success for Ruth's dream doll.

For thirty years under the Handler's leadership, an entire generation grew up knowing the joys of Mattel's creations and vision. The first generation has been doubly blessed in that as children they enjoyed the love of Barbie and now they can as adults also share that love with their children. Love and sharing – a testimony that has taken Barbie from an initial wave production of 200,000 dolls to a worldwide market in more than seventy countries. And as the world community reaches out to embrace those once behind the iron curtain so does Barbie as our Ambassador of Friendship. Born of humble beginnings, driven by the hope of a child's joyful smile, Barbie brightens the future for those that share her love.

Chapter 2

The Lady Behind the Doll

What it takes to start a corporation is a strong business sense. To manufacture any successful product requires a generous blend of imagination and an adroit skill in management. All of these characteristics describe Ruth Handler. Behind the success of the doll, is a lady confident in her product. With this confidence she shows a love of her work. Mrs. Handler always had an eye for the exact details which gave the Barbie doll the strong foundation that carried her into three decades of sales.

Born in Denver, Colorado, the tenth and last child of Jacob Joseph and Ida (Rubenstein) Mosko, she was of Polish-Jewish ancestry.

Ruth Handler, co-founder of Mattel, served as the company's president from 1967 – 1974. From Mrs. Handler's urging came the Barbie doll. Photo courtesy of the Department of Special Collections, University Research Library, UCLA.

She arrived only two short months after her oldest sister was married. Ruth's parents were more like grandparents to her. When her mother became ill little Ruth went to live with her oldest sister, Sarah, and her husband. Owners of a combined restaurant, soda fountain, and liquor store, Ruth ventured into the commercial world at age nine as she worked at the soda fountain belonging to Sarah and her husband.

Ruth's management ability stems from her sister Sarah who was a constant role model. A take charge person, Sarah was the matriarch who held her family together. She made all the decisions and took care of money matters. Sarah passed these talents to her young sister, Ruth.

By the age of sixteen, a friend introduced Ruth to a young man named Elliot Handler at a high school dance. Love blossomed instantly!

After her sophomore year at the University of Denver in 1936, Ruth took a summer vacation to balmy Los Angeles, California. There she looked up a friend of her sister who worked at Paramount Pictures and had lunch in the studio commissary. Ruth was mesmerized by the glamour of Hollywood. She went to the personnel office and successfully talked her way into a job in the Paramount Studio steno pool. Sarah was pleased with her sister's move and urged her to remain in Los Angeles. Sarah was concerned that Elliot and Ruth were becoming serious. Although Elliot was nice, he wanted to be an artist and Sarah preferred Ruth marry a doctor or lawyer.

Not long after, Elliot moved to Los Angeles and attended Art Center College of Design. He also found a job working for a company designing light fixtures.

Still discouraging romance, Sarah urged Ruth to return to Denver. Ruth went to Denver and Elliot came shortly after. Ruth and Elliot were married on June 26, 1938, joining the dynamic talents which were later to make history in the toy manufacturing world. The young couple together returned to the city both had grown to love, Los Angeles, to establish their home.

Ruth has always maintained an active part in business ventures with Elliot and was a working mother in an age when this was not the norm. Although she did not have to work, Ruth chose to because she enjoyed the challenge.

While raising her two children, Barbara Joyce and Kenneth Robert, she did all with style, and proved women can have a career and keep the home fires burning. She was comfortable in her work and had a natural ability to market what people would buy — toys. With almost a second sense about this, Mrs. Handler seemed to realize early what toys children enjoyed most and set in motion the production of these items. As a working couple, the Handlers made a compatible team. Elliot with the talent for design and Ruth the forcefulness needed for marketing, this couple seemed to have something close to the Midas Touch.

For many years, collectors have whispered the possibility of Bild Lilli being Barbie doll's mother. Not true! Ruth Handler in her low voice of confidence and poise dispels this theory. Ruth says *she* is "Barbie's Mom." Following the sale of her second business, which she founded in 1976 called "Nearly Me," she told me she had a title for her next speech. She plans to call it "The Two Lives of Barbies's Mom." An idea formed in her mind of the perfect doll, and from there pushing the project through to completion, she used the hand of a loving and instructive mother. The Barbie project was more than just a business venture, it was a creation of something very special to her. It was the realization of a dream long sought in her spirit. She put her energy wholly into this effort. Everything about the doll must be just right. She had to produce something with which she herself would love to play. This doll was what brought out the little girl in Ruth Handler. In retrospect, the doll, Barbie, has brought out the little girl in all of us.

Both daughter Barbara and son Ken were embarrassed about the dolls names, but mainly because those many doll fans made such a fuss over them. It propelled them into instant celebrity status. There seemed to be Barbie and Ken doll fans everywhere.

The 60's saw Mattel rise to the pinnacle of success with Barbie and Ken being the centerpiece of the company's empire. This success for Ruth was going to have a bittersweet end with a personal tragedy she was about to face.

In 1970 Mattel was experiencing financial difficulties the likes of which the company had not seen before, and Ruth was to face her own personal despair. Ruth found a lump in her breast. Going to the hospital for a biopsy she awoke with a mastectomy. "It was the most devastating thing that had ever happened to me," she says. She retired from Mattel in 1974 and by 1976 was continuing to struggle with the artificial prosthesis. She began research on breast design with the help of Peyton Massey. Massey was a Los Angeles based sculptor who specialized in prosthesis. Living proof that "necessity is the mother of invention," Ruth formed the Ruthton Corporation's Nearly Me with plants in Los Angeles and Dallas. The artificial breasts were sold first at Neiman Marcus. They were sold later in department stores throughout the country making women whole again. Here history

has come full circle with Ruth being first to put breasts on a doll and later making breasts for women.

Mrs. Handler is a woman of vibrant energy. Always busy and willing to travel, when the need arises, she has often appeared as a guest speaker on television programs promoting the prosthesis product which Nearly Me makes for mastectomy patients. Before Nearly Me, she says the equipment available was "dreadful." The secret to what drives this lady seems to be an ability to see a need and her efforts to fulfill that need.

A dynamic speaker and lively woman, she tells of the time she appeared on television to discuss Nearly Me. After leaving the studio and walking down the street to her car she heard screeching brakes from behind. A young man leaped from the car waving an old boxed Barbie doll and called, "Mrs. Handler, Mrs. Handler." He wanted her to autograph the box his prized doll was in. This young man had seen her on television and grabbed his doll, rushing to the studio. As she says, Barbie has propelled her to celebrity status. This comes as a surprise to Mrs. Handler, who never felt the doll would still be selling so well. Most dolls or toys have a marketable shelf life of from two to three years, yet Barbie doll has passed thirty years and is still going strong.

Another time when she appeared on a television talk show Mrs. Handler wanted to discuss Nearly Me. The hostess agreed only if they could talk

Elliot and Ruth Handler pose with a few Mattel-made toys. Note a number three Barbie doll wears Wedding Day Set. Photo circa 1959. Photo courtesy of the Department of Special Collections, University Research Library, UCLA.

about Barbie also. At the conclusion of the show, the live studio audience all on signal held up their Barbie dolls. There in the audience were hundreds of old Barbies as a surprise to Mrs. Handler.

As a list of credits, Ruth Handler served as executive vice president of Mattel from 1945 - 1967, president of Mattel from 1967–1974, was a founding member of the Los Angeles Music Center in 1965, a member of the business advisory council of the White House Conference for Children and Youth in 1970, an Associate Professor at the University of Southern California since 1967, a lecturer at UCLA, and on the board of directors of the Vista Del Mar Child Care Service. She was awarded the Outstanding Business Woman from the National Association of Accountants in 1961, the Handlers were Couple of the Year of the City of Hope in 1963, she was Woman of the Year in Business by the Los Angeles Times in 1968, one of the Outstanding Women in America by the Ladies Home Journal in 1971, recipient of the Growth Company of the Year awarded by the National Association of Investment Clubs in 1962, and received the Honor Award of the American Society of Tool and Manufacturing Engineers in 1965.

Longevity is not foreign to Ruth. Barbie may have lasted over thirty years, but the love between Elliot and Ruth has lasted five decades and is still strong. A true love story which has weathered time, trials, and business ventures, it is a symbol of true dedication.

Ruth Handler sold Nearly Me in November 1991, and once again she finds herself in retirement. Although Elliot is an avid golfer and painter, she now wonders what new interest will keep her busy again. It makes us wonder now, is it the doll, Barbie, or her mother, Ruth Handler, who is really the legend.

Chapter 3

Which is Which?

It is confusing deciding which Barbie doll is which when you buy one at a doll show, auction, or yard sale. How old is she really? Is she still on store shelves or is she one of those rare finds that you have wanted for years? Even now a 1991 All American Barbie doll wears the stamp on her back reading:

©MATTEL, INC. 1966
CHINA

After thirty plus years the 1960's date is still imprinted on her back. Simply explained, the body mold has not changed drastically in all these years, therefore, the copyright of that body does not change. Some dolls are marked on the hip, others on the lower back. This date stamp does not mean this is the year a doll was made, only patented. Only when the mold changed in some way did the date stamp change.

In 1959 the first Barbie doll came with:

Barbie TM.
Pats. Pend.
© MCMLVIII
by
Mattel
Inc.

printed on her hip. A patent for this doll was issued in 1958, the year previous to when the doll was marketed. This same date appeared on dolls until 1966. Although wording varied the date stamp remained the same. They were first printed as roman numerals but later changed to 1958.

A change in the patent in 1966 as the result of a body form change made the doll read:

©1966
Mattel, Inc.
U.S. Patented
U.S. Pat. Pend.
Made in
Japan

Dolls found wearing this imprint are the Twist 'N Turn Barbies sold between 1967 and 1971, 1967 Trade-in Barbie, Barbie Hair Happenin's from 1970 and 1971, Malibu Barbies from 1971–1972, Forget Me Nots Barbie from 1972, and numerous other Francie, Casey, Twiggy, P.J., Christie, and Julia dolls from those years.

A sure-fire way to tell whether your doll was sold in 1959 or 1961 is by weight. Only the first four dolls made are a solid torso product. The dolls sold from 1961 to the present are hollow body built. This

makes the weight of the dolls considerably different. Mattel found, though, that it was much cheaper to manufacture the hollow bodied dolls. Difference in weight amounts to .10 lbs., with .38 lbs. being the weight of the solid bodied Barbie dolls and .28 lbs. being the weight of the hollow dolls.

Mattel was never a company to waste parts and has in turn created a new avenue of confusion. This doll condition has become known to collectors as a "transitional doll." Simply put, after production of a particular Barbie doll legs or arms or even possibly heads are left over. When another style of Barbie is being made these arms, legs, or other parts are used on the new production. This was done in the early years which seems to create some interesting finds. Collectors have reported finding number three doll bodies with number one heads. Another collector has a bendable leg body with a bubblecut head. Until all the parts were used up there was some mixing that happened. Mattel made toys and never thought of these dolls as collectors items. They did not imagine thirty years later that collectors would be so exacting about parts.

Children at play have also changed the style of some dolls. I have talked with women who admit to exchanging heads on their dolls when playing as little girls. This has also put the wrong heads on bodies. Most often these dolls are found in yard sales. For collectors, this could mean finding the right doll and placing the parts in the correct order. As a collector, it is best to access any unique find as possibly the result of child's play unless the history of such a doll can be verified.

Talking Barbies of the early 1970's appeared with a 1967 date on her lower back. Living Barbie sold in 1970 and 1971 was issued with a 1968 copyright. Also with this date Walk Lively Barbie was sold in 1972 or 1973. The Busy Barbie of 1972 was found stamped:

© 1966
Mattel, Inc.
U.S. & Foreign
Patented
Other Pat's
Pending
Made in
U.S.A.

During the 1970's, dates stamped on dolls were 1966, 1967, or 1968. With little or no drastic body mold change over the years, no application for a change of patent is needed. There is more to deciding which Barbie is which than the date on her hip or back. The hairstyle, face, and even the exact wording does differ with each variety. Now after thirty plus years there are many dolls needing their exact age determined.

As an example, if a doll you hold has holes in her feet with copper tubing inside, she may have a pony-tail and high arched eyebrows. This lovely lady should carry the MCMLVIII date of a number one Barbie. Most often these first issue Barbies are an ivory or sickly white. The pigment used to color the vinyl has faded over years. In fact, this fate has affected the dolls numbered one, two, and three. Only that first doll had holes in her feet to fit the stand inside the copper cylinders.

The number two Barbie was only manufactured

A first wave blonde Barbie mint in her original box. Many of these dolls have turned an ivory color. Pigment in the vinyl of the first dolls was not colorfast, and faded.

for three months, creating fewer out there to find. She has the same face as a number one doll, but due to a change in the stand, no holes in the feet.

Another possible way to tell how old your doll is, is to notice she has an oily head. Regardless of whether she is a bubblecut or a ponytail, this doll is always a 1961. Changes in the vinyl mixtures used in the doll that year had an unstable oil concentration and now appears to be oily. This oil even leaves a stain on the sides of boxes that the doll is stored in. Some of the 1961 oily Barbies have arms and legs which also are made from the oily vinyl.

Always attempting to improve the product, Mattel had a bendable leg doll made in 1965. This doll had a pageboy hairstyle and featured legs that could be bent at the knees. She was marked in depressed letters:

© 1958
Mattel, Inc.
U.S. PATENTED
U.S. Pat. Pend.

As production of this doll continued in 1966, her imprint was changed to read in depressed letters:

©1958
MATTEL, INC.
U.S. PATENTED
U.S. PAT. PEND.
MADE IN JAPAN

As 1966 drew to a close the dolls were imprinted as above but with raised letters. Only a slight varia-tion, but it gives the collector the information about whether their doll was the first, middle, or final issue of the Bendable Leg Barbie dolls.

Another difficult era is the time called by collec-tors the "Eyelash Era." This time frame was when Mattel made Barbie with rooted lashes. Also included was the marvelous Twist 'N Turn waist. This took place in 1967 and continued until the early 70's. Apparently, this was very tedious work and so was discontinued. The Twist 'N Turn Barbie had been produced for more than one year. She had straight hair to start in 1967 but later a flip hairstyle came into being. The imprint on her back however, read from 1967 through 1971:

©1966
Mattel, Inc.
U.S. Patented
U.S. Pat. Pend.
Made in
Japan

In the case of identifying the Twist 'N Turn Barbie beyond the hairstyle, her original suit would be helpful. Swim-suits on the dolls each year were different. These dolls appeared for six years and the 1966 version wore a suit with a fishnet top. The 1967 appeared in a pink print shorts suit. The 1968 was seen in a yellow and red checked suit. She also was the first year of the flip Twist 'N Turn hairstyles. Some collectors are so impressed with the years of the eyelashes that they collect only these particular dolls. They are well made and worth the effort.

A Barbie doll that is easily recognized is the 1971 Dramatic New Living Barbie. She was the only Barbie doll produced with flat feet. That year she came with long straight hair, eyelashes, and the flat feet. Outfits sold to go with the doll had flat heeled shoes to match.

Three 1961 Barbie dolls with shiny, oily faces. Dolls from 1961 have a different oil mixed in the vinyl that over years has left an oily surface.

Another engineering accomplishment for Barbie in the early 1970's was posable wrists. Designers at Mattel fashioned wrists that were on a ball joint and could be turned and appeared more lifelike. Live Action Barbie On Stage from 1971 also had these hands and the twist waist. She was sold with the advertisement of "real dance action."

Hands were not out of the minds of the engineers at Mattel. Busy Barbie with Holdin' Hands sold in 1972, had a small television and other little accessories that the hands could hold. Busy Barbie came marked:

© 1966
Mattel, Inc.
U.S. & Foreign
Patented
Other Pat's
Pending
Made in
U.S.A.

Dolls of the late 1970's, 80's, and into the 90's will be more difficult to label without their boxes or clothing. In many cases the doll molds were the same but the outfits were different. Without those tell-tale outfits they are not of high value and it is unlikely anyone can guess which lady is which. Still in the original package with all clothing and accessories, the doll is guaranteed to increase in value yearly. Markings on these more recent issues have not changed much. As long as the body mold remains the same a patent stamp date change is not required.

Other unique Barbie dolls have become recognizable over the years. The Super Size Barbie sold in 1977 was larger than the conventional 11½". This doll was a full 18" tall. Super Size clothes were sold

Miss Barbie with three wigs and sleep eyes was sold in 1964. The sleep eyes were an invention of Dick May for Mattel.

along with a Super Size Christie doll. A Super Size Bridal Barbie sold for a brief time in 1978 as well as a 1979 Super Size Barbie with Super Hair.

Speaking of alterations in the Barbie body design, specialists at Mattel introduced Beauty Secrets Barbie in 1980. This doll had several tiny beauty items to use with the doll and her hands were designed to hold even the mini hair dryer. Push a button in the doll's back and she raised her arm to comb the long blonde hair. Beauty Secrets Barbie came marked:

©MATTEL, INC. 1979
Taiwan, 1965

This same innovation of the button in the back also appeared in 1981 with the Western Fun Barbie doll. With this button pushed, the doll winked her heavily made up eye.

In 1986 Magic Moves Barbie did not move by magic, not really, it was all mechanics. She was the ultimate in posable elegance. This doll could be twisted and turned in many unique positions. She was marked:

©MATTEL, INC. 1986
TAIWAN

A switch in her back positioned at the waistline enabled the doll's arms to move up or down. Barbie could brush back her own hair with head and arms in the proper position. Magic Moves Barbie was another example of Mattel's efforts to make Barbie more lifelike and kindle childhood imagination.

Now that collectors are more aware of the differences that exist between the dolls throughout the years, they will find it easier to purchase the doll they most need to add to their growing collections. Barbie dolls are being purchased with collecting in mind. Dolls are remaining in their original boxes at a record rate. Stores are now selling dolls listed as department store specials. They have similar markings as the regular varieties but are unique in clothing and packaging to their stores alone. Special limited issues like these are best left in their boxes. With these out of the box it would be next to impossible to judge the true identity of these dolls. These limited editions will be discussed at length in a later chapter.

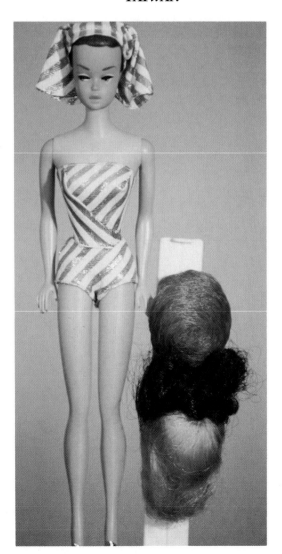

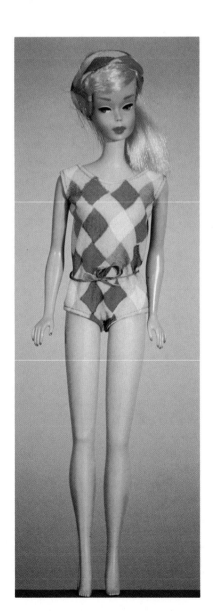

Left: Fashion Queen Barbie, sold in 1963, came with three wigs in titian, brunette, and blonde. This made the doll three dolls in one.

Right: After long research and inventive work, Color Magic Barbie was introduced in 1966. Both the color change hair and clothing were based on an invention by Ralph Dunn for Mattel.

Chapter 4

Changing Faces

One of the most often changed features of Barbie in her thirty plus years has been her face mold and the accompanying facial paint. Beginning in 1957, with the first sculpting of Barbie, the doll's head and appearance has been the focal point of concern for Mattel. It is through the face that the designers had to express Ruth Handler's dream for a doll which a child could transfer herself into in an imaginary world. The task would not be an easy one.

The first wave face for Barbie was molded and remolded by sculptors. The final result was made by Kohei Suzuki for Mattel and fashioned with Charlotte Johnson as the model.

Seymour Alder's concern with the initial work was centered on attaining the exact proportion of head to body size that had been generally lacking in other vinyl attempts. As Ralph Dunn stated, "Mattel was making every effort to work on proper proportions with the doll. Perfection with this project was everything." The demand for a satisfactory head mold resulted in Mattel's hiring of an expanded sculpting staff in the United States and a consultant in Japan.

As the Mattel staff progressed on the sculpting of the torso, arms, and legs, completion demands resulted in Mattel seeking assistance with refinements in the molding process.

The person that enabled Mattel to bring to Barbie the detailing and proper proportion was a Japanese consultant, Kohei Suzuki. Mr. Suzuki is one of Mattel's first examples of acquiring the best and the brightest stateside and internationally to complete their efforts with Barbie.

It is because of the association with the Orient, that many collectors evaluations ascribe to Barbie an oriental appearance. The description as such is more illusion than actual fact. An examination of the unpainted Barbie doll head pictured in Chapter 8 will show no oriental appearance in the molding. The effect is purely a cosmetic one.

When first produced for marketing, the facial paint on the doll was very heavy. The sharp tapering of the black eyeliner coupled with the iris being painted black in the corners with only a slight white U shaped accent creates the affect of an almond shape. Light brown eyebrows painted in an inverted V shape only enhanced the sharpness of the facial contrast, creating an image more reminiscent of Audrey Hepburn circa 1953. By the third issue doll in 1960, those arched brows were more curved and softened and the heavy black outline of the eye was not used. The molded eyelashes were painted black, the heavy underliner was removed and the eyes were given blue pupils. In this area, the face mold had not changed, just the paint job was much more refined. This became the first of many facial makeovers in the glamorous career of Barbie.

The fourth wave, as Mattel chooses to refer to production, was the doll issued which best met with Ruth Handler's original ideal doll.

For Mattel, a lack of qualified talent was never a problem. Designing the doll to appeal to a receptive buying public, not only required a master sculptor, but also a face painter who could apply the pigments in an artistic way to be aesthetically appealing to the eye. The lady who has served as Barbie's facial painter bringing out her character and charm since 1966 is Hiroe Okubo-Wolf. She first began in 1963 with Mattel as a samplemaker in the Fashion Department. By 1966 her talent with face painting was realized and her career took a new direction. Hiroe worked with Mattel sculptor, Martha Armstrong, learning the art of face painting. Within a year she was one of seven painters in the Face Design Department. Of Hiroe, Jean Ann Burger is quoted as saying she has the "unique ability to achieve a new facial look on the same molded head over and over again. Hiroe will do a different face painting, different expression, different use of colors and design."

Face design "was very competitive in those early years," tells Hiroe. Working under Erin Libby, the department manager, Hiroe says each person in the department received the same assignment. For the individual dolls each designer painted three faces and submitted them to the marketing personnel. This gave marketing twenty-one faces to choose from. They would pick one design for the doll and most often Hiroe's design was the one they liked the best. "After time," tells Hiroe, "all of the other face painters were laid off and for many years I did all the designing and paint masters myself." Now after many years alone in the workroom Hiroe has an assistant, Ei Fong. Ei Fong is responsible for all of the large dolls Mattel produces.

To begin to design a face Hiroe first finds out what look the doll is expected to have, glamour, casual, outdoorsy, sweet, high fashion, and what clothes she will wear. The color of hair and skintone are also factors in her decision. Work on the doll takes long hours. Using acrylic paint and tiny brushes, she works stroke by stroke creating a new face for Barbie. To try something different, she can wipe it off and begin again. She likes the vinyls because of the ability to erase your mistakes and change your mind. She says she "checks to see how it looks from different angles, changing a color here, a highlight there," and the outcome is a new look for Mattel's best loved doll. Often she uses the Superstar mold which was designed for Mattel by Joyce Clark. The Superstar mold has proven to be the most popular mold designed for the doll to date.

Hiroe Wolf is also responsible for face designs on all the porcelain dolls as well as Skipper, Ken, and their many friends. She designs the faces for department store specials which seem to grow into a longer list with each passing year.

Hiroe's favorites are the P.J. dolls and the oriental designs. "I also remember the first Barbie I designed entirely on my own, Sweet Sixteen, in the early seventies," she says.

By the time the dolls are ready for mass production they are painted with airbrushes. Tiny metal masks are used to cover the face as they pass along the assembly line.

Times have changed in the face design group where Hiroe has been manager since 1989. There are nine painters in her group designing faces, preparing paintmasters and specifications, painting photo, television, and sales samples, and evaluating finished heads from the plants. Over one hundred face designs each year are done by this small group of talented artists at Mattel.

Sometimes conceptual changes for Barbie were required beyond alterations of facial paint. In 1963, the innovations of molded hair and interchangeable wigs in three colors and styles were marketed as Fashion Queen Barbie. It was to assist in the development of wigs that Mattel was to find Ms. Jean Ann Burger and her presence at Mattel was destined to yield dividends over many years to come. The molded head concept made Barbie three dolls for one price while entrusting the child with the power to choose blonde, brunette, or titian. It wasn't long until Mattel took another bold step with the molded head and in 1964 began marketing a doll with the added touch of sleep eyes. In this mold, holes had to be cut in the eye socket to insert sleep eyes that closed when the doll was laid down. Designed by Dick May, the doll was called Miss Barbie. These innovative offshoots, attempts to try new ideas that would spark variety in their marketing scheme, were to become the creative trademark of Mattel. They continued to use the ponytails, bubblecuts, and bendable leg Barbies. Still the desire to make something new and exciting was ever constant in their design department.

Creating a molded head for a doll with wigs required a new sculpting. Fashion Queen Barbie was sold in 1963.

Miss Barbie, sold in 1964, required a mold be made to allow for not only wigs, but also sleep eyes.

A new look for the Barbie doll was created and sold in 1967 as the Twist 'N Turn Barbie. With a new face mold, she also was sold with rooted eyelashes.

To manufacture Barbie with rooted eyelashes required yet another new mold for her famous head. At this point in 1967, the raised molded eyelashes were gone forever. With the introduction of the Twist 'N Turn Barbie came a coy yet demure face with a mouth that appears almost ready to speak. This new mold kept pace with what Mattel produced through the end of the 1960's and into the 1970's. Raspberry red lips and rosy painted cheeks created a high cheekbone appearance for this newly issued Barbie doll. Wide round blue eyes and long feathered bangs coupled with light brown eyebrows accented those long luscious eyelashes.

Mattel was always reaching out for new innovations to embody their doll with for the buying public. Throughout the 60's and 70's Carol Spencer tells of efforts to recruit talented people to the staff to fill a wide range of positions. Mattel's efforts filled positions in the technical areas of mechanical engineering, chemical engineering, and fashion design. Maintaining technical preeminence required Mattel to be constantly on the lookout for outstanding personnel. Recruiting drives were national and international in scope. The art schools of Europe were targeted to locate superior sculptors. Mattel representatives visited art schools in London, England; Paris, France; and Florence, Italy seeking sculptors to fill the needs of a fast growing toy industry. Aldo Favilli was an art student in Florence, Italy designing sets within the Italian movie industry. Favilli's teacher recommended him to Mattel as his best sculpting student.

Speaking only a few words of English, Favilli was first screened by a Mattel representative who spoke no Italian. The representative's wife was also present and she spoke only minimal Spanish. "It was an interesting interview but not much was accomplished," says Favilli. For three years Mattel continued to talk with Favilli, finally convincing him to visit southern California and to see the Mattel facilities. "They even took me to Disneyland," says Favilli. An offer was made and Aldo Favilli joined Mattel in 1970 in the sculpting department. Since 1985 Mr. Favilli has been the head of the sculpting department.

Mattel might find itself in need of a translator periodically. The multitalented Barbie displayed her aptitude for foreign languages in 1970 when she spoke fluent Spanish. Talking Barbie and Spanish Talking Barbie were the creative offering of 1970. Both versions of the Talking Barbie were made in both Hong Kong and Mexico. These dolls came with two different head molds but were packaged in identical boxes. Spanish Talking Barbie number 8348 was made with the Stacey head mold in Hong Kong. While the same Spanish Talking Barbie made in Mexico was molded with the Twist 'N Turn face of the past. Talking Barbie number 1115, made in Hong Kong, was molded with the Twist 'N Turn face, while the Talking Barbie made in Mexico number 1115 came with the Stacey head mold.

A short lived doll called Steffie was sold in 1972 and 1973. Although her appearance on the market was brief, the head mold typifies the flexibility that slight alterations of the facial paint can have on its marketability. Dolls such as Miss America, Malibu P.J., Free Moving P.J., Cara, Kelley, #8587 Barbie, Hawaiian Barbie, Gold Medal P.J., and Deluxe Quick Curl P.J. were all made from this same head mold. In the late 80's, dolls such Whitney, Mrs. Heart, and the Hispanic Barbies, all used the old Steffie head model. The combination of the popularity of the Steffie face and limited release of brunette hair, make any doll with this combination a sought after prize on the secondary market.

Faces of Barbie again changed in 1975 as she prepared for the Innsbruck Winter Olympics. Gold Medal Barbies were issued with a head mold showing a smile undoubtedly beaming with anticipation of the gold medal performance awaiting her on the Austrian slopes. Instead of the expressionless face used in the past, Barbie was now seen smiling. Although these Gold Medal dolls featured a smile, other dolls sold in 1975 and for a very few years after still came with the expressionless face. By 1977 the face of Barbie doll changed forever. Ruth Handler's desire for the expressionless face was remolded and the doll smiled from toy shelves everywhere.

Beginning with the Steffie doll in the 70's, the Steffie face mold became a popular design for many Barbie dolls.

Mattel's most popular face mold to date is the Superstar mold which first appeared on the Superstar Barbie. The mold was designed for Mattel by Joyce Clark.

Face molds were painted in different styles because of the numerous topical Barbie dolls that were released each year. The most popular face is the Superstar mold, so named because of its first appearance on the Superstar Barbie in 1977. With her award-winning smile and dimple this Superstar face mold appears on the Happy Holidays Barbies from 1988 though 1991; Rollerblade Barbie in 1992; Birthday Surprise Barbie in 1992; Air Force, Army, and Navy Barbies during 1989, 1990, 1991; and Totally Hair Barbie dolls in 1993 to name just a few.

Beginning the International Series, the Italian face mold has been seen only on the Italian Barbie doll sold in 1980.

The Superstar Barbie doll face mold did not require a new sculpting but inserting rhinestones in the eyes gave sparkle to Sparkle Eyed Barbie sold in 1991.

Another innovation was Kissing Barbie sold in 1979. Designed with a permanent pucker, this doll had lip paint in an almost neutral beige coloring. She came packaged with a tube of lipstick which when the child applied it to the lips and pushed the button panel in the doll's back her head tilted back and the face drew up into a slight pucker. Packaged inside the Kissing Barbie doll was a form where parents could order additional lipsticks for the doll. Many found today by collectors have been all kissed out. The mechanism that performed the pucker no longer works from repetitive use. However, those mint in their original box still have the kissing ability.

Designed with the same back torso button as the Kissing Barbie, Western Barbie was sold in 1980. Her facial alterations had to be made to allow for the winking eye. The right eye of this doll closed when the button was depressed. Heavy blue makeup accented the eyes on this doll.

Beginning a new era in the 1980's with an International series also required design changes to the face molds of some dolls in this theme. Italian Barbie in 1980 came with a newly designed face with an open mouth revealing a row of perfect teeth. High cheeks tapered to a chin that gave the doll an oval face. The mold was not used beyond Italian Barbie. A similarly designed mold was created for the 1992 edition of Fantastica Barbie sold as a depart-

The Steffie face mold was used with the first issued black Barbie doll sold in 1970. Face molds can be used for a variety of dolls with a change of pigment and face paint.

ment store special. The Fantastica face has wider cheeks and less oval to the face. Vibrant face paint made a colorful presentation to Fantastica Barbie.

Another new mold of the 1980's was the Oriental. This was also created for dolls in the International and nationalities series. It appears on Oriental, Eskimo, Japanese, Korean, and Malaysian Barbie dolls of that series. The Oriental mold is a popular face mold to which collectors respond favorably. The Oriental face mold is much rounder, with a closed mouth smile. Pale pink blush accents high cheekbones which call attention to wide brown eyes. Black liner outlines the eyes and eyebrows. With this mold the eyes appear almond shaped even without the black painted eyeliner. All dolls with the Oriental mold have a head full of lush black hair.

With the exception of Miss Barbie, the Barbie has most often had painted eyes. However, in 1992 Mattel found another medium for creating unique eyes for their doll. The Sparkle Eyed Barbie doll had rhinestone insets inserted into the eye to create the effect of sparkling eyes.

As the years progress into the 1990's, head molds will continue to evolve and Mattel's design staff will be mindful of keeping pace with the ever changing world. They will be seeking to express the love they wish to share with all through the eyes of a doll.

Another example of what can be done with a change of face paint is Grandma Heart. Age lines were painted on the face and grey hair was rooted to add maturity and age to the doll.

Another face mold created for the International Series was the Oriental. It was first used on Oriental Barbie in 1981. The face mold now appears on many Oriental dolls in the Barbie line.

Introducing an all new face mold in 1992 for Fantastica Barbie gave a Mexican accent to Mattel's Barbie line.

Chapter 5

Fashions Galore

"The doll sells fashions and the fashions sell the doll." A marketing axiom that Ruth returned from Europe with and was going to put into practice in the United States. The rest is history but behind the scenes is a larger than life story. From Barbie's earliest beginnings, clothes that could only be described as meticulous and eyecatching were a part of the Barbie wardrobe. Their detail was far from accidental for Mattel was determined to produce quality in the doll and the fashion design. She was billed on the sides of her early boxes as a "teenage fashion model" because very early on was the recognition that Ruth's axiom would be a double edge sword that would carve out a large marketing share for the doll in the toy industry.

Clothing styles change from year to year and with the Barbie doll, Mattel made her clothing reflect the influential styles of the period. Her clothing is a perfect history of fashion over the past thirty years. If proper accessories required hats, gloves, shoes, purses, and jewelry, the doll had these and more. When pantsuits came into being, Barbie's wardrobe was filled with a myriad of colors. Whether it be mini or midi skirts, Mattel kept pace with a clothing design to match. Mattel sought to make their fashions a point of keen interest for teenage girls of each generation.

In 1959, Barbie's wardrobe was designed for Mattel by a freelance clothing designer and instructor from Chouinard Art School, Charlotte Johnson. Neither mimicry nor fad governed these garments, they were drawn from timeless fashion, the effort to anticipate the changes in fashion has kept the design staff in constant reevaluation of the trends. Like Balenciaga, Dior, Givenchy, Balmain, and Castillo, the fashions for Barbie were up to date miniatures that in and of themselves were an impressive collection. Charlotte told her staff these garments should be tiny replicas of fashions of the time. Each of these creations bore titles to identify them. Made with great care, they had zippers, linings, buttons, gloves, hats, and jewelry, all to make Barbie doll look the part of a real fashion plate.

Such tiny zippers were hard to come by. Mattel found a company in Japan who made these miniature clothing accessories called "YKK." Made by Yoshida Kogyo, who also made tiny snaps for Barbie size garments, these came in extremely large lot amounts. Frank Nakamura, who also served as Mattel's Japanese

A number one Barbie models one of the rarest of the early 1959 outfits, Roman Holiday Separates.

Ruth Handler's first list of requested garments to Charlotte Johnson included something for the ballet. The first ballet outfit sold for Barbie between 1961 and 1965 was Ballerina.

translator and negotiator arranged with Yoshida Kogyo to purchase smaller lots in those early months.

Not only did Mattel seek out fashion insights from the great fashion houses of Europe but Seymour Adler says, "Ms. Johnson gleened many of her fashion ideas from a Sears Roebuck catalog which sat on her desk at Mattel." He says, "She often looked through it and took a skirt idea from one and jacket or blouse from another for Barbie outfits."

Some of these beautiful fashions were not mass produced in large quantities. In fact, some are very rare and hard to find today. Some outfits were sold in only certain areas of our country, making the task of finding a particular outfit in some regions extremely difficult. Reasons for one area of the country receiving a particular outfit while another did not is simple, some outfits were made for a very short time. A limited number were made during that year's production and as shipping orders were filled, they ran out

quickly. This fact left other areas of the country never to see this particular rare Barbie collectible. Now with collectors buying these outfits on the secondary market, they are becoming more scattered throughout the country. The difficulty and complexity of making the outfits may also account for their small numbers. Those that are harder to find are number 916 Commuter Set, number 964 Gay Parisienne, number 966 Plantation Belle, number 967 Picnic Set, number 968 Roman Holiday Separates, number 971 Easter Parade, number 981 Busy Gal, number 985 Open Road, and number 982 Solo In The Spotlight. These outfits found now mint and complete are priced extremely high. Fashionable clothes made this three dimensional doll as versatile as any paper doll. She could be played with and changed depending on the fantasy. It was no wonder that by 1960 Mattel had seen the necessity of marketing a plastic carrying case to hold all those clothes, shoes, gloves, and other paraphernalia.

Plantation Belle, an outfit introduced in 1959 at the Toy Fair, is now one of the seven rarest outfits.

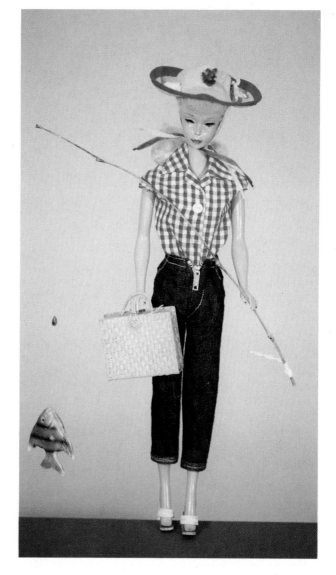

This outfit called Picnic Set is hard to find. Note the tiny plastic frog and flowers on her hat. The outfit pictured was sold with a molded plastic fish. Earlier outfits came with wax fish.

There is more to fashion than clothes, shoes, and jewelry. Makeup is as much a part of the costume as the color of dress or style of shoes. Teenage years are a time of awakening for young girls. Experimentation with cosmetics is a major interest to these budding young ladies. Mattel, in their infinite wisdom, kept the doll's face paint as up to the minute as all the fashions. The late 50's was a time of heavy eyeliner and blue shadow with flame red lips. As the bubblecut doll came into marketing, new fashions in lip colors were being seen. Pale lip colors were the new fashion and Barbie doll was no exception. Pink, peach, coral, and even white lip colors were sold. The doll appeared on the market with these new shades. Some dolls have even appeared over years looking like they never had painted lips, indeed, that is always possible because red lip color had come and gone. Each of these dolls were painted by the Japanese staff who stroked all the finishing touches to the doll. With loving hands and small brushes they applied the face of the elegant lady — Barbie.

Like any fashionable garment, these wonderful outfits came with tiny designer labels printed

Barbie®
©By Mattel

For Mattel, one label on one piece of the outfit was sufficient to denote their manufacture of the outfit. Placement seemed to vary. As an example, Easter Parade had a label sewn only in the coat as did Roman Holiday Separates. However, Enchanted Evening had the label in the side seam of the gown near the hem. The key to deciding the label location was where visibility would be the highest. One tag was living proof of Mattel authenticity. This brought the fact to an official state, these were real Barbie doll fashions. Even in the early days, copycat outfits were on toy shelves and attempting to pass as real Mattel garments.

The garments appear to have been completed even including zippers before the labels were installed.

A redhead swirl ponytail models Open Road. With glasses and road map, she is ready for an exciting trip.

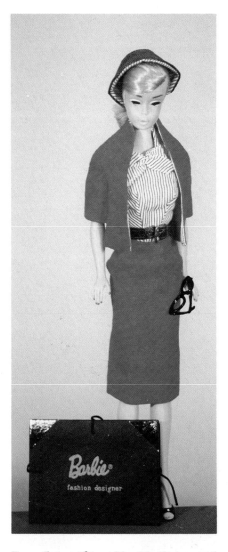

Busy Gal outfit, sold with the second wave Barbie, is considered rare. Busy Gal made the doll a fashion designer and came complete with her own portfolio. Sketches were also included.

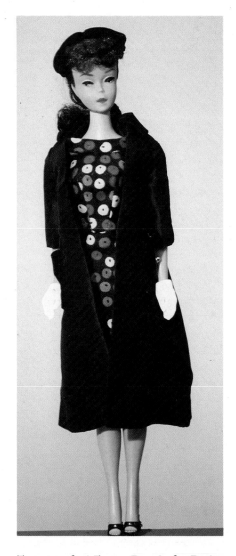

Trying to find Easter Parade for Barbie collectors is sometimes difficult. Seen in the first fashion booklet, this was an extremely elegant outfit.

Observation of stitching bears this fact out. Pak items were never labeled with only one exception, if an item was once a part of an ensemble and transferred to "The Kingdom of Pak" later they then had the label. For an example, Yachtsman and Barbie-Q reached this status and sure enough, they had labels.

Labels were a woven continuous ribbon with selvage edges. White threads run the length of the ribbon with interlocking black threads caught at intervals to spell out the words. To inhibit fraying, a glue was applied at intervals to coincide with the woven message. Not water or play proof, the glue came off and labels have frayed over the years. How much the label has deteriorated is one of the criteria that determine the pristine condition of any outfit which in turn reflects its market value.

During 1959 an extremely rare outfit called Gay Parisienne was sold. This was inspired by a bubble dress created by Hubert de Givenchy in the mid 1950's. Another haute couture gown was inspired by Charles James, a famous fashion creator. Balenciaga was a major fashion influence with his pill box hat which was seen in many outfits of the 1960's. Three of these Barbie outfits were Theatre Date, White Magic, and Red Flair. Another Balenciaga inspired ensemble was an outfit sold in 1963 called Career Girl. This striking suit had a matching cloche hat with a rose. Hats were a regular part of the early Barbie fashions. Women of that era wore hats and gloves for many occasions and so did the doll. On The Avenue was a 1965 tailored suit inspired by Dior. A tight fitting pink satin gown with full train called Enchanted Evening was sold in 1960. This Castillo influenced gown was once seen on a 1949 Vogue Magazine cover which shows that Mattel sought to evaluate fashion beyond the scope of the immediate trends. The Enchanted Evening outfit was marketed for the doll between 1960 and 1963. It came with three rhinestones at the hip. Another version of the same gown also sold during that time had a pink fabric rose at the hip. Both versions available were sold as outfit number 983.

With fashions of this nature, it is evident that Charlotte Johnson consulted more than the Sears Roebuck catalog. She also browsed through many fashion magazines and publications of that time gleaning ideas for this doll. Women's fashions of the period have been a driving influence on the doll's clothes. Mattel has obviously kept one eye on the fashion scene and the other on the toy market. If bright colors are in style, as in the late 60's and early 70's, so were the clothes Barbie doll wore. Mary Quant, an English fashion designer, introduced miniskirts in 1965. She was the creator of the "Mod" era fashions for young women. Andre Courreges brought go-go boots to the fashion world. The Barbie outfit called Zokko sold in 1967 was a mini dress with matching go-go boots. Tiny pearl earrings were no longer fashionable. Barbie wore bright plastic geometric shaped dangly earrings to match her new mod clothes.

Another very rare 1959 outfit is this Gay Parisienne modeled by a number two Barbie.

A 1961 titian bubblecut models Career Girl. Finely detailed fashions were the trademark of Charlotte Johnson and her staff. Mimicry was not the name of the game. Fashion was the watchword and not fads. Charlotte Johnson maintained strict values about garment production.

The Enchanted Evening outfit was sold in two versions. One gown came with a satin rose at the waist, the other had three rhinestones at the waist.

Always the top selling garment of the Barbie outfit line is the wedding gown. The first wedding gown sold in 1959 was called Wedding Day Set. Here a number one Barbie models her Wedding Day Set.

A number one Barbie and flocked hair Ken model wedding attire from the early years.

Mattel creates a little girl's dream with their many bridal gowns. The 1959 version was Wedding Day Set. This dreamy mass of lace and satin appeared in the very first fashion booklet. It sold between 1959 and 1962. Of all clothing sets sold, the wedding gown each year is the best seller. When found today, the gown of Wedding Day Set most often has a split down the center of the dress bodice. Lace, with age and handling, becomes very fragile. Every little girl dreams of the perfect romantic wedding and Barbie makes that fairytale come alive.

Themes were a plus when those early outfits were created for both Barbie and Ken. A campus theme made school a popular make-believe during playtime. Ken was designed an outfit called Campus Hero in 1961. This featured white pants and shoes, and a multicolored striped sweater with a felt "U" or "M." The outfit also included a State

A second wedding gown, sold between 1963 and 1965, was called Bride's Dream. A number one blonde Barbie models Bride's Dream.

A 1962 outfit called Icebreaker has the Barbie doll gliding over the ice.

Drum Majorette was sold in 1964 and 1965. A corresponding outfit for Ken was sold separately.

pennant. The rarest of these is the set with the "M" on the sweater. In 1963 an outfit called Touchdown gave Ken the opportunity to play football. Also that same year Playball was introduced for Ken to play baseball. An always popular item was called Graduation and was made for both Barbie and Ken. This was the traditional black robe and mortarboard. The school theme continued in 1964 with a Barbie ensemble called Drum Majorette. Barbie doll could lead the band in style along with her favorite beau Ken who wore Drum Major. To cheer Ken on to victory during the big game Barbie could wear Cheerleader. This outfit was sold also in 1964.

The student exchange program opened up new vistas of travel for the youth. Teenagers were going to foreign countries for schooling and Mattel was busy designing the right travel clothes for Barbie. Even a doll can see the world and visit new lands.

Ken along with Barbie, had vibrant colorful costumes created to simulate pretend travel.

These travel costumes were designed for Mattel by Dorothy Schue, Aileen Zublin, and Kay Carter.

The first costume for Barbie was Barbie In Japan a creation for 1964 that did not include a companion Ken outfit. Barbie In Mexico had a matching Ken fashion called Ken In Mexico. A colorful travel pamphlet was included with each outfit. Barbie In Switzerland and Ken In Switzerland brought the couple to the Swiss Alps. Ken's outfit even included a beer stein and pipe. Doll-sized lederhosen with red suspenders were a part of the Swiss Ken outfit. They were an alpine delight! Barbie In Holland and Ken In Holland were lovely recreations of a dutch girl and boy in the Netherlands. To complete the travel set was a Barbie In Hawaii and Ken In Hawaii. Apparently, the dolls spent their spring vacationing in our fiftieth state!

Ruth Handler requested something designed for Barbie to wear to the game. Charlotte Johnson fashioned a Cheerleader outfit which is modeled by a straight leg Midge doll.

Ready for a Halloween masquerade is Barbie, Ken, and Skipper wearing their costumes of Masquerade. Tutti's clad in Clownin' Around. Todd models a clown suit from Germany.

Every teen loves a party and Mattel created matching outfits called Masquerade for Barbie, Ken, and Skipper. These were very popular ensembles during 1963 and 1964. They featured a black and yellow color theme. Masks, clown type suits, and hats were a part of the costumes. A party invitation was also included in each ensemble. This outfit with more of a Halloween flavor, was popular and is easily found by collectors today, although finding these outfits complete is more difficult. Small pieces to the sets have frequently been lost and the nylon panty hose in Barbie's costume sometimes splits. Often hardest to locate in Ken's Masquerade is a white cotton skull cap to be worn beneath the clown hat.

Over the years, hundreds of fashions have been made for the doll. During the early years, incredible detail was devoted to creating elaborate fashions for her. An example of this detail would be a 1963 ensemble called Sophisticated Lady which commands a high price complete and mint today. This pink formal gown has a rose velvet coat with a stand up collar. A tiara for her dainty head, a pink pearl necklace, long white gloves, and tiny pink shoes made her a princess set for the ball. This outfit also is noted for being the last of the 900 series garments marketed.

Another novelty in doll clothing manufacturing was the system in Japan in the early 60's. Factories were not constructed. Doll clothing was made under a cottage industry system in that country. Frank Nakamura tells that the system was operated like a chain. The fabric supplier was at the beginning of the many link system but under him was a subcontractor. Under this subcontractor was yet another subcontractor who has the cottage industry. In Japan there were many apartment complexes and housing areas

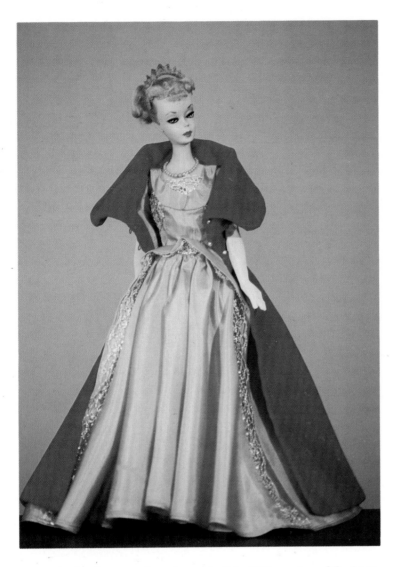

Barbie looks the part of a princess in this 1963 version of Sophisticated Lady. The outfit is being modeled by a number two Barbie doll.

the American market. All necessary documents were filled out, and forwarded to the bank in Japan. In preparation for this, a Letter of Credit from Mattel had previously been received by the bank. The bank paid the supplier who in turn paid the subcontractor who in turn paid the next subcontractor. The seamstresses were paid as the last link in the chain.

"In those days, you had to be very careful that there were no mistakes," says Jackie Leighton, "because these people were copy experts. They would copy the mistake if what we sent was not perfect. Everything had to be made so that these women could follow the pattern. Instructions were written, patterns were made, pictures were taken and sent along with several completed samples of the outfit. These sample outfits had to be made and sent for the people to see what was expected and the look of the final product. It was a very exacting job." There was always alot of mailing samples of fabric and outfits back and forth between Japan and California. Jackie says, "Mattel was very strict about keeping the quality up."

The Japanese ladies stitched each garment and then sewed the outfits to cardboard backing which later was placed inside the packaging with a cello front. Although much more sophisticated today, it is somewhat similarly accomplished but stitched in factories.

Jackie Leighton spent only one year in the Barbie doll fashion design department. She was transferred to the doll department and designed for every doll except Barbie. Some of the items she created for Mattel were rag dolls, puppets, and stuffed animals. She even designed small animals for Liddle Kiddle dolls and Skipper.

Another Leighton feature was a line of children's clothing for Mattel. The clothing was very unusual because they considered Barbie doll in the design. These very colorful garments had pockets where the children could put their Barbie doll. At the last minute, Mattel chose to not market this line of clothing.

By 1964 Mattel moved on to the number 1600 series fashions. Many of the 1600 numbered outfits are more difficult to locate than 900 numbered garments. Larger amounts of the 900 series outfits were produced than 1600 ensembles. A beautiful rose pink satin outfit called Satin 'N Rose sold in 1964 is rarely seen. With this fashion, pink rhinestone stud earrings accompanied the pink satin skirt, blouse, pants, jacket, hat, and pale pink mule high heel shoes.

Satin was used in many outfits during this time

where people lived. These subcontractors were in charge of the women who lived in these areas. The suppliers would receive the work from Mattel and in turn give the work to the subcontractor. They in turn took the work home to the women and at the end of the week returned it to their boss. He would inspect and sort the work giving out new work to these ladies. The subcontractor then gave the finished work to the next subcontractor who would inspect the work. At this area the clothing was packaged in cardboard boxes with cellophane fronts. When this was completed the boxed garments were taken to the fabric supplier along with a bill for the packaged goods. The supplier collected the packaged outfits sending them to the shipping dock where containers were waiting in a warehouse. All merchandise was gathered at the dock where it was packed for shipment, sealed, and shipped to California to be sold in including the White Magic ensemble, number 1607, sold in 1964. A white satin coat, pillbox hat, white gloves, and silver clutch purse made Barbie the best dressed doll in America.

As another example, number 1622 called Student Teacher was a career oriented fashion. Here a dress with red bodice and red check skirt came with red pumps, black rimmed glasses, globe, geography book, and pointer stick.

Skaters Waltz number 1629, is very hard to find today for many collectors. This pink skater costume came in a rose pink knit and felt fabric. A fleecy fabric collar and mittens to keep tiny doll hands warm were accompanied by nylon tights. Plastic white ice skates were molded with gray blades.

On The Avenue number 1644 was fashioned from a Christian Dior tailored suit. The fabric was gold and white knit and featured a large wide collar. This style suit was a popular design in 1965, the year Barbie doll wore this ensemble. With a change of accessories this same outfit became Sunday Visit number 1675 in 1966.

A brunette bubblecut Barbie is modeling Golden Elegance sold by Mattel in 1963.

Fine detailing of the 1600 series garments have made them highly sought after by collectors. Pictured here is a 1965 bendable leg Barbie modeling the outfit Fashion Luncheon from 1966.

Pink came in many shades for Barbie. Satin 'N Rose from 1964 is seen here on a 1965 bendable leg Barbie doll.

Many career opportunities were depicted with the doll. Here a bendable leg Barbie models Student Teacher which was sold in 1965.

Some 1600 series outfits are deemed rare, as is Skaters Waltz from 1965.

A titian hair, bendable leg Barbie doll models On The Avenue sold in 1965.

Many gowns, dresses, suits, and other appropriate garments were included in the 1600 series. Eighty-three outfits carry the 1600 series numbers during the years between 1964 to 1967.

With each passing year at Mattel the clothing for Barbie has gained momentum. Starting with twenty-two outfits in 1959, the variety for buyers to pick has increased tremendously. Each year a new line is introduced but those from the previous year are still seen on store shelves for a period of time. Every career imaginable was anticipated and Mattel's fashion designers created a fashion for each. Outfits for every possible occasion, you can name were available.

Until 1970, dolls were sold in swimsuits with only a few boxed as dressed dolls. During the 1970's dolls came dressed rather than in swimsuits and began a trend which continues even today. As the years have progressed, however, the dresses and gowns sold on the dolls have become much more elaborate. The fashions of the 70's lent themselves to fewer ensemble pieces. Furs, lace, and vibrant colors were the dictates of the day. Bellbottom pants and big floral prints kept Barbie doll in the groove. Although the dressed doll has caught on, still each year one doll is sold in a swimsuit reminiscent of the original designs.

Many of the 1600 series outfits are extremely glamorous. The Black Magic ensemble sold in 1964 was designed for Mattel by Carol Spencer.

Before coming to Mattel, Carol Spencer designed women's lingerie fashions. Here is a lingerie fashion she designed for Barbie doll which sold in 1967 called Underprints.

Designers at Mattel created gaucho pants, madras, and an array of peasant clothes for our doll, Barbie. Bellbottom pants and granny dresses were a popular trend in the 70's, and Mattel made an assortment from which children could choose. The 1970's doll fashions were fashionable and colorful. Outfit number 1798 called Rainbow Wraps sold in 1970 came with a dress made of satin in blue, green, orange, and pink geometric print. This dress with a green velour top came with a satin print shawl with melon colored fringe. A pink petticoat and blue shoes completed the set.

In 1971, Golfing Greats number 3413 was a yellow bodysuit with a multi-colored plaid skirt in a wrap design. A plaid hat to match, aqua knee socks, and aqua shoes were accompanied by, yes, a golf bag with two clubs and two balls. Those tiny plaid prints were very hard for Mattel to find and had to be special woven just for use as Barbie doll clothes.

Remember Cher and her fur vests? Wild Things number 3439 was another 1971 fashion. It came with a green nylon bodysuit and white fake fur vest with flower trim. A blue vinyl belt and ankle high blue boots were Barbie's finishing touches.

Design in the 1980's reached record breaking proportions. With dolls such as Rocker Barbie and her friends, Western Barbie, Dream Glow Barbie, and many others over the years Mattel made sets of additional outfits sold separately for each of these dolls. Usually, there are approximately six separately sold outfits to be used with each specially dressed doll. For collectors this amounts to a large number of outfits each year to buy.

For example, My First Barbie doll has some very simply designed clothing made each year for the very young doll enthusiast. Approximately six in number, they are made so that they can be easily pulled on and off the doll. Dolls like Dream Glow Barbie from 1985 came with outfits in a variety of colors all designed to glow in the dark. That same year a series of outfits for Astronaut Barbie came reflecting a space age theme. There were five in this series designed for Mattel by Carol Spencer. Perfume Pretty Barbie doll in 1987 came with a collection of outfits which were scented. California Dream Barbie doll from 1987 was sold with a collection of outfits suited for the beach. With the large collection of theme directed dolls released each year many outfits are required. This calls for a large staff at Mattel to produce the doll designs as well as the necessary garments.

Designer outfits were made in the early 80's beginning with only a few each year. These quickly caught on with collectors and children alike and now each year from four to six are produced in exclusively designed boxes. Boxed outfits are a plus item and several varieties of outfits come sold in boxed packaging. These vary in cost from $7.00 to $9.99 each. Mattel has attempted to keep their outfits under ten dollars each. Most companies know what parents are willing to spend on toys for children each year. Knowing about cost concerns, Mattel stays within a budget.

In the early 60's Mattel went on recruiting drives like the aerospace industry to locate exceptional talent for their design staff. They were canvasing the country to locate engineers who would be well qualified to design toys for Mattel. In November, 1962 Carol Spencer answered an advertisement in one of the recruiting drives. She did not hear from them. She was anxious to relocate away from the ice and snow of the upper Midwest to the sunny climate of California. She was a designer of teenage sportswear who had fallen in love with California. With her lease up in Milwaukee she packed and moved to Los Angeles. She again began searching for employment in the Los Angeles area. In the process of considering several options, a friend suggested that she again apply at Mattel. Mattel had begun running the recruitment advertisements again. She sent Mattel a telegram and they immediately responded by making an appointment to talk with Carol for Friday morning at 11 a.m. That same week by mail she received a note to contact Operator 25 in Wisconsin. When she called she found the application she had sent from Wisconsin was not lost. They too wanted to see her, in Chicago, Illinois, on Friday morning at 11 a.m. In

Los Angeles, Carol accepted an offer and joined the staff of Mattel to assist in designing the new Barbie doll and her wardrobe. Carol was delighted and decided to give it a six months try. She joined the staff of Charlotte Johnson in the design department on April 29, 1963. She felt if she did not like the job she could always do something else. Those six months have long since passed and Carol Spencer has remained with Mattel's design staff as a steady inspiration. She says it has been, "an exciting experience which I do not regret."

Charlotte Johnson was manager for the department where Carol designed fashions and accessories. Carol was one of eleven people in Charlotte's department. She joined designers Dorothy Schue, Aileen Zublin, Kay Carter, and several sample makers and assistants.

Carol came to Mattel with both experience and education. After receiving a Bachelor of Fine Arts Degree from Minneapolis College of Art and Design,

Travel costumes were marketed in 1964 beginning with Barbie in Japan. With the student exchange program, Barbie too, enjoyed traveling.

she worked in infant and children's wear, ladies lingerie, junior sportswear, and was guest fashion editor for Mademoiselle Magazine.

During the years Carol worked with Charlotte, names were given to each outfit. Each designer prepared a list of possible names for her designs. Charlotte submitted the ones she liked to the copywriter who went through the formal process of obtaining rights to use the names. Unfortunately, this practice of naming outfits, says Carol Spencer, ceased in 1973.

The effort was made to make toys that were safe for children and that parents would be happy with. Fad designs were considered taboo at Mattel because fads are short lived. Style survives much longer.

Carol has been responsible for the simplistic fashions for My First Barbie and the more complicated and sophisticated designer original fashions.

Carol Spencer's credits from the 1960's include her first assignment, designing the Sew Free fashions which were outfits a child could make for her doll without sewing. Glue strips in the seams held the garments together. Other designs by Ms. Spencer were the number 1609 Black Magic, number 1639 Holiday Dance, number 1666 Debutante Ball, number 1655 Underfashions, and number 1685 Underprints. The two latter designs were results of her past experience in designing women's lingerie. When the mod era arrived she dressed Barbie in number 1823 Jump Into Lace, number 1844 Extravaganza, and number 1799 Maxi and Mini among many others. She even designed the bulk of the Sears and Montgomery Wards exclusive releases. Tutti and Todd outfits are to the credit of Ms. Spencer, as are Liddle Kiddles. Some of the Spencer creations were only seen in pictures such as

Although Ken did not travel to Japan, he too traveled to Mexico, in Barbie and Ken in Mexico. Each outfit was sold separately in 1964.

The Alps were a second home to Barbie and Ken in Switzerland. Note Ken has his pipe and beer stein.

Becky from the *Collectors Encyclopedia of Barbie Dolls and Collectibles* by Sibyl DeWein and Joan Ashabraner on page 222. This doll is also seen in chapter eight of this publication. This doll was seen in 1971 on the back of Francie outfit packages.

Work for Carol at Mattel has also required some travel overseas. In 1986, when Mattel entered a joint venture with Ma-Ba, Carol traveled to Japan to oversee the design of the Ma-Ba dolls. In 1988, Carol was transferred to Hong Kong to direct the design of fashions sold through the Arco Toys division of Mattel.

Mattel gave honor and credit to Carol Spencer's work in 1992 with the introduction of the first in the Classics Collection called Benefit Ball Barbie doll. Along with this doll Carol also designed two special outfits. These outfits are called Fifth Avenue Style and Hollywood Premiere. Fifth Avenue Style is a silver metallic mini dress with a ruffled white and silver coat lined in pink. Rhinestone pantyhose, a purse, and shoes accompany this outfit. Hollywood Premiere is a pink suede-look skirt and jacket worn with a black bodysuit. Pink pantyhose and matching boots make this outfit appear to have stepped out of the space age. Both special issue fashions come with zippered closures like outfits from 1959 through the mid 1960's.

Outfits from the late 50's and early 60's had real snaps and zippers. In an effort to make fashions easier for little hands to fasten, Mattel changed to velcro closures according to Carol Spencer.

Working for Mattel has been a fulfilling experience for Carol Spencer. When designing the clothes for the Color Magic Barbie doll she worked with a textile expert testing many fabrics. She says it was alot of fun working with so many types of fabrics. She even recalls making silkscreen and applying designs directly onto fabrics through this medium. Back in the early years she says, "we did not have all the right fabrics and trying to find the right quality, we did not have the right finishes. The things we can do today are amazing with the fabrics that will accept all this. We just did not have all of the technology that exists today."

Carol confides that her favorite fashion era was the Mod styles of which she says, "we got to try all these fun styles, like miniskirts, transparent coats, and weird shapes."

A step to make dressing Barbie dolls easier was taken in 1962 with an invention by Bill Robb for Mattel. A clear coating that when dry, left a slick finish on the body, was applied to the dolls. This made clothing slide over doll arms and legs much easier.

The veil of secrecy that cloaks the world of industry and fashion also extends to toys and, of course, Barbie and her ensembles. Work on the fashions for a doll are a top secret venture which is

The sound of wooden shoes on cobblestone streets rang in Barbie and Ken In Holland. These outfits were sold separately.

protected from the competition. Industrial espionage is still a cloak and dagger business even in the toy business.

Although an abundance of garments have been made over three decades for Barbie, only a small number can be mentioned here as examples. *Barbie Fashions Volume I* featuring the years 1959 through 1967 by Sarah Sink Eames, shows full color photographs with written descriptions of each garment. The book is a complete listing of all fashions made during those years.

Fashions make more to collecting than accumulating dolls. As a colorful addition, the fashions have gathered a following of collectors who are as interested in locating them as in locating the dolls. Over the years, trends change and styles may vary but fashions add spice to a popular hobby.

In the spring a young student is ready for vacation. Barbie and Ken spent their spring vacation as Barbie and Ken In Hawaii.

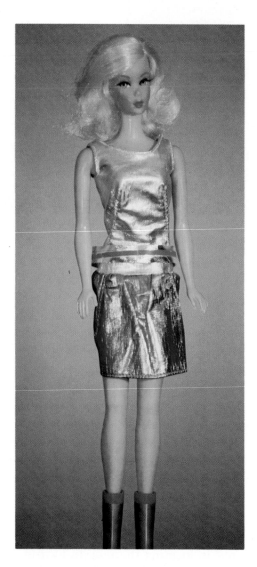

Zokko was a popular fashion in the late 60's. A Twist 'N Turn Barbie models the 1968 outfit.

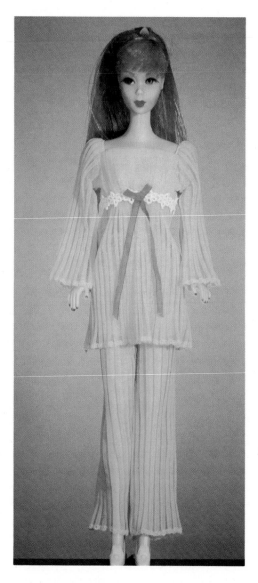

A rare 1967 redhead Twist 'N Turn Barbie models Lemon Kick from 1970.

Chapter 6

Barbie Footwear

Who has more shoes than any individual on the planet? Forget Imelda Marcos! We are talking about a true shoe fetish here. Barbie doll stands alone in the number and varieties of footwear. With most of those Barbie outfits came matching shoes. Among those outfits there were seventeen that were sold with what collectors call the number one shoes. These shoes were designed as high heeled slingbacks for the dainty doll feet. In a rainbow of colors to match the particular outfit that they were sold with, these shoes had one differing mark – a hole. This hole was found in the sole of the shoe at the ball of the foot and was designed to accommodate the number one doll stand. The holes in each shoe were exactly positioned so as to fit at the hole location on the bottom of the dolls' foot. The holes in both the doll's feet and shoes made it possible for the doll to be displayed on the stand with all those glamorous costumes and shoes.

By the second issue doll, the stands were redesigned and dolls no longer had holes in their feet. The shoes also sold this second year were minus the holes. However, these shoes with the holes are highest priced to replace when found on the collectors market. They are rare and not easily located. Being sold for only a part of one year, there were many more shoes made without the holes.

Mattel sold shoe packs in a rainbow of colors separately. Other accessory packs came with purses, gloves, and extra shoes.

The Shoe Wardrobe was sold as number 1833 between 1964 and 1965. This packaged set featured thirteen pairs of shoes in varying styles and colors. Another packaged set called Costume Completers sold at this same time, contained long gloves, short gloves, two pair of shoes, and two purses all in white and black.

Mattel recognized the fact that the first items lost from any outfit were most often the shoes. For those people trying to find shoes to put an outfit

A view of a first wave Barbie's feet shows the holes with copper tubes for the two pronged stand. Shoes came with holes in the soles for the first wave outfits.

Shoes for the first wave Barbie. Note the holes in the soles to allow for the doll stand.

"Let me show you something in a Reebok," says a 1991 All American Barbie to a first wave Barbie from 1959. All American Barbie was sold with two pairs of Reeboks just her size.

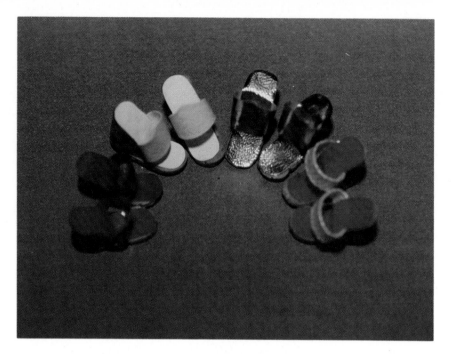

Treasured by collectors are these examples of cork wedgies which accompanied some of the 900 series outfits.

popular costuming in the late 60's and early 70's. Shorter boots such as those with Zokko were seen. Zokko came with grey plastic low top boots just right for the fashionable girl of that year.

Other shoes seen in those early years were ballet shoes found in 989 Ballerina. Other years featured a ballerina outfit and shoes to accompany. Various designs of ballet shoes were used over the years. Some of these ballet shoes came with attached ribbons to tie on the doll while others were a slip-on style. Even a pair of terry cloth slides were found in 988 Singing In The Shower. Several mediums were used in making footwear for America's favorite teen doll: cloth, plastic, and lamb. In the mid 80's a night gown was even sold with fuzzy slippers.

Barbie was truly a fashion plate all the way down to her shoe apparel. Mattel was very detailed with each outfit and made the appropriate footwear to match whatever doll was being featured. The outfit Icebreaker has a pair of ice skates to match. This wintertime ensemble was a popular item in those early years. No sport was beyond this doll's realm. In 948 Ski Queen, Barbie could sail down the snowy slopes of any child's imagination.

Shoe styles of the featured period have had a strong influence on the type used with outfits. However, in travel costumes sold during 1964 Barbie had some unusual styles of footwear. In 0821 Barbie In Japan, the dress was a Japanese kimono. Shoes with this were socks which had been attached to tiny golden thongs. These footwear items have had difficulty surviving over the years. The thongs were very fragile. Another travel costume was Barbie In Holland number 0823. This featured tiny wooden shoes. Although they look wooden, the shoes were really molded plastic.

back to mint and complete is a challenge. Some garments like number 951 Senior Prom, have a pair of green shoes with tiny inset pearls. This was the only outfit with this style shoe. Those outfits sold with basic black or white shoes are easily replaced. Cork wedgies are difficult to locate in the right color. Several outfits came with cork wedgies, however, they were all of different colors. Cork wedgies are something many collectors admire and wish were still sold with outfits. They were a detailed shoe and prone to be expensive to manufacture.

Other unique shoes were black mules with gold and black pompoms sold with number 944 Masquerade. Number 965 Night Negligee and the 973 Sweet Dreams were sold with matching mules which also had pompom decorations. Tennis shoes came with Tennis Anyone and with other Barbie doll outfits in the early 60's. Those tennis shoes were a molded plastic shoe which fit neatly over the doll's high heeled foot. It completely covered the foot to hide the fact her feet were really designed for high heels. There were specially designed shoes for the Little Theatre costumes such as Arabian Nights which had gold lamb slippers and Cinderella which came with glass slippers. Those glass slippers were really a clear molded plastic with glitter flecks throughout. Guinevere's costume also had blue and red stitched cloth slippers.

A large variety of boots has emerged over the years with the outfits designed by Charlotte Johnson and others after she retired. Boots were a

Early 900 series mules that accompanied Barbie doll outfits.

44

Malibu dolls sold in the 70's and early 80's were some of the small number of Barbie dolls which came packaged without shoes. Most dolls came with a small plastic bag in the box which included a comb, brush, and shoes. More recent dolls sold with bathing suits in the tradition of the Malibu Barbies still come minus shoes. Also sold without shoes are the Fun To Dress dolls who come dressed in undergarments.

Recent years have brought other unique shoes into the world of Barbie doll. Those wonderful International Series dolls came with shoes not sold in package sets or with other style dolls or outfits. Some of these shoes featured straps across the foot while others were simply fabric like the shoes sold with Eskimo Barbie in 1979 and again in 1991. Cowgirl boots were sold with Horse Lovin' Barbie and Western Barbie sold in 1982 and 1980 respectively. Another more recent design was in 1985 with the first issue Rocker Barbie doll. High heeled white closed toe shoes were sold with the doll along with a lamb sleeve which slipped up the foot and leg creating a boot type apparel. This was a type of high heeled boot. The 1985 Astronaut Barbies came with super high top boots to send them into the space age spirit. These silver grey boots were very form fitting and nearly impossible to put on the doll's foot, but when worn they were very striking. Six outfits were also sold separately for this particular astronaut doll. They each came with unusual footwear to make this doll a fashionable space explorer.

Another low top boot came packaged with Animal Lovin' Barbie in 1988. This boot was similar to the boot sold in Zokko from 1967. These boots packaged in Animal Lovin' were a molded pink plastic and made Barbie well outfitted to be a jungle explorer or zoo keeper.

As a sports enthusiast, Barbie even went skin diving in 1964 and a part of this outfit was a pair of green plastic swim fins. This has not changed over the years as even today similar ensembles are sold with colorful plastic swim fins for the Barbie dolls of the 90's.

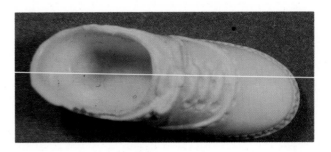

Tennis shoes were seen in outfits such as Tennis Anyone and Cheerleader. Cheerleader tennis shoes were sold in red.

The first ballerina outfit sold was called Ballerina and came with slippers that tied.

Ski boots were a part of Ski Queen sold in 1963 and 1964.

Other mules from 900 series outfits. Lingerie came with shoes that had cotton pompoms as decorations.

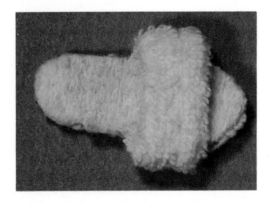

Barbie shoes varied as with this slipper that came with Singing In The Shower.

Footwear is important to the collector as well as the child who plays with the dolls. A 1988 Mattel release called Barbie Step 'N Style Boutique number 2769 was a shoe store for the little doll who loved to shop. This boutique came without dolls, but was filled with thirty pieces for shopping delight. Included in the box were shoes in an array of colors, hats, scarves, purses, three stack shelves to display the merchandise, cash register, two seat bench, and foot rest. Even the shoe sizer, credit card for the shoppers of the 90's, and punch out money were included. Barbie doll and her many friends could shop for any accessory to make their fashions complete. All shoes included in this shop were Mattel made and sized just right for Barbie and her friends tiny feet. Nothing too large or too small would be found in this shop.

In the doll world this fact stands out, even small things mean a lot.

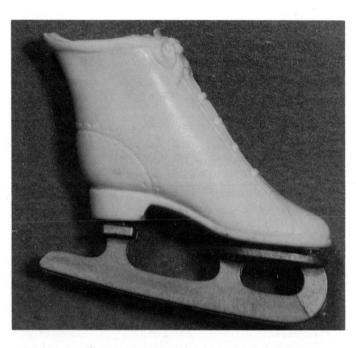

White skates with silver blades were a part of Icebreaker sold in 1962, 1963, and 1964. The fine detailing is what kept Barbie a step ahead of her competition.

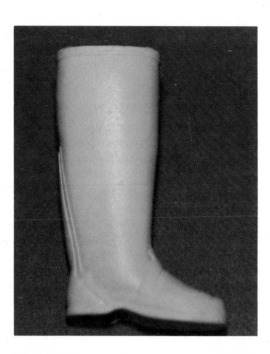

Boots came with Rain Coat sold in 1963. The boots were molded rubber and remain soft even today.

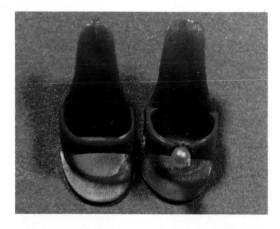

Green mules came with only two 900 series outfits. Plain green mules were with Theatre Date. Green mules with a single pearl were with Senior Prom.

SHOES WITH HOLES IN THE SOLES

Colors	Outfit Numbers
Black	917, 971, 976
Brown	911, 915, 961
White	912, 962, 969, 972
* Navy	968, 918
* Purple	916
Pink	966
* Midnight blue	964
Pink w/pompoms	965
Light blue w/pompoms	973
* These shoes look black.	

900 SERIES FOOTWEAR

Colors	Outfit Numbers
Black	917, 918, 968, 971, 976, 934, 955, 977, 978, 979, 982, 984, 954, 923*
Brown	911, 915, 961, 937, 992
Navy	916, 981
White	912, 962, 969, 972, 947, 923*, 986, 987, 991, 931, 956
Red	939
Pink	966, 993, 923*
Blue	957
Green	959
Light blue with pompoms	973
Black with yellow pompoms	944
Green with pearls	951
Pink with pink pompoms	965
Dark blue	964
Red tennis shoes	0876
White boots	0875
Cork wedgies	963, 967, 975, 985, 940, 946
Clear with gold glitter	983, 958
Terrycloth slippers	988
White ballet	989
White tennis shoes	941, 0889
White skates	942

White hightops boots	949
Black Ski Boots	948
* Denotes an accessory set.	

1600 SERIES FOOTWEAR

Colors	Outfit Numbers
White mules	1604, 1606, 1646
Pink with silver glitter	1611, 1676
Mustard mules	1610
Green mules	1612
Clear with silver glitter	1632
Red mules	1614, 1616, 1667
Brown mules	1615
Blue mules	1617
Green closed toe pumps	1620, 1625, 1643
Red closed toe pumps	1621, 1622, 1631, 1640, 1663, 1664,
Pink flats	1623
Red tennis shoes	1624
White closed toe pumps	1626, 1627, 1639, 1644, 1649, 1653, 1661, 1675, 1665
Orange closed toe pumps	1628
White ice skates	1629
Fuchsia closed toe pumps	1633
Light blue closed toe pumps	1634
Aqua closed toe pumps	1635, 1672
Light blue with pompoms	1636
White tennis shoes	1637
Fuchsia mules	1638
Pink with blue pompoms	1642, 1674
Clear with gold glitter	1645, 1660, 1666
Brown closed toe pumps	1647
Aqua flats	1648, 1671
Brown zip boots	1641
Black closed toe pumps	1652, 1678
Light blue closed toe pumps	1654
Pink closed toe pumps	1656
Rose closed toe pumps	1658
Brown high boots	1668
White with melon pompoms	1669

Chapter 7

The Hair Has It

Hair for the first Barbie was designed in a ponytail with curls and overwrap. Curly bangs also accented the face. The first design was fashioned for Mattel by Larry Gemaine from Universal Studios.

During Barbie doll's earliest beginnings styling doll hair was an art beyond the Mattel staff's expertise. They called on people beyond their staff to create the proper coiffure. In 1956 the Handlers sought the talents of Larry Germaine from Universal Studios to design a style for their new doll. Mr. Germaine styled the hair of many Hollywood stars so why not the star of America's doll world. Germaine was asked to design a hair style for the Barbie doll which would be fashionable with both formal wear and sports attire. His creation was the ponytail with top wrap and short curly bangs. Later styling was created by Charlotte Johnson and Ella Waltz Brown as Barbie continued into the ponytail and bubblecut era. No specific doll hair styling department existed at Mattel for those first years. For two years the personnel staff searched for the perfect person to establish such a department for Mattel.

Jean Ann Burger tells of the times working as a beauty stylist when she kept feeling, "somewhere out there is a job looking for me." Answering an advertisement in the *Los Angeles Times*, Ms. Burger interviewed for the job as stylist for Barbie doll at Mattel. She says she felt from the beginning that the job was her's. Her new career of creating superior crowning glories for the Barbie doll began on January 28, 1963. The first few days on the job proved she had the "right stuff." Ms. Burger was asked to create a new hair style like the ponytail but

with an air of elegance. Displaying her dexterity and imagination she fashioned the swirl ponytail in only ten minutes. It was marketed in 1964.

Jean found that Barbie was a wonderful customer with which to work. She neither complained if the rollers and pins were too tight nor did she move the wrong way. In fact, Barbie cooperated in everyway.

In 1961 Barbie doll was sold with a new shorter hair style in a bubblecut.

Mrs. Handler recalls those years with Jean Ann Burger fondly: "Ms. Burger was a very talented person."

It was a challenge establishing a new department at this major toy company. Jean had to teach herself how to root doll hair. With Barbie, different styles of hair requires that rooting patterns be performed differently. The scalp holes placement is different for each style. Imagine the child's surprise when they took down the hair of a swirl ponytail doll and found that it was only rooted around the edges of the scalp. The doll was totally bald on top. This was done to make styling the hair simpler to accomplish.

She gave the Mattel staff at least four to six hair designs to choose from for each of their new lines of dolls. Because she lined these doll heads up on a shelf over her work area, Mattel officials referred to this as "Jean's chorus line." Each newly designed outfit required new hair styles. These were used in both the Mattel catalogs and television advertisements.

Ms. Burger's routine was to design hair styles and Mattel would select the one they wanted. She then took pictures of the hair style and wrote out rooting and grooming instructions, giving the exact tolerance levels. This meant she gave the factory the amount of stitches per inch required to produce this style. Shipment to the factory included two heads of the same style, one for them to keep as a control model and one to use for a daily production comparison. They also received the pictures of the hair style and the written rooting and grooming instructions in one package. This format would be the same with any new hair style. Time studies were run on each step and listed on the sheet of instructions. Every detail of hair grooming and rooting were seen to by Ms. Burger. Instructions were given as to hair length, however, tolerance levels were flexible and because of this some dolls have been found with short tresses and others with extremely long. This is especially true with the number three dolls marketed in 1960. They have been found with ponytails that reach almost to their waist and others shoulder length. Bubblecut dolls also came with shorter bubbles as well as longer fluffier versions. Even versions with a part on the side have been found in the bubblecut and bendable leg dolls.

Bendable leg dolls were made with the new pageboy hair style which was fashionable in 1965. Styled by Jean Burger, this came with a part down the center of the doll's head. The pageboy came with a longer fluffier version and curls that curved up around the face. A shorter version made with hair that hung straight with fewer strands was also seen.

Ms. Burger recalls that the 1965 center part hair style sold on the bendable leg Barbie doll was the easiest to design. The type of bendable leg doll that attracts the most excitement is the one with the sidepart hair style. A few dolls with more densely rooted hair that curls and turns out all around the head, have been found both in the United States and Japan. The center part bendable leg dolls were designed by Jean Burger as were the sidepart hair style dolls. It required much more time to root this glamorous style. Designed to accent the elegant ballgowns which Mattel marketed for Barbie doll in the mid 60's, the dolls with this hair style were made in much smaller numbers. Some were marketed in blonde and brunette. About three or four titian haired dolls were made. These were designed for the photography staff at Mattel to be used in television and catalog advertising only. Many collectors to date doubt the existence of the redhead sidepart dolls, but in the 1966 Mattel catalog pictured on plate 21 is a titian sidepart Barbie doll modeling number 1639 Holiday Dance.

Even at best, sidepart bendable leg Barbie dolls are in limited supply. Doll dealers such as Marl Davidson of Bradenton, Florida, sees only one or two a year. Joe Blitman, a dealer in Los Angeles, California, has found only one in his many years of dealing.

Other rare exceptions to the standard hair rule is a bubblecut rooted in a sidepart style. This head was rooted with every intention of making a part down the side of her bubblecut. Regular bubblecut styles were rooted in a swirl around the top of the crown leaving no appearance of a part. Heads with the sidepart style are extremely rare and as Mellie Phillips, presently head of the hair styling department says, the sidepart of any style is designed as a glamorous accent for gowns. Because of the time and cost of manufacturing any sidepart style their use is limited. This might mean a limited edition doll.

Designed for Mattel in 1963 by Jean Ann Burger the swirl ponytail was sold in 1964.

Another design by Jean Ann Burger was the style on the bendable leg Barbie doll sold in 1965. This style is called the American Girl hair style by collectors.

Bendable leg Barbie was sold with two styles of hair in 1966. Extremely rare, the sidepart hair style was designed to contrast with elegant evening gowns which were marketed by Mattel for Barbie that year.

A variation to the sidepart is the sidepart bubblecut Barbie sold with bendable legs shown here in her original box. Photo courtesy of Glenn Mandeville.

Three basic colors of blonde, brunette, and redhead did not remain so basic. By 1964 the main colors varied almost as much as the hair on those children who bought the doll. Blonde was no longer just blonde but there were reddish blondes, ash blondes, honey blondes, platinum blondes, and several shades in between. Colors of brunette ran the same variation. Some were black, others more brown. Redhead dolls came in a variety of strawberry and even a Lucille Ball red that was a real eyecatcher. By the time of the Twist 'N Turn Barbie doll, hair colors had taken names such as chocolate bon-bon, go go co-co, sun kissed, and summer sand. Some of these names resembled flavors in an ice cream shop more than a hair color.

The 1967 redhead Twist 'N Turn Barbie is a lady who has raised many questions. According to the Mattel catalog for that year, only two shades of brown and two shades of blonde were made. But a rare redhead is sometimes seen. The question of whether this is an oxidization problem with some of the brown hair colors was presented to Ms. Burger. "Certainly not," she says, "this was more likely a case where the company who did their rooting for the doll ran out of the hair colors in a 50,000 head order and just made some to complete the order in the titian color from older hair stock supplies." Ms. Burger says, "occasionally this did happen and Mattel did not hear about it until people in the stores would call saying they had a bright redhead Barbie and this was not what the store ordered." As previously stated, Mattel would not allow anything to go to waste and if a different hair color was needed to complete an order, it was substituted.

Twist 'N Turn Barbie doll was sold in 1967 and listed in the Mattel catalog with two shades of blonde and two shades of brunette hair. However, shown here is a rare titian haired 1967 Twist 'N Turn Barbie doll.

The wonders of Mattel's imagination can be seen in the array of changes Barbie doll went through each year. Just when you think engineering is the only requirement to toy making along comes new needs requiring chemistry.

In 1962, a resident chemical engineer was needed to create new fun playtime creations for Barbie doll. Ralph Dunn joined Mattel's staff on March 26, 1962, to produce some interesting toy designs. Mr. Dunn says they were thinking of making a Barbie doll on which children could use dyes to color the hair. He says, "it occurred to me that there was no way you could give a child something to dye hair with without them dyeing everything else." Mattel was also trying to avoid using anything which could be toxic. He remembered his days in school at Berkley they had a large chart of pH indicators hanging on a wall. "It was so amazing to change the chemical nature of something by adding a little base or a little acid which would make the item change colors. There was something magical about that as I used to gaze at the chart," he recalls. Dunn suggested the pH indicator possibilities to his supervisors who immediately liked the idea. Along with John Jones, who worked out a method to get the indicator to stick to the hair fiber, they proceeded with the project. It was a difficult process because the indicators are not normally used as fabric dyes. He tells that they began using methyl red which turned to yellow and then alizarin was used to change from yellow to purple. Constantly on the lookout for new dyes, Mr. Dunn says they put a blue dye into the hair shaft with the yellow and hair would change from green to purple. "Those first experiments," he says. "did bleed alot and by todays standards they would not be acceptable in terms of toxicity." But as Wanda Clearwater, a former chemical engineer for Mattel mentioned, "once the methyl red is in the hair shaft, its toxic qualities are masked."

These experiments yielded a unique hair play innovation in 1965 with the introduction of the "NEW" Barbie Color 'N Curl Set in the Mattel catalog. This toy set came with two doll heads, one Barbie and one Midge from the Fashion Queen and Molded Midge molds. Designed so they could be placed on any existing doll the children had, this set also included four wigs, rollers and curlers, comb, brush, hair dryer, hair pins, hair spray, clear activator solution, and instruction booklet. This was hair play at its finest. When the wigs were treated with a clear acidic solution of vinegar and water they would change from gold to lilac, redhead to brownie, topaz to brunette, and flame to carrot top. Another bottle of a clear saline base would return the wigs to their original colors. As advertised, these products were perfectly safe with no mess since they did not include any dyes. The contents of the bottles were biologically safe for children even if they did swallow or ingest them. Hair play could go on for hours because with the curlers and pins little hands could style and restyle doll hair at will. The hair dryer operated off two "D" batteries removing the danger of using electricity during playtime.

The next year Mr. Dunn and others began work with dyes which could also stick to cotton or rayon fabric fibers. Powder methyl red was made by only one company in the United States and Mattel purchased all they had in stock. They soon needed more and found only one additional company in England who produced this chemical. Again, Mattel purchased all that was available. "At one time," Mr. Dunn states, "Mattel had bought the entire supply of methyl red in the free world." Mattel employees wore oxygen masks while working with the fine powder chemical. The chemicals used in this doll production are considered a carcinogen by today's health standards, but in the 60's were considered perfectly safe.

A full two years went into the research to develop the doll called Color Magic Barbie. Color Magic Barbie came in blonde which changed to scarlet flame and midnight which changed to ruby red. Here too the dolls came with two bottles of changing solutions. The acidic solution was a mixture of vinegar and water and the saline solution combined washing soda and water. The instruction booklet which accompanied this doll also included directions for making additional amounts of the changing solution if the child should happen to run out. The hair was not all that changed color with the doll. She was wearing a swimsuit with a diamond print. The same solution could be wiped on the suit with an applicator and the diamonds on the suit changed

colors. A series of outfits were sold separately featuring color changing abilities.

The packaging for Color Magic Barbie was different. It was a rigid box with a clear plastic front and sides. After the doll was removed this box could be used as a standing closet for the doll's many outfits. A patent for the Color Magic process is held by Mattel.

Hair play was always a big issue with Barbie doll. Steve Lewis of Mattel's preliminary design department asked for a doll with an easier curling method. The first idea presented by other employees was to have the child wet the doll hair with water and use a plaster or plastic mold to fit down over the doll head to press the hair into a style. Product development felt this was much too messy. While working at an electronics firm, prior to his days at Mattel, Ralph Dunn remembered seeing a coil of very fine wire laying on his work area. It had been cross cut and together it was almost like hair. "When you pushed them they stayed where you had put them. It had a strange feel to it." Dunn had an idea to use this wire system in doll hair for an instant styling. He went to the Mattel electronics lab for a fine wire. He then presented the wire to Jean Ann Burger and asked her to root the wire in a doll head. Ms. Burger recalls sending him to her assistant Mellie Phillips who rooted a doll head with this tiny wire. Ms. Burger says, "the doll head came out looking more like Medusa."

Steve Lewis liked the idea and sent Dunn back to Mellie with orders to root a yarn of hair and wire

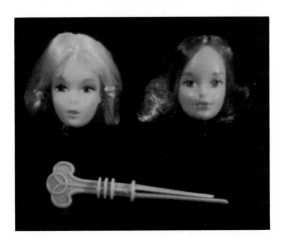

Ralph Dunn created a hair style for Barbie called Quick Curl with wire rooted into the doll's head along with a yarn of hair. These doll heads are prototypes of the Quick Curl Barbie and Kelly sold in 1973 by Mattel. They have never been on a body. Photograph courtesy of Ralph Dunn and Gerry Leistikow.

Quick Curl hair was again sold in 1981 with Golden Dreams Barbie. Although the U.S. versions came with Quick Curl hair those found in Europe did not.

Showing that Quick Curl hair could create some unique styles, Golden Dreams Barbie was also sold with a hair design collectors call the "monster hair style."

issued with short hair. The bubblecut Barbie was issued the most with such short hair.

Barbie hair has not always been rooted. Wigs were popular for women in the mid 60's. A doll called Fashion Queen Barbie was sold in 1963 with wigs. The doll hair was painted on and wigs fit down over the head. Fashion Queen had wigs that were brunette, blonde, and titian. These came on a white wig stand. Mattel was not finished with the wig concept. Miss Barbie was the doll of 1964 and she too had three wigs. This bendable leg Barbie also had painted hair which the wigs neatly fit over. (Miss Barbie is more famous, however, for her sleep eyes which were designed by Dick May.) Each of these wigs were styled differently and made these two dolls three in one. It depended on the mood of the child as to which hair color her Barbie doll had.

It would seem that Mattel only missed finding a way for Barbie's hair to grow. Not so! In 1971 Growin' Pretty Hair Barbie was sold with hair that really grew. This unique feature was a hole in the top of her head with a hair piece inserted in that spot. This hair piece could be pushed in or pulled out at will. This innovation was also designed by Dick May.

Jean Ann Burger looks with pride at her contribution of the Hair Fair Set and the many hundreds of styles she designed for Mattel between 1963 and 1974. Her last design for Barbie which she describes as her "crowning glory" was a large doll head on a stand, called Barbie Beauty Center which made hair styling and make-up fun and easy for little girls. A doll head of this type is still sold today. Included in this toy were bobby pins, rubberbands, barrettes, ribbons, brush, comb, and rollers. Other items such as stick on eyelashes, wash away blushers, lip gloss, and eyeshadow were also included.

The 80's brought a new hair fiber called kaneklon to replace the old saran hair. A new innovation of hair with two colors appeared on the doll. Women during the this period wore their hair frosted. This process bleached or colored sections of darker hair. Barbie dolls such as Golden Dreams Barbie had hair frosted with two colors, blonde and golden. Golden Dreams Barbie opened the 1980's with this new feature. By 1983 Sun Gold Barbie also had this style of hair coloring as did Wet 'N Wild Barbie in 1989. Another doll called Beach Blast Barbie in 1989 had hair which when placed in direct sunlight turned pink. Needless to say, Mattel has not always just varied the styles or the color of hair but has found new ways to present the hair as the most fascinating feature of their doll.

The 90's have brought more creativity to the hair on Barbie doll. A department store special in 1992 for F.A.O. Schwarz called Madison Avenue Barbie featured platinum blonde tresses styled in an Ivana

together into the doll head. One wire and one hair was rooted together. With the completed head Mellie used a wooden dowel to roll a curl which would stay. They found the hair and wire held together very well and made a nice curl. "At that time," says Dunn, "the wire was already available in colors which made it even more desirable." Colored wire could make redhead and brunette dolls available. A blonde color had to be special made for Mattel. This wire and hair rooting system became Quick Curl Barbie doll sold in 1973. Mattel Toys holds the patent on this invention. All new innovations for the doll had to be patented by the person who developed them. The patent such as Quick Curl Barbie is then assigned to a company, in this case, Mattel Toys.

After considerable surveying of young girls, Mattel found that the longer the hair the better they sold. Because of this not many dolls have been

Trump upsweep. Another first was in 1992 when the Barbie with the longest locks ever marketed, called Totally Hair Barbie, was sold in both blonde and brunette and as a black doll with long raven black tresses. The hair on this doll came down to her heels and was in a crimped wave the full length of the hair.

Mermaid Barbie doll of 1992 continued the color change concept but this time with a twist. Thermal sensitivity is the key to this innovation. Long blonde locks in cold water turned a rainbow of colors. In Mattel's television advertisement, a little girl is seen with an ice cube, running the ice down the hair fiber and showing the color changes happening. Another scene in the same commercial shows the doll being totally submerged in cold water and the hair as it fans up above the doll head turning a rainbow of colors.

The 90's have brought back the redhead Barbie dolls which had been missing from store shelves for ten years. Teen Talk Barbie came with a variety of longer hair styles as well as two eye colors.

Stylable doll hair was a wonderful invention. A child can play with numerous beauty shops that have been created to enhance the possibilities for styling and arranging and to stimulate the child's imagination. Give a child a comb, brush, and Barbie doll and they are content for hours. When it comes to the fascination for Barbie, the hair has it.

Streaks with more than one color hair was the style for this Sun Gold Malibu Barbie sold by Mattel in 1984.

Hair was always a marketing plus with Barbie and the longest hair sold on the doll was in 1992 with Totally Hair Barbie. The doll was sold in blonde, brunette, and black. The dress for the doll was designed for Mattel by Carol Spencer.

Chapter 8

What is a Prototype?

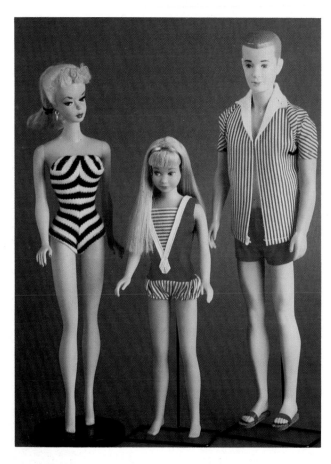

Prototype of a number one Barbie doll is shown here with prototypes Skipper and painted hair Ken. Notice the white head and right leg of the Ken doll. Vinyl used to make the prototype Ken was the same used on the first three issues of the Barbie doll. They also faded. Photography by Barry Sturgill, dolls from the collection of F. Glen Offield.

The value of any doll is governed by the quantity produced and by its desirability in the eye of the collectors. Whether an old or new design, the value index is respondent to the numbers produced. Barbie doll collecting is not immune to the law of supply and demand as these examples show. In the early 60's there were approximately 6,000,000 bubblecut Barbie dolls produced over a four year period. Because of this the prices on bubblecuts have remained reasonably low. The Miss Barbie of 1964 maintains a higher price on the secondary market. Because it was not one of Mattel's best sales, they discontinued production after only one year, limiting quantity. Now as collectors attempt to locate these scarce dolls the price continues to climb ever upward. Low sales, however, are not always the reason for a shorter manufacturing cycle. In

recent years dolls, such as the Pink Jubilee Thirtieth Anniversary Barbie were designed for the doll's big three-0 celebration. Mattel made only 1200 to present to those who attended a party held in 1989 at Lincoln Center, New York City. Yet another short run was the Canadian Thirtieth Anniversary Barbie of which only 500 were made. Both dolls are rare additions to any collection but none of the above truly shine as unique.

In recent years the revelation of a rarer Barbie and family dolls has caused a stirring among collectors. This truly unique Barbie is the prototype doll. These are dolls made by Mattel as a test model from which designs are later patterned. As Barbie doll production expanded and evolved, a great number of experimental prototypes were required. Some of these experiments were later mass produced yet others never were. What happened to these old prototypes is only now coming to light. The source of many of these older Barbie prototypes has been former Mattel employees who salvaged these experiments from the garbage dumps of extinction. California Barbie collectors such as F. Glen Offield have devoted considerable time to searching for and then purchasing these precious jewels as they are discovered. Glen Offield has spent the last five years studying the prototype style, which gained him the distinction of the foremost collector of Mattel prototypes. Glen's discoveries have expanded the insight into not only Barbie's production and development but also to her family and friends. Developmental dolls fall into three categories:

The difference between a prototype, mock-up, and a sample doll is very misunderstood. "The prototype is an original hand-made doll," says Jean Ann Burger. They are the dolls with a hand-made body, painted face, and personalized rooted hair. She has even worked with wax prototypes. The prototype is a doll created to see if it will sell well and if they want to manufacture it. They are to show what the doll will look like. Mock-ups are dolls that are made from the prototype, usually copies. Samples are dolls which are first wave runs of production that employees use in their work. Samples are used by the fashion design staff to assist in the design of new garments.

Unless a collector is certain of the past history of a particular doll and is sure it is a prototype, it is best to assume that it is not. In the days of the number one Barbie dolls many tests were made with various types of vinyl and plastic in the mold. Some number one prototypes are being found today made of a very hard brittle plastic. An unfortunate fall to the floor could cause them to crack or shatter instantly. Each test case was an effort to determine which vinyl would be the best and the most durable. Since these dolls were being produced as only a trial they were never marked on their back sides and nothing on the doll itself indicates these were from Mattel. Prototype experts like Offield can see that they are number one Barbies in a different type material. With the appearance of these dolls we find doll manufacturing becomes a science of repeated experiments until a marketable product is obtained. Remember, doll designers are industrial engineers for very good reason. Creating a doll such as Barbie is an engineering feat. To create a doll who is manufactured and accepted by the buying public for over thirty years is an accomplishment by Mattel surpassing other toy companies.

The artistic hand which applies the acrylic face paint to these dolls is as attentive to detail as any make-up artist, for Barbie emulates the fashion model image. As a one of a kind creation, these dolls have colors more vibrant than those found among the store bought variety. Like a fashion model, these dolls were also styled to model their one of a kind fashions. Dolls sold in stores were mass produced and less time could be allowed for each doll. These ladies and gentlemen are special creatures and individuals all their own.

Over years of Barbie doll collecting there have been many hair colors but the varieties did not appear until 1962. Mattel apparently was considering something different, such as a redhead, because a prototype of a reddish brown haired 1959 doll exists. Pictured in *The Wonder of Barbie* by Susan Manos, this lady wears a black and white jersey swimsuit like her sister dolls of that year. The legs on this beauty are a mismatched work. The right leg has the hole for fitting the number one stand inside, but the left leg is designed like the number two Barbie doll. No hole for a stand here. Face paint appears to be like that of the first Barbie doll sold in 1959. Stand her beside another 1959 doll and the hair color is far from similar. Brunette number one dolls had extremely dark brown locks, this lady was meant as a redhead.

In 1972 Montgomery Ward & Co., sold a reissue of an older style Barbie to celebrate their one hundredth anniversary. The pictured prototype is a black haired doll which was rooted but not painted. Without the face paint, detailing of the face mold is visible. Photography by Barry Sturgill, doll from the collection of F. Glen Offield.

A Montgomery Ward & Co. prototype doll from 1972 with rooted hair and face paint. Photography by Barry Sturgill, doll from the collection of F. Glen Offield.

Visions of how these dolls came to exist kindles the desire for a time machine. Mattel employees are sitting in their offices, boxes of heads, arms, legs, and bodies all around. At one desk a woman sits threading strands of hair through a machine into rooting holes in a dolls head. At another desk a lady paints features on a doll. With gentle strokes she paints on brows and heavily mascaraed eyes. Bright ruby lips make a colorful contrast against the pink tone vinyl body. If they want something different a change of hair rooting or a different paint color creates a prototype for a future design.

Mattel stores the prototype dolls in plain white boxes very similar to the ones in which the dolls originally came packaged. Those dolls with simple outfits are seen in smaller and narrower boxes, but those larger boxes are reserved for the formal outfitted dolls. On the ends of each box, usually hand written, is the name of the doll and the outfit in which she appears.

Some early number one through four dolls have been found in pink boxes. These boxes, marked with silhouette pictures similar to the familiar white ones, have been a great mystery. Many collectors choose to believe these dolls were prototype Barbies. Others felt they were designed to be given to store managers to encourage the sale of the doll. Yet others felt they were display material only. I presented this question to Ruth Handler during our interview and even she found them difficult to remember. Soon she did recall the situation after I described the boxes to her. She tells that the company hired to manufacture boxes for their new Barbie doll made both pink and white to let the Handlers decide which color would be aesthetically best. Mrs. Handler says they wanted Barbie to look her best and the final choice was for the white design. The company presented the white design with drawings of Barbie doll in an array of separately sold outfits. The pink box was covered with dolls in these outfits but done only in silhouette. The white box gave much more detail to the outfits which would serve as advertising Barbie doll's available clothing. As time for the 1959 International Toy Fair drew near the white boxes were not shipped to Mattel. With delivery late and the need to be ready approaching, those pink boxes were still in the office. The Mattel staff began putting Barbie dolls into the pink boxes. Mrs. Handler says even "some dolls arrived at the toy fair in hand glued white boxes. Samples of the white boxes were still in the office. As the final hours of the toy fair drew near these boxes were needed to insure the proper amount of dolls were presented at the fair. Collectors, somewhere out there are a few hand glued boxes containing number one Barbie dolls. These dolls went to the International Toy Fair in 1959 with the Handlers and their entourage. After the toy fair in 1959 those pink boxes came back to the Mattel office.

Prototypes of Skipper have been found. This never produced variation of the Twist 'N Turn Skipper models a prototype outfit. Photography by Barry Sturgill, doll from the collection of F. Glen Offield.

In the late 60's Stacey was sold by Mattel as a friend of Barbie. The marketed dolls came with long blonde or titian hair. A prototype Stacey is shown here with red bubblecut style hair. Photography by Barry Sturgill, doll from the collection of F. Glen Offield.

They still found a use for these by packaging dolls wearing outfits. These uniquely boxed dolls had the doll name and outfit she wore printed on the end flap. They were then sold to store owners to use for display purposes only. Catalogs with outfits available from Mattel also showed these dolls. These pink boxed dolls were considered samples in those early years. Upon the completion of the promotion of Barbie in 1959-60, the store managers sold these display models to the general public. Therefore, dressed numbers one through four are found in pink boxes. Barbie doll is not the only prototype dolls found, there were test copies of little sister Skipper made also.

Prototype Skippers are missing the familiar markings on the back side of the doll. Interestingly, these dolls have more rooted hair than the dolls which were sold. Larger groups of hair strands were placed into each scalp hole to give the doll a much fuller and fluffier head of hair. After all, this was a test case doll and possibly more care was put into making her. Leg molds must have been quite different on the prototype Skippers than those sold in stores. They all had a wider stance and the feet are not only larger and better sculpted but had a slightly higher incline in the top of the foot at the arch. Prototype Skipper dolls with never before seen hairstyles are now surfacing. Prototype dolls of friends of Barbie doll such as her boyfriend Ken have also been found.

Ken prototype dolls are very interesting. Shortly after release of that first Barbie doll, the planning stages for a friend for her began. Apparently, the old vinyl used for numbers one through three Barbie dolls was still present. Those early prototype Kens have limbs which are faded like those early Barbies. Ken's head and one of his legs have faded badly to an ivory white. His arms are faded in a splotchy pattern. Poor Ken appears to have gone through a long spell of sickness. The legs on these prototype Kens have more detail. The sharpness of the knee and calves are much more distinguishable than with later manufactured knobby knee dolls. Ridges and dimples in the calves and ankles stand out and are much more noticeable. His feet are 2.6 centimeters where the later marketed Ken's feet were 2.4 centimeters long. Possibly the reason these prototypes were made from the fadable vinyl was Mattel's way of using up this left over material. They had already found the early Barbies were fading and were producing the dolls with the new vinyl that did not loose its color. Arms and hands of this Ken are also different. Fingers are deeply grooved and lines in the palms of the hands are also pronounced. Even those lines inside the fingers to distinguish joints are very visible.

Ken like this has the marked torso of a flocked haired Ken and the legs of a knobby knee doll. Rather sickly in appearance, he too has the larger feet and detailed legs and arms.

Prototype Barbies run a wide gamut of experimental design. Bubblecut dolls have been found in hair colors not sold. Other dolls were painted with more of a smile than those later marketed. More recent Mattel prototypes have included hair color and style experiments. Can you imagine Barbie with yarn hair or how about pink or golden hair. One prototype Happy Holidays doll in 1988 was made with raven black hair. This was a show stopper! A Barbie with blue hair wore a blue dress to match and the doll with the pink hair, wore a pink dress. Does purple hair and a dress to match sound marketable? There was a prototype made but never sold.

Not all prototype items will be dolls. Mattel designed many outfits for their doll and among these were clothing that never were reproduced. These are also considered prototype items. Mrs. Handler tells us Charlotte Johnson made and

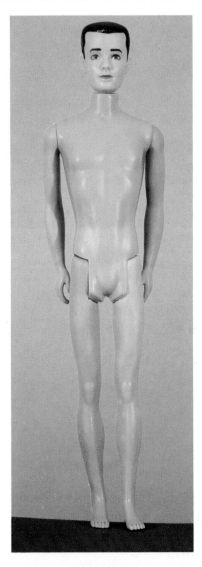

A closer look at a prototype Ken doll shows a white head and splotchy white right leg. The prototypes were hand made and therefore hands and feet are more detailed. The feet are also larger than the marketed dolls. The Ken doll pictured has a body of a flocked hair Ken but legs of the third wave Ken with knobby knees.

designed many more outfits than were sold. Similar items made and sold in the 60's were sewn by Mrs. Johnson out of various fabrics. Even different hat designs were created. Apparently, when the item was made a particular fabric was chosen that appealed more to Ruth Handler. She had the final say on all designs for Barbie. For example, a number 981 Busy Gal outfit has been found with a dotted

hat and a number 1647 Gold 'N Glamour was also made from plain brown cloth. The original outfit sold was a tweed material. Another find has been a white version of number 982 Solo In The Spotlight which appeared in the 1959 booklet. This outfit, when mass produced, was made in black. Some outfits made in the prototype stage were never manufactured, probably because of cost of production. In the early years, Mr. Offield tells us that Mattel attempted to keep the cost of each outfit down to 17 cents for the materials excluding labor, marketing, and packaging costs. This would insure the profit of the garment and still hold price down to within what people were willing to pay.

Some extremely glamorous gowns and outfits have been among the collections of former employees of Mattel. Mr. Offield says these rare outfits, many times, did not have labels but still a Mattel item is easily spotted.

Three prototype bubblecut Barbies from the version sold in 1961. Photography by Barry Sturgill, dolls from the collection of F. Glen Offield.

Charlotte Johnson and her staff designed many outfits that for one reason or another Mattel did not choose to market. She is wearing one of the outfits never produced for market. Photography by Barry Sturgill, doll from the collection of F. Glen Offield.

Another view of the three bubblecut dolls shows the delicately hand painted faces. Finer detailing could be accomplished with the prototypes than with those factory produced. Photography by Barry Sturgill, dolls from the collection of F. Glen Offield.

Mattel's own Charlotte Johnson fashions designed for Barbie were made so that a veteran could easily recognize her work. "Mattel used the smallest setting on their sewing machines and number ten needles," says LaRue Diniakos, a former Mattel supervisor. Ms. Johnson designed fashions with a touch of elegance brought only by a gifted designer. Every detail has been seen to and all threads completed. Often Offield says the outfits came sewn to the doll. As a test copy, there are no fasteners put on the garment. The outfit is stitched onto the doll and remains a unique discovery.

In 1965 when Mattel marketed the Little Theatre series there were costumes made that were for one reason or another ruled out. One unfortunate costume that was never seen is a Ken prototype costume of Napoleon and it is assumed there was a consideration of Barbie wearing Josephine. Another prototype was of Peter Pan with a miniature Barbie wearing wings as Tinker Bell.

At the 1989 Barbie Doll Collectors Convention held in Los Angeles, California, a large display of Mattel made prototypes were the star attraction.

These prototypes were a part of the collection of F. Glen Offield. Among them were variations of some of the most collectible 1600 series outfits that dazzled the crowd. These garments, high priced even as the original fashion, are now sold on the secondary market at extremely high prices. Other outfits in the exhibit were never produced styles of the 1988 Happy Holidays gown. Jeweled gowns which were too expensive to mass produce were also there. A Little Theatre version of Alice In Wonderland with her own deck of cards drew a lot of attention. Also seen were 100 doll heads with never produced hairdos. Such styles were bubblecut Francie, a hippy style Midge, and Barbies with puppytails, updos, flips, shags, curls, and an assortment of bobs.

Although a mystery, prototypes are fascinating mostly because they were never marketed. Viewing these opens a window into the world of toy manufacturing. It is all a matter of what will sell and what will be rejected by the buying public.

When the new Barbie releases began appearing in 1971 a doll was seen on packages and booklets called Becky. She was to be a friend of Francie and

Many times cost was the factor involved in why a fashion was not marketed. This prototype fashion is modeled by a 1965 bendable leg Barbie. Photography by Barry Sturgill, doll from the collection of F. Glen Offield.

A prototype of a Charlotte Johnson designed outfit which was never marketed is pictured here modeled by a 1965 bendable leg Barbie doll. Photography by Barry Sturgill, doll from the collection of F. Glen Offield.

No longer in "Beckyland" she is still only a prototype of a never produced doll called Becky. Photography by Barry Sturgill, doll from the collection of F. Glen Offield.

clothes were intended for both. On clothing packages the note read for "Francie and her new friend Becky." This doll appeared in the 1971 booklet modeling outfits numbered 3444, 3446, 3449, and 3450. In 1973 she also modeled one of the Sew Magic Fashions in the catalog on page 40. Of course, collectors asked Mattel what happened to this doll when she did not show up on toy shelves. The company explained that this doll was once intended for production but was later cancelled. It was always assumed that one or two prototypes of Becky existed somewhere. This doll was made with the Casey head mold. She had shoulder length flip hair in a dark blonde. With the part on the side, the hair was held in place with a dark rose headband. Now after many years of existing in what collectors call "Becky-land," this illusive doll who exists only as prototype, has been found. Becky is alive and well living in her vinyl world with her good friend F. Glen Offield in California.

Reflecting back to those pink boxes brings to mind the changes made in the packaging of present day Barbie dolls. Mattel is still designing new boxes and has produced more colorful box art in recent years. At the "Once Upon A Time" Auction held in Washington, D.C. in August, 1991, two prototype boxes for Rocker Barbies were sold. They never contained dolls but were considered by Mattel's management for their Rocker Barbie line. These were the rejected designs. One of these boxes was very colorful with pink, blue, and green. The other, a pink and grey version, was filled with circles and lines. The latter appeared hard to read because of the geometric patterns that may account for its demise.

Some more recent prototype dolls have appeared in boxes, such as the previously mentioned 1988 Happy Holidays Barbie which was designed with black hair. Possibly, Mattel had recognized the value of these dolls and their collectible nature. They do appear to be packaging these and taking greater care of those once unnoticed prototype versions. Mattel has given notice to the ever growing volume of collectors and their endless appetite for the unusual. Those collectors who once amounted to only a small group of people have grown to an army of devoted followers of the doll, and her many family and friends. Collectors dream of owning these one of a kind gems which have appeared in even greater numbers in recent years. It is safe to say that they truly add sparkle to any collection.

Twist 'N Turn Barbie had long straight hair in 1967. The prototype twist and turn Barbie has flipped puppytails. Photography by Barry Sturgill, doll from the collection of F. Glen Offield.

A prototype of a 1970 Dramatic New Living Barbie. Photography by Barry Sturgill, doll from the collection of F. Glen Offield.

Marketing in the Orient was planned in advance. A prototype set of Oriental Barbie, Francie, Skipper, and Tutti dolls that were never produced. Photography by Barry Sturgill, dolls from the collection of F. Glen Offield.

Doll makers have tried creative ideas with hair colors and Mattel has been no exception. Pictured are prototypes of a Barbie with pink hair and one with blue hair. Each doll wears a matching prototype outfit. Photography by Barry Sturgill, doll from the collection of F. Glen Offield.

Left: Doll ideas sometimes overlap as does this prototype of a cross between a Twist 'N Turn and the bendable leg Barbie hair styles. Photography by Barry Sturgill, doll from the collection of F. Glen Offield.

Right: A hand-painted prototype of the Mattel-made 1972 Miss America doll wearing her prototype outfit. Photography by Barry Sturgill, doll from the collection of F. Glen Offield.

Chapter 9

Ken

The creative spirit was still with Ruth, and in the kingdom of Barbieland, princess Barbie was very lonely. Designers in the workshop at Mattel set out to create a boyfriend that was just right for Barbie, his name was Ken. It is a long process to create, but well worth the effort where Ken is concerned. The completed doll was named after Elliot and Ruth Handler's son. The first issue was twelve inches tall and was a slender but realistic friend. Like the first Barbie doll, Ken had an expressionless face for children to imagine whatever pretend play they wanted. The doll had flocked hair, which was sold in both blonde and brunette. The flocking was a glued on process which was soon abandoned because it rubbed off and came off in the tub or swimming pool.

Working with the flocking for Ken doll was an experience. Jean Ann Burger tells of how Charlotte Johnson and other employees talked of those flocking days. Ms. Burger says the flocking was a feathery powder-like substance which was very sensitive to static electricity. Glue was painted on Ken doll's head and then flocking powder was applied to the area. Ms. Burger tells the flocking got stuck on everything. Arms and hands among other areas became coated with the flocking which was difficult to get off. It was soon replaced by painted hair which was more durable and less messy to apply.

He was sold with red swim trunks with a beach jacket, sandals, booklet, and towel, with a collection of other clothing available separately. The beach jacket was a red and white striped garment with a terry cloth collar. The terry cloth was bonded onto the striped material. Some issues of the jacket came with the terry cloth stitched to the striped material. Those first swim trunks were of a red fabric with a white stripe. Due to "copycat dolls" being produced to look like Ken dolls, Mattel sold Ken doll wearing a wrist tag declaring "Genuine Ken T.M. Mattel." Ken was first seen at the 1961 American International Toy Fair in New York City. This first Ken came marked on his lower back:

Ken T.M.
Pats. Pend.
©MCMLX
by
Mattel
Inc.

Like Barbie doll, Ken has had an exciting life for three decades. He has played baseball, football, and tennis. He has skied, and even served as drum major. His careers have covered astronaut, airline captain, fountain boy, doctor, soldier, sailor, and business person. Life in the enchanted Kingdom of Barbieland has been fulfilling for Ken. As with Barbie, Ken too was destined to evolve and change

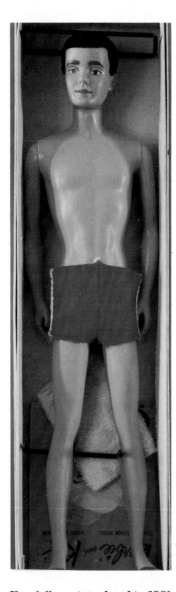

Ken doll was introduced in 1961 as a flocked hair doll. Mint in his original box, the doll was sold with stand, towel, booklet, sandals, and red swim trunks.

A blonde first issue flocked hair Ken doll was later issued with a striped jacket.

physically. All these were improvements on the prince of the doll world.

The second issue Ken was sold with painted crewcut hair. This second issue doll was marked the same as the first because the same body mold was used.

Just as Barbie continued to change so did Ken. The third issue in 1963 also had painted hair but the body was one-fourth inch shorter from the previous twelve inches. He had very pronounced kneecaps and the legs jointed at the hips were very loose. Number three Ken was marked:

Ken®
©1960
by
Mattel, Inc.
Hawthorne
Calif. U.S.A.

Mattel soon found that little girls were not the only fans of Ken. Many little boys bought the doll. They played with him and his football, tennis, and baseball outfits. These Ken dolls held a special place in the lives of both young girls and boys. A gamut of play patterns evolved with Ken and the romance of the first prom and date. With the longevity of this product, Mattel has shown how popular Barbie, Ken, and the array of family and friends have become.

Over the years the body build and facial features of the doll have changed. In 1969 Ken was made with a new body. He took a hiatus from store shelves in 1968 but the redesigned doll was most impressive. The makeover was a total body transformation. He came with a new head mold, muscular body, pinker skin tone, bendable legs, and he could even talk. The hair mold was an Edwardian hair style which was molded and painted medium brown. This Ken was marked:

©1968
Mattel, Inc.
U.S. & For. Pat'd
Other Pat's
Pending
Mexico

Although Ken was back to twelve inches tall, all those clothes made for the earlier Ken dolls would no longer fit this more muscular and robust frame. Larger size Ken clothes were issued to fit the new design.

Less noticeable changes to Ken have occurred. A 1972 Busy Ken came with hands designed to hold small items. The Talking Busy Ken also issued in 1972 was much like that of Barbie doll. Talking was achieved with a pull string apparatus. The talking mechanism was first made for the Mattel doll Chatty Cathy then reduced to fit into a Barbie and Ken doll. Because of the body changes necessary to insert the talking mechanism into the doll the patent was also changed on the back of the doll to read:

©1968
Mattel, Inc.
U.S. & For. Pat'd.
Other Pat's
Pending
Mexico

A 1973 Mod Hair Ken was the first with rooted hair. Teenage boys were wearing their hair longer and so did the doll. Longer hair continued through 1976

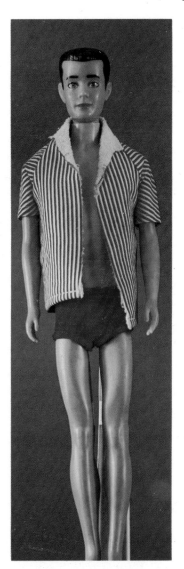

The third wave Ken doll had knobby knees and was one-fourth inch shorter. Painted hair replaced the flocking by the second wave.

Charlotte Johnson and her staff designed a football uniform for Ken which was sold in 1963.

with Now Look Ken who also came with rooted hair. This Now Look doll also had a decal beard, side burns, and two mustaches packaged in the box. Little boys could emulate manhood yet again in 1980 with Sport and Shave Ken. This doll had longer rooted hair and a substance rubbed on the face that could be shaved off. A tiny plastic razor was included in the packaging.

In the 80's physical health became a priority with the American public and weightlifting was popular. In 1982 All Star Ken was sold with a set of weights and a new body. Mattel designed Ken to be movable so he could exercise. The neck was designed with a ball joint and could rotate. Similar arm joints were made. Articulated wrists were a part of this Ken design. Hands could be positioned in any desired direction. Hands were molded to hold barbells. An unusual two piece body connected by a rubber strap made it possible for Ken to turn from side to side and bend over. Legs were jointed so they too could bend in any direction. A very soft vinyl was the material used to make the body of this Ken doll. The 1982 Ken doll was marked:

©Mattel, Inc. 1980
TAIWAN

In recent years most changes on the Ken doll have not been to the body itself. Most have been in the clothing line. Many dolls, with exception of the Malibu and Swim Party type dolls, have come dressed in a complete outfit. These outfits have also been designed to match a theme of a particu-

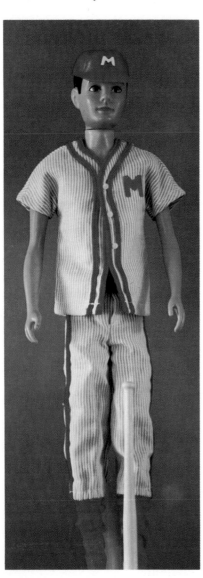

Baseball was another sport for Ken doll. The fashion design staff made the outfit complete down to a baseball and wooden bat.

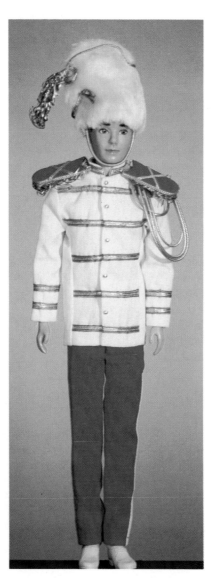

Ken was a busy doll. He served as Drum Major while Barbie was Drum Majorette. The Drum Major outfit is difficult to locate in some areas of the United States.

NASA was not the only organization with astronauts. Ken was ready to travel to the moon in his 1965 Mr. Astronaut.

lar Barbie doll. These outfits have been extremely elaborate in nature.

In the early 80's, Mattel was expanding its outreach to all the ethnic backgrounds and many new friends joined the Barbie family. Prior to that time, she had friends that were black, but in 1982 a black Ken was introduced to the market. A black Barbie doll was introduced in 1980. Mattel's ethnic sensitivity sought to fulfill the desires of all children. It was greeted with immediate success. The body mold for the black Ken was the same but the head typified African-American facial features. Shortly after, this black version was followed with an Hispanic Ken.

Mattel chose to honor the thirtieth anniversary of Ken doll with the creation of a porcelain Ken to accompany the porcelain Barbie doll in 1991. The porcelain Ken was a reproduction of the first doll with brunette flocking. Made only in the one hair coloring, this doll had a reproduction of the 700 series outfit called Tuxedo Set. With this version designed especially for the porcelain doll, two items of clothing were made new to the garment. These pieces were a pair of boxer shorts and sock garters.

The 90's brought new head molds for Barbie's beau, Ken. The 1992 line sports two new molds used for the doll. Sparkle Surprise Ken doll for 1992 has molded hair with a longer style. The molded hair reaches almost to the shirt collar and is in a sandy brown color. He comes dressed in a tuxedo set for a party with his hair slicked straight back on the front and sides. This same head mold is used for the 1992 Rappin Rock Ken.

Ken was an avid hunter and provided adequate meat for his table in Goin' Hunting from 1964 and 1965.

Costumes came with the Barbie and Ken Little Theatre from Mattel. Dolls were sold dressed in the costumes. The garments were packaged separately as well. A box dressed Ken wearing The Prince is shown here.

My First Ken and Ski Fun Ken come with the old head mold. The byword for 1992 is new and Totally Hair Ken released that year with rooted hair is yet another new head mold. This Ken doll has hair which is long on top and able to be combed over to the side. This style is reminiscent of the early 60's when men wore longer styles and slicked the hair back such as television star Ed "Kookie" Byrnes in the detective series "77 Sunset Strip."

Longevity and change has made Ken a collector's dream. Changes in the dolls are what makes collecting important. Ken too has grown in his place as the prince of the doll world.

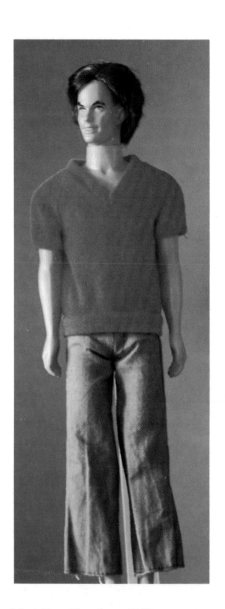

Mod Hair Ken from 1973, note the combable rooted hair.

Ken came with more than blonde and brown hair. In 1983 Dream Date Ken was sold with painted black hair.

Sold only in Venezuela in the late 80's was this Llanera Ken.

Chapter 10

Midge

Barbie doll as a successful marketing venture, was sweeping the nation and it was evident that she could be more fun if a friend could be made to create conversation during play. Barbie had passed the sales test and Mattel set to work to design the perfect friend for their doll. It seemed much more advantageous to make this new friend with the same body style as Barbie, therefore, the two dolls, like real life friends, could share clothing. It was an excellent marketing procedure since parents were more willing to buy doll clothing if their child could use it for more than one doll.

Ruth Handler says soon after the release of Barbie their company received mail from mothers and children asking for a friend for Barbie. The designers at Mattel set to work and in 1963 Midge doll was released.

Like Barbie, Midge was an 11½" doll with molded high heeled feet. She was designed to wear Barbie clothing. Midge came in three hair colors, blonde, brunette, and redhead. With shoulder length hair, which flipped up at the ends, she sported a generous sprinkling of freckles.

Midge was marked on her lower back:

Midge T.M.
©1962
Barbie®
©1958
by
Mattel, Inc.

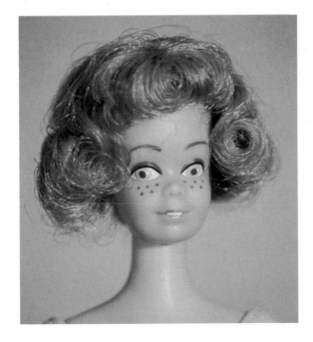

A closer look at Midge with teeth shows bright blue eyes and well placed freckles. She wore the same swimsuit sold on the straight leg Midge sold that same year.

Midge was Barbie's first friend introduced in 1963. Midge models Barbie fashion Theatre Date also sold in 1963.

Hiroe Okubo-Wolf tells that, "Mattel wanted to try painting teeth on Midge without changing the head mold." The result was Midge with teeth which sold in 1963 along with the first issue Midge. Mattel was not pleased with the results, so very few were made.

The same year, Midge came with a slightly altered paint job. Mattel's face painters tried another look for Midge, with a brush of white paint applied to the doll's lower lip some Midges were sold with teeth. Marked the same as the other 1963 Midge dolls, this doll was dressed identical only painted slightly different. Midge dolls with teeth are found today in all three hair colors and are considered extremely rare. Even with the Midge doll variations to the theme were attempted from the beginning.

These same Midge dolls remained for sale on store shelves, but in 1965 the evolution of Barbie doll's friend began. That year she was issued with a new bouffant hairdo and bendable legs. This Midge doll came with intaglio letter markings reading:

©1958
Mattel, Inc.
U.S. Patented
U.S. Pat. Pend

The bendable leg doll was manufactured in the new vinyl that was softer and made dressing the doll more difficult. Clothing did not slip over doll limbs as easily. However, the new vinyl made the bendable leg mechanism much more workable. This was an engineering feat which put Barbie doll and her friends in first place in the doll world.

Another innovation in the doll making world occurred with Midge in 1964. At this time a molded head Midge was being marketed. This doll was sold with three wigs; a titian with double ponytail, blonde swirl and curl, and a brunette topknot pouf. With the innovation of the wig, Midge could be three dolls in one. If the children wanted a redhead doll all was needed was to pop on a titian wig and she had one. Although the bendable leg Midge was sold in 1965, the wigged Midge also continued to be available with straight legs like the first doll. She was marked:

Midge T.M.
©1962
Barbie®
©1958
by
Mattel, Inc.
Patented

By 1967 Midge was no longer being marketed by Mattel. Two decades had passed since Barbie and Midge went their separate ways, but in 1987 Mattel chose to reissue some of the age old favorites, and among those was Midge. Still looking much the same as in years past, Midge had new up-to-date hair designs. The designers of the new Midge doll settled on a titian hair shade that accented her new green eye color. In the 60's the doll had blue eyes.

After a twenty year absence, California Midge appeared on store shelves in 1987 to again befriend Barbie doll. Continuing on with the Midge line Mattel issued Cool Times Midge in 1988, All Star Midge in 1989, and Midge from Barbie and the Beats in 1990. In 1991 Midge doll was not sold in all stores. She did however, appear in the Toys 'R Us stores as Ski Fun Midge, a department store special. This doll

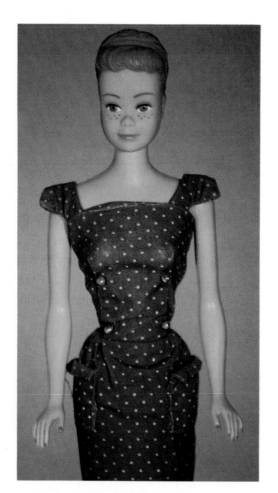

To compliment the Fashion Queen Barbie in 1963 was a molded Midge doll. She came with three wigs in blonde, brunette, and titian.

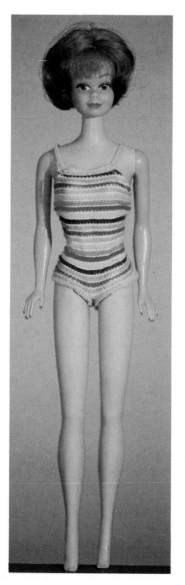

A 1965 bendable leg Midge was a part of the 1965 Barbie line by Mattel.

was sporting a brightly colored ski outfit and skis to glide down mountain slopes with her friends Ski Fun Barbie and Ken, which were found in all stores.

As an established friend of Barbie doll, she continues each year with a new issue. New outfit and hairdo are also a part of each year's introductions. The 1991 issue doll most talked about was a bride. Issued both individually and in a huge boxed set of six, Midge was finally after all these years, the bride. She had Alan with his redesigned head mold as her groom. The bridesmaid was none other than long time friend, Barbie. Ken served as best man. All older issues of the Alan doll were spelled "Allan." With the new issued groom Mattel changed the spelling by eliminating one of the "l's" in his name. The flowergirl was a little girl named Kelly and ringbearer was Barbie doll's baby brother Todd. Collectors are assuming Kelly is the renamed Tutti doll from previous years. Along with this wonderful set came a bridal trousseau for Midge to wear on her honeymoon. Other honeymoon clothing were made and sold separately. There were four individually sold clothing outfits for Midge to accompany the wedding fantasy. This was the first time Midge had clothing outfits made exclusively for her.

Bringing Midge back into Barbie playtime, gives mothers and daughters a link that unites each generation. Over time we all go our separate ways but the bond of friendship transcends both space and time forever.

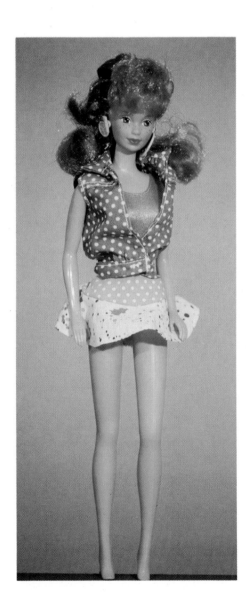

After twenty years absence from the Mattel line Midge was back with a new face mold, titian hair, and freckles in 1987. She was called California Midge.

Cool Times Midge was the 1988 release. Midge had alot of long red hair for children to style.

All Star Midge was glamorous with a head full of crimped red hair in 1989.

Ski Fun Midge was a department store special sold in 1990 at Toys 'R Us stores only wearing a colorful ski outfit.

Chapter 11

Sisters

Skipper was first introduced in 1964 as an extension of the Barbie family. She is Barbie doll's little sister.

Like any good parents who has found themselves blessed with a five year old prodigy, Elliot and Ruth Handler were faced with the desire to create yet another sibling to follow in the "mold" of Barbie doll. The Mattel designers again churned off the drawing board a little nine inch girl doll which they called Skipper. Marketed for the first time in 1964, she was an immediate success. Billed as Barbie's little sister, Skipper could be played with along with the 11½" doll. As Ruth Handler tells, Skipper doll was named by members of the Mattel design staff.

Over the years, the face mold of this doll was changed. She has become a collectible in her own right. She was originally marketed in blonde, brunette, and titian hair colors. Even though she is the little sister of such a famous doll as Barbie, she has not lived in a shadow. Having her own

wardrobe, furniture, and friends has made her a person to be admired and identified with by younger children during play.

The first Skipper doll in 1964 had straight legs, long straight hair, and was marked:

Skipper
©1963
Mattel, Inc.

Depicted as the little sister of Barbie with the round face, wide eyes, and pixie bangs, little Skipper was not sold with polished nails and eye makeup. She was a juvenile sibling to the teenage fashion model.

As updating is a part of Barbie so was it with Skipper. The bendable leg Skipper came marked:

©1963
Mattel, Inc.

Like Barbie, the bendable legs on Skipper sold in 1965 were a wonderful invention. She too, became more lifelike. The hair on this doll was different than the first issue. A silkier texture to the hair is evident. Again the three hair colors were featured in a longer waist length style with bangs. The same face mold as the first Skipper was used on this new bendable leg frame.

When Barbie was given a horse of her very own little Skipper also had a horse, named Honey. Little girls have found playing with their Skipper a joyous experience. Imaginary fun could reach new dimensions. Skipper doll and her friends could make pretend cookies, go skating, swimming, or just play dolls with her very own minature Barbie doll. Skipper's little Barbie doll was a two inch tall plastic replica of the blonde ponytailed doll. Hair and the red swimsuit were painted on. A pink checked gathered skirt came with the tiny mannequin. Marvelous outfits came with endless tiny accessories which over the years have become extremely rare.

Many of the Skipper outfits were made to coordinate with her big sister's clothes. These outfits were made with the same eye for detail as the Barbie clothes. They were sold in the 60's with gloves, shoes, and socks. Tiny accessories were also present. A checkerboard with miniature black and red checkers, croquet set, even miniature hair rollers were sold. In Cookie Time a bowl, rolling pin, box mix, spoon, and cookbook accompanied the dress and shoes. Skating Fun came with a pair of ice skates and warm muff to protect tiny doll hands on a snowy day. As a fashion conscious doll, she went into the Mod Era with outfits which kept pace with current trends.

Evolution of the doll continued into the late 60's and Twist Skipper was introduced with a twist and turn waist. This doll came marked:

© 1967 Mattel, Inc.
U.S. Pat'd
U.S. Pats. Pend.
Made in Japan

Along with the improvements in Skipper's body came a new hairstyle and pinker skin tone. Her hair was parted in the center and fastened with rubberbands. Long banana curls were the finishing touches. Orange hair bows were tied in each side of the hair to match the orange and pink checked swim suit Skipper wore. As was customary of the Twist 'N Turn designed dolls, this little pixie girl also had rooted eyelashes.

A bendable leg Skipper was a part of the 1965 Barbie doll line. She is pictured wearing Me 'N My Doll sold in 1965.

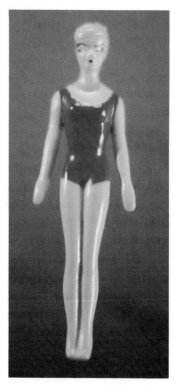

A closer look at the Barbie doll sold with the Skipper outfit called Me 'N My Doll. Even Skipper had her own Barbie doll to play pretend with. Actual size of the doll is two inches.

With the 70's came yet another design for the Skipper doll. This year was the Dramatic New Living Barbie design and Dramatic New Living Skipper came with new engineering accomplishments as well. A much shorter hair style set in sidepart pigtails with very curly ends was all new for Skipper. She still retained the rooted eyelashes and twist and turn waist. Bendable legs also remained to assist her in holding a pose, however, articulating wrists were all new for the doll body. A jointed wrist made it possible for the doll's hands to be turned in many directions. Living Skipper doll came marked:

©1969 Mattel, Inc.
Taiwan
U.S. & For. Pat'd.
Other Pats. Pend.
Patd. in Canada 1967

One year a controversy arose when Growing Up Skipper appeared on store shelves. This marvel of doll production sold in 1975 was designed in such a way that when you turned the doll's arm she grew in stature and developed breasts. Growing Up Skipper doll was designed by Mattel inventor Dick May from an idea submitted by members of the preliminary design department. Some parents were upset. However, the doll shows the marvelous engineering of the Mattel staff. Growing Up Skipper was marked:

©1967
Mattel, Inc.
Hong Kong
U.S. & For. Pat.

Skipper has had her own share of boyfriends. First on the scene was Ricky. Another was a skateboarding fella' named Scott. More recent is a doll named Kevin who has been on store shelves since 1990.

Girlfriends have been numerous over the years starting with Skooter in 1964. Skooter was a little nine inch doll with an impish face and pigtails. She came in three hair colors of blonde, brunette, and redhead. In 1965 when Skipper developed bendable legs her friend Skooter also came with lifelike legs. By 1970, Skipper's girlfriends were Pose 'N Play Tiff which is a very rare and hard to find Mattel creation. Another friend was Living Fluff who came with a bright yellow skateboard to match her blonde hair. Fluff came with a twist and turn waist, bendable legs, and the articulating wrists. Growing Up Skipper also had a friend called Growing Up Ginger. Ginger was a brunette doll with long hair tied in a sidepart ponytail. She had the same maturing ability as the Skipper of that year.

The 1969 Twist 'N Turn Skipper wore long banana curl puppytails. Like the Twist 'N Turn Barbie, she too had long eyelashes.

Dramatic New Living Skipper was introduced in 1970 with redesigned puppytails. She featured a bendable waist, wrists, legs, and a rotating neck.

Unfortunately, when the brunette and titian hair colors disappeared from stores shelves for Barbie they likewise did for Skipper. For her too the blonde color sold more frequently.

The first black version of Skipper was introduced in 1988 when Homecoming Skipper was sold in both color variations.

On the international scene, dolls were the same as here on our own U.S. shores. Although, in 1989 the Style Magic Skipper was sold only in Canada and Europe. Collectors have managed to locate some of these through doll dealers.

A department store special in 1990 for Toys 'R Us featured Dream Date Skipper. These were found only in that store. No mention of the department store special appeared on the packaging. In 1991 Beauty Pageant Skipper was also a special sold only at Toys 'R Us. Unlike her sister Barbie, who has several department store specials each year, there are few for little Skipper. The 1992 toy season at Toys 'R Us featured a Totally Hair Skipper and Totally Hair Courtney that coordinated with the Totally Hair Barbie sold in all stores. However, the Skipper and Courtney only were marketed in the Toys 'R Us store as department store specials.

Another first for Skipper was in 1992 with Sun Sensation Skipper. Never before had Skipper been sold wearing earrings but this doll came with large gold earrings to match a necklace also on the doll. A

Toys 'R Us department store special in 1991 was the Disney Barbie and Friends Gift Set which included Barbie, Ken, and Skipper set for a trip to Disney World.

Mattel began a Babysitter series in 1991 called Babysitter Skipper. Along with Skipper was a small blonde haired baby and tiny accessories to keep baby content for hours. Sold separately was Skipper's friend Babysitter Courtney. A friend Kevin was sold separately but not really a part of the Babysitter series.

Pets were the feature for 1992 and Skipper was sold as Pet Pal Skipper with a white fluffy dog. Her friend Pet Pal Courtney came packaged with a kitten and Pet Pal Kevin came with his own dalmatian puppy.

A doll set that is not a department store special but still not found everywhere is the Sharin' Sisters Set. This three doll set features Barbie, Skipper, and a new baby sister called Stacie.

The newest sibling in the Barbie family, Stacie, joined the group as a 7½" fashion doll in 1992. Sold first singularly and billed as Barbie doll's little sister, she was brightly attired in a costume consisting of nine pieces which could be mixed and matched to make three different looks. Like big sister Barbie, Stacie is born to shop and one of the looks is shopping along with party and school. Stacie is listed as new on page 36 of the 1992 Mattel catalog. After over thirty years the Barbie doll family still continues to grow and bloom.

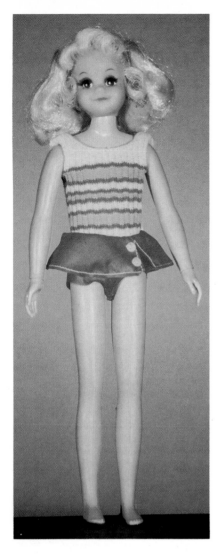

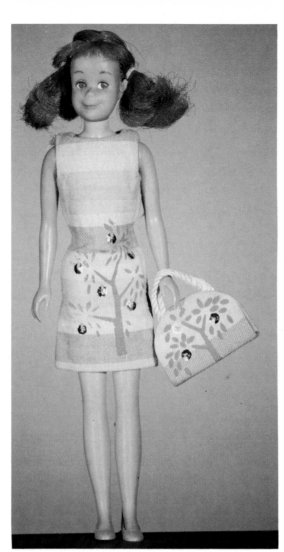

Living Fluff, a friend of Skipper, was sold in 1970. She is considered extremely rare today.

Skipper had friends to share play time with such as a Skooter doll sold in 1965.

Another Skipper friend sold in 1965 was Ricky who models his outfit called Sunday Suit.

Left: Kevin is a boyfriend sold in the 90's. Mattel has found creating friends for the dolls makes play a group fantasy.

Right: Another friend for Skipper in the 90's is Courtney.

A black Skipper issued in 1988 was sold as Homecoming Queen Skipper.

Horse Lovin' Skipper was sold in 1983 as a part of the Horse Lovin' series.

Left: Cheerleader Skipper was a 1987 doll with blonde streaks through her hair.

Right: A 1986 issue of Jewel Secrets Skipper came with cute Shirley Temple curls.

Style Magic Skipper was sold only in Canada and Europe in 1989. Boxes that the doll was packaged in were printed in French as well as English.

A 1990 Toys 'R Us exclusive doll was Dream Date Skipper. The dress sold on the doll could be worn a multitude of ways to make varying looks.

The 90's brought a new little sister called Stacie sold in 1992. The family continues to grow with personable additions by Mattel.

Chapter 12

Tutti and Todd

Barbie's twin baby siblings were sold in 1966. The baby sister was Tutti. She was only 6¼" tall.

Twin boy doll, Todd, was a part of the Barbie family during the 60's. An array of outfits were offered separately for these dolls. They were designed for Mattel by Carol Spencer.

We continue our journey into Barbie's past with the growth of the family of dolls. The series of family members became a masterpiece of design when in 1966 Mattel introduced Tutti and Todd, Barbie's tiny twin baby brother and sister. Sold both in Europe and the United States, these dolls were six inches tall. Made of soft rubberized vinyl, their construction was somewhat different from that of big sister, Barbie. Having rooted hair in three colors – blonde, brunette, and titian, they had a wide eyed expression of impish playfulness. The latter hair color was available only as a department store special. A one part body was still posable due to the internal wires in the arms and legs which allowed limbs to be bent into desired positions. Hair play was encouraged here, too, with Tutti having tresses which hung her lower torso. A fringe of bangs across her forehead accented her face. Chubby cheeks and a hint of pink blush gave Tutti a pleasant expression.

Todd had a boyish Beatle style haircut which was topped with a red hat sewn to the dolls head. Todd's wide brown eyes were a contrast to Tutti's bright blue eyes.

Mrs. Handler says the design department named Tutti but Todd was named by her after Barbara's son, Todd.

Tutti was sold wearing a little pink dress and

Todd wore red shorts and navy blue shirt. An array of outfits were also sold separately for the dolls over the years. These tiny garments were designed for Mattel by Carol Spencer for use on Tutti and Todd.

Friends were an important part of the dolls social structure and Mattel added another six inch doll in 1967 named Chris. As a friend of the twins, Chris, had the same body as Tutti and Todd. She had a slightly different face mold than Tutti, with less chub to the cheeks and less smile on her lips, but still she was a recognizable persona. Chris had waist length hair in both blonde and brunette. Wide brown eyes accented her tiny face. Other friends for Tutti and Todd sold by Mattel in 1968 were Buffy and Mrs. Beasley, a doll based on the television show, "Family Affair." The show starred the late Anissa Jones as Buffy. This doll had the same body mold as Tutti and Todd and the same face mold as the Tutti doll. She had blonde hair tied back in puppytails accented with red hair ribbons. Buffy's doll, Mrs. Beasley, fit neatly in the doll's arms and wore glasses which are hard to find for the collector of this doll. By 1970 three new dolls joined the line called: Lori 'N Rori, a blonde doll holding a brown teddy bear; Nan 'N Fran, a black doll holding a black toy doll; and Angie 'N Tangie, a brunette doll holding a blonde toy doll. All of these dolls were marked:

©1965
Mattel, Inc.
Japan

Dolls were not all sold individually, some came as sets. For example, Todd and Tutti were sold in a set called Sundae Treat. The set featured a redheaded Tutti and Todd along with a small table and chairs. This same titian haired Todd and Tutti were sold in a Sears department store special issue of the Tutti Playhouse. Tutti's Playhouse was also sold in department stores other than Sears without the dolls. These were the only redheaded Tutti and Todd dolls available and the only occasion they came packaged together.

Other Tutti sets were Walkin' My Dolly, Night-Night Sleep Tight, Me and My Dog, Melody In Pink, Cookin' Goodies, and Swing A Ling. These sets came with doll and swing, doll and stove, doll and doll carriage, doll and bed, doll and dog, and doll and piano.

Tutti, Todd, Chris, and the other friends were no longer available in the United States after 1976. For many years after, Americans visiting Europe were surprised to find these tiny toys still available in foreign countries through 1981. Clothing unique to Europe was made for these dolls by Mattel and sold overseas along with those also found here in the United States. Sold in Germany, those cute doll clothes came with such elegant names as Ballspiel an Strand, Blumen-reign, and Mein Rosa Schlafanzug. The Tutti, Todd, and Chris dolls are highly collectible in Germany and other European countries. They were even purchased to be used in other doll houses in those areas.

The demise of Tutti and Todd as Bill Robb, former Mattel inventor tells, was due to a late 60's quality control effort. Always concerned with safety, Mattel discontinued all toys which had bendable wire arms or legs which would break after frequent bending. They felt there was danger of a child being punctured by the wires if they should break through the vinyl skin of the doll. "Mattel was always painfully cautious of having only safe toys for their customers," says Robb.

Now over a decade after these tiny playthings disappeared from store shelves a new doll set was released by Mattel in 1991. Simply called Wedding Party Set, this large box collection came packaged with Midge as the bride, Alan as the groom, Barbie as bridesmaid, Ken as bestman, Tutti (renamed Kelly) as flowergirl, and Todd as the ringbearer. Bride, groom, bridesmaid, and bestman were sold separately as well as in the set. However, only in rare and selected areas did Mattel sell a two doll box set of Kelly and Todd in wedding attire.

As additional small links in the Barbie family chain, these tiny dolls are considered collectible on the secondary market.

The twin dolls needed a friend and Chris was on the doll market in 1967. She was sized right to wear Tutti's clothes. Here she is seen in her original outfit.

Chris came with long straight blonde or brunette hair. Here she models a Tutti outfit number 3602 called Ship Shape. Doll from the Debbie Fernow collection.

Little Tutti and Todd also had friends. Pictured here is Buffy and Mrs. Beasley. The doll was patterned after a popular television show of that time. Doll from the Debbie Fernow collection.

One little Tutti outfit called Let's Play Barbie featured a miniature Barbie doll. A blonde Tutti doll models this outfit. Doll from the Debbie Fernow collection.

Offered as a part of a set in Sundae Treat and in Tutti's Playhouse by Sears department store was this redheaded version of Todd. Both sets featured the same outfits. Doll from the Debbie Fernow collection.

Tutti from Sundae Treat and Tutti's Playhouse was also titian haired. Note the different hair style of this Tutti doll. Doll from the Debbie Fernow collection.

New for 1991 was this Wedding Party Midge Set with the flowergirl and ringbearer returning as Todd and Kelly. Little Tutti had a new name change but was still the same size doll from the 60's.

Chapter 13

Friends

Barbie had Midge as a friend and Ken had Allan as a friend. Allan also served as Midge's boyfriend for double date fantasies. Allan was only made for eighteen months beginning in 1964.

Francie was not only a friend for Barbie, but also her cousin. Shown here is a no bangs Francie sold in 1971 with the Twist 'N Turn waist. Doll courtesy the Mid Ohio Historical Museum.

"Life is to be fortified by many friendships." Mattel was going to heed the words of the writer Sydney Smith by surrounding Barbie with a pantheon of friends. By the close of the first year, a surge of orders for Barbie amassed to nearly a three year production requirement to fill orders. Mattel was also flooded with letters to add playmates for their female phenomena. With a twist, real life was dictating more realism in the fantasy world of the friends for Barbie. The production of Ken and Midge did not satisfy the public craving for more. The direction of how the demand for more friends would be addressed had Mattel again calling upon the insights of mother and marketer, Ruth Handler. Recalling the play of her daughter with paper dolls, Mrs. Handler sensed the need for a well balanced mix of male and female, sister, siblings, and friends that express the racial diversity of the communities.

Midge needed a male friend and Ken also needed someone with whom he could share experiences. Allan appeared on store shelves in 1964. He had the same markings as the 1964 Ken dolls and the same body mold. He had molded red hair and brown side glance eyes. Dressed in blue trunks, he wore a multicolored striped beach jacket and tan sandals. Allan could wear Ken doll's clothing. Allan appeared again in 1965 with lifelike bendable legs. Although marked the same as the 1964 issue, these dolls had bendable knee joints. Only these two issues of Allan ever appeared until his reissue in 1991. With the reissue Allan experienced a spelling change and became Alan.

With those first three friends came greater expansion of the Barbie doll family and in 1966 a Barbie doll cousin called Francie was introduced. The concept of Francie has its roots in the developmental age of the straight legged body so she was sold with both straight legs and the newly marketed bendable legs that first year. Although the same scale, she was less shapely and had flat feet. Francie was indeed a stylish debutante doll with her own persona. Sold in both blonde and brunette, the bendable variety had rooted eyelashes. The straight leg variety had painted eyelashes. The swimsuits on the two versions of Francie were not alike. Straight leg Francie was sold wearing a red and white two piece swimsuit where the bendable leg Francie wore a one piece aqua suit. Francie was 11¼" tall making her one forth inch shorter than Barbie. This was a beautiful doll and some collectors claim to love her more than Barbie. A whole line of clothes were manufactured for Francie between 1966 and 1975. Outfits totaled 182 between those dates for Francie. The doll has not been available except on the secondary market since 1976 when they disappeared from toy shelves. The first straight leg Francie and bendable leg Francie came marked:

©1965
Mattel, Inc.
U.S. Patented
U.S. Pat. Pend.
Made in Japan

Other Francie dolls made during the period were Twist 'N Turn Francie, Hair Happenins' Francie, Colored Francie, and Malibu Francie which were marked:

©1966
Mattel, Inc.
U.S. Patented
U.S. Pat. Pend.
Made in
Japan

An issue of Growin' Pretty Hair Francie came marked:

©1966
Mattel, Inc.
U.S. Pat. Other
Pats. Pend.
Pat. Canada
1967
Japan

A Busy Francie which came equipped to hold small items in her small doll hands was marked:

©1966
Mattel, Inc.
Hong Kong
U.S. & Foreign
Patented
Other Pat's

Growin' Pretty Hair Francie sold in 1970 came with hair pieces to style.

P.J. was a Barbie friend from the 80's. Shown here is Sweet Roses P.J.

81

Barbie's cousin and friend in the 90's is Jazzie. Jazzie is made with the Francie body mold and has flat feet.

Pending
The issue of Quick Curl Francie was marked:

©1966
Mattel, Inc.
Taiwan
U.S. & Foreign
Patented
Other Pat's
Pending

The late 60's was a time of great challenge for the Mattel design department. They had to create a diverse number of friends which were unique in their character. A doll called Casey was sold in 1967. She too came in both blonde and brunette. This mod doll wore one earring in her left ear as if she were making her own fashion statement of the 60's. Fashionable that year were teenagers wearing one earring. Although she was the same size as Francie, Casey had a different head mold. A broad smile with molded teeth gave her a very pleasant expression. She was marked:

©1966
Mattel, Inc.
U.S. Patented
U.S. Pat. Pend.
Made in

In the Island Fun and Tropical series Barbie had a Polynesian friend called Miko. The Oriental face mold was used to make an ethnic friend for the doll.

Japan
She too had bendable legs and rooted eyelashes. Mattel did not dispose of the Casey mold because the Twiggy doll sold that same year also had this same head mold. Twiggy was a doll friend of Barbie but was also a character doll. In London, England, Twiggy was one of the top fashion models of that time. She was paid top dollar for her modeling talents. Twiggy was a girl with a short cropped haircut, shapeless figure, large eyes, and very stark features. The doll Twiggy, came with short blonde hair and heavily made up eyes. She had rooted upper lashes but painted lower lashes. Twiggy's markings were:

©1966
Mattel, Inc.
U.S. Patented
U.S. Pat. Pend.
Made In Japan

A black friend in 1968 was Christie. She came

82

wearing a green knit top over rose shorts. She had a light brown skin tone and wore dark brown curly hair parted on the side. She was marked:

©1966
Mattel, Inc.
U.S. Patented
U.S. Pat. Pend.
Made in
Japan

1968 also brought a doll called Twist 'N Turn Stacey. She came with either blonde or titian long straight hair and molded teeth. Other assets were rooted eyelashes and bendable knees. The TNT Stacey doll was available between the years of 1968 and 1971. Another Stacey sold the following year was called Talking Stacey. This doll was marked:

©1966
Mattel, Inc.
U.S. Patented
U.S. Pat. Pend.
Made in
Japan

Talking P.J. joined the Barbie friends in 1969. The small group was a growing collection of friends meant to appeal to all children. P.J. was made from the old Midge head mold. She too had rooted eyelashes, bendable legs, and long straight blonde hair with bangs. She had an interesting hair style. It was divided into two sections and each section was decorated with strands of beads. She was marked:

©1966
Mattel, Inc.
U.S. Patented
U.S. Pat. Pend.
Made in
Japan

By 1970, in the fine tradition of Mattel, Christie needed a boyfriend. They created Talking Brad doll who was a friend of Ken doll's and also a boyfriend for Christie. He was marked:

©1968
Mattel, Inc.
U.S. & For. Pats
Other Pats.
Pending
Mexico

These dolls were made in two issues that year. The first was made in Mexico and the second in Hong Kong. This was a time when Mattel was trying new areas to have their dolls molded.

Barbie had a new friend in 1972 in the body of Walk Lively Miss America number 3200. This doll was a character design based on Laurie Lea Schaefer, Miss America 1972. Her wardrobe was a gold and white gown and red cape trimmed in imitation ermine. The doll had brunette hair and was made from the Steffie

face mold. Another Miss America doll was offered this same year with Kellogg Corn Flake tops and $3.00. The Kellogg doll was number 3194-9991. The Miss America dolls came marked:

©1967 Mattel, Inc.
U.S. Pat. Pend.
Taiwan

Miss America returned in 1973 minus the Walk Lively body but with regular bendable legs and twist waist. Dressed the same as the 1971 version, this Miss America was called Quick Curl Miss America number 8697. Although in 1973 she was brunette, in 1974 the doll was released only as blonde. The 1973 Miss America doll came marked:

©1966
Mattel, Inc.
U.S. & Foreign
Patented
Other Pat's
Pending
Made in
Taiwan

The Miss America dolls are very misunderstood. Many people consider these dolls to be Barbies but they were made and intended to be only her friend. These dolls were available through 1975.

Action was the name of the game in 1972. Dolls were being sold this year on a Walk 'N Turn stand.

The Oriental face mold has proven a popular creation and was used here for Barbie friend, Dana from the Barbie and the Rockers series. The Rocker series dolls featured a new dance action, twist the waist and the arms moved.

They were a part of the Walk Lively doll series. Along with the regular Barbie and friends line was a doll called Walk Lively Steffie. Steffie was an 11½" tall and had long brunette hair with flip ends. She had brown eyes. Although not a long series of Steffie dolls was made, the face mold has been used numerous times over the years. Even today Hispanic Barbies are made from Steffie's old face mold. Steffie was marked:

©1967 Mattel, Inc.
U.S. Pat. Pend.
Taiwan

In 1974 Mattel introduced the sports line with Sun Valley Barbie and Ken, Newport Barbie, and a new friend Yellowstone Kelley number 7808. With long straight red hair, this doll had lovely suntan skin. She had bendable legs and a twist waist. An adventurous friend, she came with sleeping bag and camping gear. She was marked:

©1966
Mattel, Inc.
U.S. & Foreign
Patented
Other Pats.
Pending
Made in
Taiwan

Kelley doll also wore the Steffie face mold.

Another black doll joined the friends of Barbie in 1975. She was called Cara and was sold as Free Moving Cara. Mattel used the old Steffie face mold here also. She had long brown hair tied in puppytails with orange ribbons. Along with Cara was a boy doll called Curtis. Curtis was also of the Free Moving line. He was made from the Brad face mold. Curtis was marked the same as Brad.

©1968 Mattel, Inc.
Taiwan
U.S. Patent
Pending

The Free Moving girl dolls were all marked:

©1967 Mattel, Inc.
Taiwan
U.S. Pat. Pend.

Remember the Steffie face mold? In 1983 it again appeared with the introduction of a bridal pair of Barbie friends, Tracy and Todd. This was the only appearance of these two dolls. Todd was made from the Ken mold and was a brunette boy doll as well as a Ken look alike. Tracy, as the bride, was a brunette with the Steffie face mold.

Rocker Barbie came in 1986 with the advent of female rock groups such as the Go-Go's. Friends in

With the same Oriental face mold and different paint, Mattel designers can create a different character and all new look as is evident with Kira. Kira was sold in the late 80's and early 90's.

Mattel sought perfection as is seen with the ethnic mold made for Barbie's friend Dee Dee from the Barbie and the Rockers series. She too had real dance action.

this line were Dana, Dee Dee, Derek, and Diva. Diva doll brought memories of Midge but in much more colorful clothing. Derek was a boy doll and very similar to Ken but with different hair mold. Dee Dee, a black doll, was much like Christie of years past. Dana was an Oriental friend with a face mold used in the Japanese Barbie and Oriental Barbie dolls from the International Series.

Other friends of Barbie were a set which began in 1986 and sold as the Heart Family Set. These came as a father, mother, and twin baby girl and boy. The sets were sold all four dolls to a box or in a two box set with mother and daughter, and father and son. Outfits were sold separately for these dolls and in the same fashion mother and daughter outfits were packaged together. Mr. Heart and son clothes were also boxed together. The most interesting set which was even discussed on television was the Heart Family New Arrival Set. Yes, Mrs. Heart had a tiny baby doll which was held to her waist by a tied ribbon. Clothing for the doll was a maternity dress, an after birth dress, suit case, and baby accessories. Even a bouquet of roses was included for Mr. Heart to give to his wife and new baby. Mrs. Heart was made from the popular Steffie head mold and Barbie body. Mr. Heart was a Ken doll with suit and tie. Even a set of Heart family grandparents made a short appearance.

The entire Heart Family and grandparents were sold both as white and black families.

Whitney joined the friends line in 1986 but was a short lived doll. She was sold as Jewel Secret Whitney, Perfume Pretty Whitney, Nurse Whitney, and Magic Curl Whitney. Whitney was a vision of loveliness with brunette hair and the always favorite Steffie face mold.

An Island Fun series of dolls found Miko as a Polynesian friend of Barbie doll. Miko was made from the Oriental face mold like the International Series dolls. Also among the Island Fun line was Teresa, an Hispanic friend and Steven a black doll. Steven was matched with the reissued Christie in the 1987 line.

The California Dream Barbie series reintroduced Midge in 1987. The California line featured roller skates and the fun lifestyle of California's beaches.

Another rocker series called Sensation came in 1987 and in this we met Becky, Bopsy, and Belinda. These dolls were the members of Barbie's newest rock group.

Animal Lovin' series in 1988 had a new Oriental friend, Nikki. A similar doll to Miko, Nikki came with a pet and was dressed for a jungle safari.

The Barbie family had not been expanded for some time. P.J. had been off the market for a few

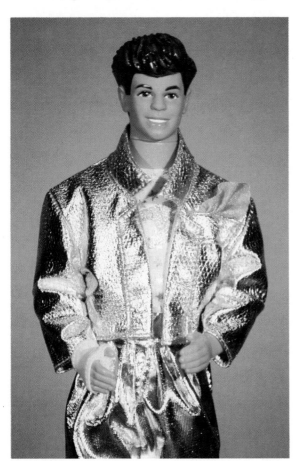

The Rockers series featured Derek with a unique new head mold. Sculptors at Mattel were at work redesigning the characters in Barbie's world to bring more attention to their creations.

Redheaded children were still being marketed to with Diva from Barbie and the Rockers. Diva was manufactured with titian hair and a Midge likeness.

years. Mattel introduced another cousin, Jazzie, for Barbie. She was sold with a line of sports clothes for her also. Even a Jazzie car was seen on store shelves. Several Jazzies were available called Cheerleader Jazzie, Swim Suit Jazzie, Teen Dance Jazzie, High School Jazzie, Workout Jazzie, and Sun Lovin' Jazzie. Jazzie was a doll who also had friends called Stacie, Dude, and Chelsie. Dude was a Derek look alike and was made from his mold. Jazzie was available into the 90's.

In 1989 yet another rock group came on the market called Dance Club series. Barbie's new friends were Kayle, a Midge look alike and Devon. Devon was Derek under yet another name.

When Barbie and the Beats came on the market in 1990, who were the Beats? Would you believe Midge and Christie? Old friends were back and still as popular as ever.

Hawaiian Fun dolls were issued in 1990 and the Polynesian friend for Barbie here was Kira. She looked like Miko under a new name. The Oriental face mold was again used on Kira. Kira also appeared that same year in the All American series of 1991. These same friends were all back in 1992 with the Rollerblade series, Sun Sensation series, and the Rappin' Rockin' series.

As the popularity of Barbie has grown, her outreach has touched the hearts of many a child around the world. Though vinyl of body, Barbie's spirit embodies the gift of sharing that binds friends together with the golden thread that entwines the hearts of all the world.

A black friend was Steven who appeared in the Island Fun series and Tropical series. Here again the face mold was specially designed with the exactness for which Mattel is noted.

Teresa was a friend who represented the Hispanic culture in America. Using the popular Steffie face mold, large wide eyes were accented with a full head of long crimped hair. Pictured is All American Teresa from 1991.

A friend from the 80's is Whitney. Shown here is Jewel Secrets Whitney. The doll was named after rock singer Whitney Houston.

An example of the Mattel made black ethnic dolls is this beauty called Dance Club Devon.

Nikki was an Oriental friend of Barbie's seen in the Animal Lovin' series.

Barbie's black friend Christie has been a popular doll in the line for two decades. Shown here is All Star Christie.

Chapter 14

Developing the Bends

Whether through the detailed examination of anatomy by Leonardo da Vinci or through the imagination of Collodi in Pinocchio, capturing the essence of the human form and expressing its nature in the medium of the artist's choice has always been the ultimate challenge. Severing the bonds of inanimate existence and reaching a state of life like expression was an obstacle the inventors and designers at Mattel seemed destined to face. To transform the rigid mannequin of Barbie to a "lifelike" figure would require far greater wizardry than Geppeto's work-

shop and an anatomical understanding that would rival the engineering of artificial protheses of the time. The preliminary development department's first call for lifelikeness came in the request for a bendable and posable knee.

The production of such a knee would consume nearly two years of the research and development staff's time and test the patience and innovative talents of each and every inventor. The fact that Barbie was advertised as a fashion model established the first criteria that had to be met. The leg must retain its shapeliness with no exposed rivets, screws, or hinge mechanisms, therefore, the designers had to create an elastic skin. One would think this first step would be an easy task in the age of synthetic rubbers and vinyls. Such was not to be the case. The first efforts as Ruth Handler describes, "they were ugly with large balls at the site of the bend." As the work progressed in thinning out the elastic skin and flexibility of the "rubberized/vinyl" compound negated the balling effect, Ralph Dunn says the research and development department's attention turned to the "swollen arthritic joints of the mechanism." The head of the research and development department, Jack Ryan, kept up the clarion call of urgency for the completion of the project as each inventor took up the challenge. The staff of inventors produced twenty-four variations of the bendable knee, each

"With lifelike bendable legs" was an invention which required almost two years to develop. The successful design was the creation of Dick May for Mattel and sold in 1965

Dick May, inventor of the bendable leg sold on Barbie in 1965, changed the path that the doll had taken. Photo courtesy of Dick May.

met with a varying degree of success. Inventor Dick May took an interesting perspective in starting his research on the posable leg. He sought to evaluate the number of required poses that would be asked of the mechanism by taking his camera out and photographing women's legs in seated and walking postures. Armed with the insights gained from the photos, he was able to enter the lab with specific expectations for his mechanism. The resultant product was a knee that not only bent properly, but also permitted the legs to be crossed, duplicating the real life poses of the photos. Dick's effort inserted into the lower end of the thigh and upper end of the calf, pieces of plastic that were to act as connecting armatures to the mechanism that was to perform like the pseudo knee. Two disks with cog teeth and a metal gripper spring were the secret to the locking of the knee into the various poses. Another of Mattel's inventors, Bill Robb tells of the insightful way in which they assessed the mechanism's performance. "The initial leg was done in clear plastic. The encased armatures and the knee mechanism were red plastic. This was done so the mechanical engineers could visibly evaluate how the parts meshed together and were able to locate any tiny flaw and correct it quickly." The true genius of the mechanism lies in its simplistic form which performed the posability requirements, and the minimal number of parts which over came the arthritic joint effect that befell the other efforts. It was a success that made Ruth Handler beam with delight because the first string was forever cut from the rigid form of Barbie. The greatest accolade for Dick May's creation is that thirty years after the knee's initial development, the most cherished sound to the collector of American Girl Barbies is that distinctive click of a yet functional knee.

An oddity concerning the marketing of a doll with posable joints arose as Mattel took opinion polls. The public showed moderate-to-little enthusiasm for the concept. Ruth's intuitive sense of what the public would buy kept the idea alive even when the polls were to the contrary. In 1965 when the Bendable Leg Barbie was released it affirmed Ruth's confidence in the doll by selling out of the stores as quickly as the doll could be stocked. Its success was attributed to the very words that Mattel advertised on the front of their product with "Lifelike Bendable Legs," a truism in marketing that remains a part of Barbie to this very day.

The new and improved Barbie doll with the bendable legs had knees which clicked into four positions. She was not alone with this new feature. Mattel marketed her family and friends with the new joint also. Midge, Ken, Allan, and Skipper were all sold that year with the bendable legs. The following year in 1966 Barbie's cousin Francie came with bendable legs.

Though being a very durable design, the joint can be broken by the equivalent of hyperextending the knee. Do not try to flex it beyond the number four position and avoid leaving the elastic skin in a constantly taut state of straight leggedness. Store the doll at the first click bent position which reduces the possibility of splitting the plastic.

Still further efforts were made in the area of articulating joints, Ralph Dunn tells of "an attempt to apply a similar technique as found in the knee with the ankle." This mechanism was marketed in 1970 with the Dramatic New Living Barbie who came with flat feet. A one click joint placed ankles into a pose. Another effort identified by Bill Robb "as an implanted piece of soft metal into the joint site to make it a moveable joint" was not used.

Dramatic New Living Barbie was the doll that moved in all directions. She gave "lifelike" all new meaning with the innovations that were packaged into her. A waist that was more than just twist and turn, it was wobbly and would bend and turn with

The reason for Dick May's design being Mattel's choice from the twenty-four bendable legs invented is how the doll appeared seated with legs crossed. After nearly 30 years these legs are still workable.

ease in all directions. A new style hip which appeared more like a sheath made this waist possible. Legs socketed into the hip were on a rotating ball that made them flex in many directions. The Dick May bendable knee provided the flexibility desired for posing legs. As a bevy of innovations were gathered into one doll, Dramatic New Living Barbie was given a one click ankle which gave Barbie movable feet. Another click joint made a bendable elbow possible. The ball joint neck made her head posable in any direction. Pinocchio's strings were no longer needed to bring Barbie doll into a new era of doll animation.

A design developed but never produced was the Walking Barbie. The doll's inventor, Egon Gorski, designed this doll with a windup mechanism to walk across the floor or table. By name, the doll infers a freedom for Barbie like Geppeto's wish, yet Mattel did not pursue the design. Dick May gives the reason being that "the walking action was not in keeping with Barbie's character."

As the research and development department focused its attention on the new innovations that would make the wishes of many a child come true in the decades to come, Barbie's "lifelikeness" was destined to take many twists and turns.

The ultimate movable doll was the 1970 Dramatic New Living Barbie. Seen with a rotating neck, bendable arms, posable wrists, bendable legs, and posable ankles. Note the flat foot and one posed.

A twist waist was marketed on Twist 'N Turn Barbie in 1967 along with rooted eyelashes. Note Barbie both twists her waist and can bend the legs.

Chapter 15

Fantasy Foldouts

A folded Barbie Dream House designed for Mattel by Gordon Shireman. Not all house designers are architects, Barbie's Dream House was designed by a graphic artist.

From 1959 to 1961, the success and popularity of the teenage fashion model, Barbie, provided Mattel with a strong marketing identity upon which further avenues of development could be extended. The next venue to be targeted was the wholesome image of home life. Mattel sought to capture the fold out fantasies of the ever popular pop-up books in a medium to which every child and parent could relate. The "Mainstreet" family of the 60's had one subject that was the center of conversation around the supper table or while watching evening television, the attainment of the American dream, to own a "Dreamhouse."

To provide the child with an extension of their parental discussions, Mattel sold Barbie's first home in 1961. The Barbie Dream House, number 816, was produced by Standard Plastics of New Jersey and went on the real estate market for the incredibly low price of $8.00, a mere three weeks allowance, of course, the lot (livingroom floor) and sales taxes would be covered by the parents. What more could be desired by the child for a paperland foldup structure that held all the amenities of home?

An inviting studio home, the 1961 Dream House folded out to reveal bright yellow walls with red and blue window blinds. A built-in book case and cupboards were included along with a built-in dressing table. Clothes closets with tiny hangers were ready to house Barbie's abundant wardrobe. A fold down floor was designed in white tile with red and yellow area rugs to decorate this fantasy world. Paperboard furniture was also included in the home, such as a bed, couch, chair, television set, coffee table, ottoman, footstool, and even a lamp. Printed both on back and front, the home, when folded up, appeared like the exterior of a house. A handle on the top was included for easy carrying.

For three wonderful years Barbie lived and built up equity in her small but efficient home, yet for a doll designed with such three dimensional character her dream house was just too two dimensional and left her feeling quite flat. It was time to find herself an architect that could justly reflect her persona in a multidimensional way. The architect she chose for this job was Gordon Shireman. Shireman had been with Mattel since 1961 when he joined the staff after answering an advertisement in the *San Francisco Chronicle*. Mattel was searching for a graphic designer to create store displays and point of purchase materials. Barbie was looking for the right man for the job of designing her dream house and who better to fill this than a talented graphic designer. Shireman's design became Barbie's New Dream House, Number 4092, which sold in 1965 for $7.50.

Compared to her previous studio quarters, this was a mansion. The two homes by outward appearances are quite similar. They both portray the exteriors of the home in detailed multicolored graphics and in the portable state of easy to carry and easy to store, the overall sizes of the carrying cases are comparable. It is when the child opens the Shireman designed home that his genius shines. Like the fold-out storybook that stimulates the depth of a child's imagination with every turn of its 3-D pages, the Shireman designed Dream House offers new settings to explore with every change of the child's line of sight. The secret to these multi-faceted alcoves is a unique engineering design and astute eye for angles that enhance the perception of depth. Contained within the chipboard structure is not only a change of wall decorum to provide distinctly separate room settings but also the use of a collapsible wall to partition off the various settings. Every 90 degree turn allows for a change of setting that makes its form so functional as the child goes from play in a bedroom to kitchenette to livingroom to the cozy den with corner fireplace. Each setting is uniquely separate for individual play yet closely linked to the others so that interactive play with friends is not lost. Barriers, no matter how small, like the wall partition, are given an opening. The space above the oven is open to permit easy transfer of play from room to room. A sliding patio door off the bedroom provides an excellent transition of play between the outside and inside. Once again, Mrs. Handler's axiom of paying close attention to detail, as displayed in Gordon Shireman's design, helped launch him into a thirty year

career with Mattel providing him opportunities to express his many artistic talents.

To avoid sibling rivalry, little sister Skipper was also rewarded with a wonderful room design by Mr. Shireman. The NEW Skipper Dream Room was also sold in 1965 listed as number 4094. The Dream Room and the Dream House were done to identical scale so the two structures could work together.

The Dream Room is all that Skipper's heart could desire. As a matter of fact, hearts are everywhere! White wallpaper with red and smaller pink hearts adorn the walls. Three chairs, a small ottoman, and assorted pillows all display Skipper's fancy for hearts. After examining the many pieces of furniture that decorate the room from T.V. to tables to the dust ruffles of the bed, one finds oneself captured by the depth of the design. From a folded size of 5" x 18¼" x 16" the carrying case transforms into a suite containing an alcoved table adjacent to a functional walk-in two door closet, a spacious area for the bed opposite a work area for a student's desk and chair. All of which draws the child to the center of the room. With two short right angle turns of the wall inside the carrying case, the pink floored area becomes a beautiful bay window. The perfect spot for Skipper to play with a miniature Barbie Dream House and a miniature Barbie doll. All reduced in scale to meet the playful needs of Barbie's admiring sister.

Mattel's appetite for Shireman designs led into the kitchen with the release in 1965 of a Kitchen-Dinette, model number 4095. Barbie's Kitchen-Dinette had everything to cook up a party or just meals for her and Ken. Tables, chairs, step stool, counter stools, cookbook, and telephone book, all made of cardboard were included. A built in stove, refrigerator, dishwasher, and counter all came with functional doors. The counter area was decorated in

Even a doll needs a place to call home. The new Barbie Dream House came with three room areas and also an outside play area. Sold in 1964, the Dream House was everything a doll needed.

patterns of the 1965 era. The chipboard structure was printed on both back and front so that both indoor and outdoor activities could be imagined. Everything to outfit a modern kitchen was included such as plastic pots, pans, toaster, toast, dishes, coffee percolator, casseroles, lids, telephone, glasses, tray, cooking spoon, and spatula. Metal items in the set were knives, forks, and spoons. Special cloth items for the kitchen were three potholders, rug, apron, placemats, and curtains for the windows.

The Kitchen-Dinette set featured a new creation, the Sew-Free Fabric curtains, table cloth, napkins, and apron. These Sew-Free designs were a new innovation for little girls to cut out and use to furnish the kitchen. Being a fabric innovation, Shireman collaborated with Mattel's fashion designer Carol Spencer to create these Sew-Free accessories.

When curtains were needed for the NEW number 4092 Barbie Dream House and number 4094 Skipper Dream Room, Carol Spencer again answered the call and created just the right feminine touch for these special structures.

To own these structures now the price was much higher. Doll dealers all know the life expectancy of any paperboard toy is short. Unfortunately, some lost their pieces and others became too damaged during playtime and were thrown away. What has survived are in short supply. With the limited amount of these dreamy scenes, the price does continue to climb on the secondary market.

Shireman was not finished in the imaginary world built for Barbie. The year 1965 was to be the biggest yet for this teenage fashion model and what more could a model want than her own fashion shop. A Gordon Shireman designed shop could only be the best possible for Barbie. Sold as number 817 the NEW Barbie Fashion Shop was a beautiful replica of a dress shop boutique of the 1960's. Made from a chipboard medium, this was the place where Barbie and Midge could "shop 'till they drop." The exterior of the portable toy was designed with a brick look featuring a large display window with mannequin and an oval corner window with a cardboard head for hat displays. Interior flooring was large enough to extend outside the building and patterned to appear like a sidewalk around the shop when opened. Step inside the shop and Barbie found a panorama to please any young shopper. The Barbie size cardboard mannequin was the correct scale to fit any Barbie doll fashion a young girl wanted to display in the window. Built in shelves and functional cupboards stood ready for tiny accessories. A built in clothes rack held all those outfits ready for the dolls to buy. Being a teenage fashion model meant the shop was fitted with a stage and curtain for fashion shows. A large standing three-way mirror helped the dolls see how they looked in the glamorous outfits sold in the shop. Cardboard furnishings in the shop included a two shelf display case, chairs, table, fashion show announcements, and three magazines for the Barbie size table. Small plastic hangers were included in the shop to hang those many garments on the clothing rack.

Preventing the loss of the many assembled pieces was yet another focus of the structure's design that would not be overlooked by Mattel. Recognizing that missing parts translated into reduced playtime satisfaction, the structures were designed not only as an object of play but also a self-contained storage case for all the assembled pieces. A diagramed placement of where to put these parts in the case while in the portable state was enclosed with the structures. Try putting away a complete set of pieces to the Kitchen-Dinette without memoriz-

Another Shireman designed structure was this Skipper's Dream Room. Furniture and playthings inside were made of cardboard. Curtains for the Dream Room were designed by Carol Spencer.

ing the diagram! Such engineering detail brings the gratitude of many collectors as structures are still being found with all pieces in place. A fine testimony to Mattel's concern with keeping a functional toy for not only years but generations to come.

With all the developments and insights that went into the production of the structures, how could one man or even a production staff put so much thought into the numerous structures and release them all in the fabulous marketing year of 1965? The answer is found in the cliche — "timing is everything." The first fruition to Mr. Shireman's work was patented in 1962, as the Barbie Fashion Shop. But the World of Barbie was not ready for its marketing debut. The problem was not with the structure but with the doll.

Mrs. Handler was in search of more lifelike characteristics for Barbie and by her recollections the preliminary ideas for flexible joints were between two and three years in creation. As the development of the knee progressed other marketable spinoffs were quickly coming on line. Accessories like stools, chairs, and sofas all left the straight legged doll in an awkward position. A new furniture line called Barbie 'N Skipper Go-Together Furniture included: number 0408, a sofa-bed; number 0410, chaise lounge; number 0411, lawn swing; number 4010, a diningroom kit; and number 4012, a livingroom furniture group. All were poised for a 1965 release incorporating a newly patented Sew-Free Fabric system and the Cut 'N Button decorator accessories. Everything was ready except the belle of the ball, Barbie.

Dick May recounted that the year prior to the release of the bendable leg doll was a very hectic one, "Development of the bendable knee made stops on the desks of each inventor at Mattel. I just couldn't understand why there was all the pressure on its development." The cog that Mr. May was to invent would become a keystone in Mattel's flexing its corporate muscle in the toy industry of the 60's. Barbie was preparing to stride center stage with a myriad of other Mattel toys in a Total Go marketing blitz that would eclipse the competition for the next decade to come.

Mattel, to this day, strives to coordinate the release of Barbie with new innovations in her accessories. Many times the patenting of inventions will supercede its release date by several years so the patent date of a product can not, as a rule, be used as an indicator of marketing release. The next structure to be discussed is an exception to this rule. Sometimes on a rare occasion, a product can be so impressive in the quality of its craftsmanship and stylish elegance that it merits command of the center stage alone.

Unfortunately, Mattel has no records of who designed the Barbie and Ken Little Theatre. Even Gordon Shireman himself says the original idea was not his, although he did work on the project. The theatre made of chipboard, was complete with stage, seating, and six backdrop scenes that could set the mood for whichever fairytale they wished to produce. Tickets to sell along with the script book and cardboard furniture for settings were included. Of the structures sold, the theatre is the one considered by collectors as the rarest and hardest to locate. So few of these have survived and even fewer are complete and in mint condition.

The Barbie and Ken Little Theatre, as the structure was called by Mattel, was a panorama of theatrics both from inside and outside. Set as a theatre it had an outside view of a poster of Barbie and Ken announcing their production. Openning the structure revealed a stage set with antique gold trim and

Mattel was hooked on graphic designs by Gordon Shireman. A Barbie's Dream Kitchen-Dinette Set was all new in 1965. As a foldout playset, the Kitchen-Dinette unfolded to reveal two interior areas and an outdoor scene for doll play.

even fold out box seats. The overflap opened down to reveal seating for a large audience. The stage was designed with chipboard backdrops in layers to create the feeling of depth. Any of the six backdrops could be inserted to show either the palace, a cabin for Little Red Riding Hood, a Mediterranean street scene for Arabian Nights, even a woodland scene. Cardboard furniture was included with the structure to add additional realism to the settings. To close the playtime, a curtain fastened to a cardboard roller could be dropped signaling the success of yet another Barbie and Ken theatre production.

The Handlers used this theatre to launch an acting career for their doll, Barbie. The theatre was sold in 1964 only, with costumes marketed separately. The costumes were designed around childhood fairytales and were still available through 1965. Although costumes for Arabian Nights, Little Red Riding Hood, Cinderella, King Arthur and Guinevere were fashions, they were made to be used in the Little Theatre. The costumes were designed by Dorothy Schue, Aileen Zublin, and Kay Carter for Mattel. The three women, in most incidents, collaborated on these costumes, but Dorothy Schue was the sole designer of the Guinevere ensemble. Four sets of stunning costumes make up the theatre series. The outfits were designed to sell the Little Theatre and the theatre sold the costumes. The combination of outfits and theatre sold the dolls.

Guinevere, number 0873, was a long royal blue velvet gown with red and gold trim. A hat with wimple and fabric shoes to match was perfect for any stage. Ken's costume was called King Arthur number 0773. This was a silver metallic fabric complete with helmet, sword, shield, boots, and spurs.

The costume for Cinderella was really two in one but sold as a set. As number 0872, Cinderella was a poor dress in brown burlap with white sleeves and black vested top. No shoes came with the poor dress. Princess Cinderella was a royal gown of yellow taffeta with silver bodice. Barbie even had a tulle veil to wear with her gown and clear closed toe shoes with silver glitter. Ken was a royal prince in number 0772 in a gold and emerald green suit with matching cape. A white ruffled collar and cuffs and a gold velvet hat with a white feather matched his gold tights. Emerald green velvet shoes added to his ensemble. For Ken to be the perfect prince charming, Mattel gave him a magenta velvet pillow with gold braid and tassel trim to carry the glass slipper on.

Continuing the theatre set was Barbie doll's costume called Arabian Nights number 0874. A great amount of work had to go into the design of this ensemble. The skirt was pink chiffon with a matching pink satin blouse. A veil of pink chiffon trimmed in gold wrapped around Barbie's head. Even jewelry in the form of a necklace of pink and turquoise pearls, gold drop earrings, and three snake bracelets of gold and turquoise were with the set. Gold lamb slippers protected Barbie's dainty feet. To summon her beau Ken, she merely needed to rub a gold plastic lamp and poof, he appeared. Of course, Ken appeared in number 0774 which these talented ladies designed. Wearing gold and white knit pants topped by a rich red velvet coat trimmed with gold braid, Ken was the perfect Arabian skeik. A white and gold belt held his coat. A gold and white knit hat with jeweled pin fit atop Ken doll's head. For shoes he wore red velvet and gold braid slippers.

Barbie could portray Little Red Riding Hood in

The folded Kitchen-Dinette even featured a counter, stools, and family room area for entertaining guests. As a part of a large thrust Mattel brought their company to the public eye in 1965 with dynamic toys and a coast to coast advertising campaign.

number 0880. In this costume both Barbie and Ken doll's outfits were sold together. Her blue and white dotted swiss dress was accented with a black felt corset. A red fleece cape with hood tied under her chin kept Barbie warm from the forest chill. White socks and black plastic flat soled shoes completed her ensemble. She carried a basket with a red and white napkin and wax rolls. Ken came on the scene as the wolf. He had a granny cap and a red and black plaid hat to accompany his wolf mask.

As in hair designing, face painting, or any other department, more costumes were designed for the theatre than were manufactured. Prototype outfits have been found of Alice In Wonderland and Peter Pan which never made the production line.

The theatre was like the other mentioned structures in its fine detail and workmanship. With such elegant structures and glamorous costumes, it is no wonder Barbie has remained the star of the Mattel show for over thirty years.

The structural creations by Gordon Shireman were a large part of the 1965 line. The Barbie Fashion Shop was a miniature example of a dress shop in the mid 60's. Barbie could not only purchase clothing here but hold fashion shows.

A variety of 60's Barbie dolls have a fashion show in the Barbie Fashion Shop. Midge serves as sales clerk in the shop.

A 1992 All American Barbie is showing Plantation Belle to a 1959 Barbie in the Fashion Shop.

Although not a Shireman design, Mattel marketed the Barbie and Ken Little Theatre in 1964. Another fold-out play structure, the Theatre came with many cardboard pieces.

The stage to the theatre was a colorful array with a Gothic design.

One side of the folded theatre reveals a stage door for the actors to enter.

The Prince and Princess dance to the strains of music at the ball. Costumes for the theatre were sold separately and designed by Aileen Zublin, Kay Carter, and Dorothy Schue.

Scenery, furnishings, tickets, and playbook were part of the Barbie and Ken Little Theatre. The theatre is considered extremely rare today.

Arabian Nights was a glamorous costume designed for Barbie. Ken was also a part of each play.

Guinevere, as portrayed by a 1960 brunette ponytail Barbie is elegant in royal blue velvet. The Guinevere costume was designed by the late Dorothy Schue.

Little Red Riding Hood was portrayed by Barbie with Ken as the Wolf. Even a woodland scene accompanied the theatre.

Costumes were boxed and sold separately. Shown is the Arabian Nights costume for Ken doll sold in 1964.

Ken's King Arthur costume was a dazzling outfit making him a knight in shining armor.

Chapter 16

Eyelash Era

Eyelashes first appeared on the 1967 Twist 'N Turn Barbie doll. The swimsuit for this doll was designed for Mattel by Dorothy Schue.

Never has a doll over time evolved to show new inventions the way the Barbie doll has. The late 60's for Barbie doll is called the Eyelash Era. The popularity of the Eyelash Era carried it into the early 70's, for a good reason. During this time in doll history, Mattel attempted something unheard of in a doll of this size – they gave her rooted eyelashes.

Mattel took this time to update Barbie's whole face, to draw attention to the new innovation, and to keep pace with the times. The facial makeover was introduced in 1967 with another first, the lifelike innovation of a Twist 'N Turn waist for Barbie. The Twist 'N Turn head mold exemplifies Mattel's efforts to focus the buyer's attention on it's newest innovation. From the slender tapered jawline and chin, the attention is drawn upward past the pursed lips to the perky upswept nose. Framed by the pale rose red rouge accenting the upper cheekbone and a wisp of bangs, the wider and brighter blue eyes peak out beneath a luscious row of Barbie's newest adornment, eyelashes. The tan skin tone was replaced by a pink flesh tone vinyl coloring. Arms on the new doll were straight as in previous years. The body mold was the new twist waist designed for Mattel by Jack Ryan. This body was molded in two parts and fastened together so the two pieces could rotate from side to side along a level mid-axial body line giving the doll greater freedom of movement. Legs on the Barbie doll were

the bendable legs which had proven so successful in 1965. This doll, more posable than ever and with it's added human feature of eyelashes, drew one step closer to accomplishing the lifelikeness that Mattel sought.

Jean Ann Burger recalls that making those eyelashes was a difficult and tedious process. "The rooting machines were designed differently than sewing machines," she says. Sewing machines have a needle that goes down into the material, but rooting machines have a needle underneath. The doll head goes down over the post and a needle comes up and pulls the hair inside the scalp. Problems were encountered when doing the eyelashes. She was working on a convex curve with a very small arc not a flat surface. Where the eyelid protrudes beyond the area of the pupil was where the rooting had to take place. As rooting begins, the machine operates fine until the center of the eye is reached. Here the shape of the face changes going towards the nose. In this area, the working surface flattens slightly causing the rooting machine to jump about an eighth of an inch. At this point of the eyelash rooting process, she would have to hold back on the head so the skipping did not occur. A much thinner needle and thread were used on eyelash rooting than hair rooting. Adding to the problem of the narrow confines of the facial shape, the vinyl was thicker than the vinyl in the scalp and skull cap area. "Needles and thread were often broken," says Ms. Burger. "With all the struggles involved, it became too expensive to continue rooting eyelashes."

Ms. Burger's specifications required that the eyelashes be shorter, but production factories did not take time to trim the lashes after rooting. This has given collectors longer more luscious eyelashes on some dolls. The trimming of these lashes was to be done by hand. Ms. Burger says some of the first issued dolls did have the lashes hand trimmed, but time became a factor and the trimming was dropped.

May 1967, featured another advertising campaign first, a trade-in doll offer. The plan presented children with the opportunity to trade in their old Barbie doll plus $1.50 and Mattel would return, by mail, a new Barbie. This doll was the Trade-In Barbie and featured the new Twist 'N Turn style body. According to figures published in the *Collectors Encyclopedia of Barbie Dolls and Collectibles* by Sibyl DeWein and Joan Ashabraner, during the month of May 1967, no less than 1,250,000 old dolls were traded. Collectors estimate that many of these were the 1959 vintage doll, and this would explain the shortage of all those first issues. Yet other collectors feel that the dolls traded were possibly only bubblecuts and bendable leg Barbies. This is an issue still under debate with collectors.

The hand-rooted eyelashes appear on Twist 'N Turn Barbie dolls for 1967, 1968, 1969, and 1970. The eyelashes were also featured on the Talking Barbie doll, Dramatic New Living Barbie of 1970, Live Action Barbie from 1971, Growin' Pretty Hair Barbie of 1971, and Barbie Hair Happenin's which was a limited edition department store special from 1971. The 1972 Talking Busy Barbie doll continued the line of rooted eyelashes.

All the Twist 'N Turn Barbies from 1967 through 1971 came marked:

©1966
Mattel, Inc.
U.S. Patented
U.S. Pat. Pend.
Made in
Japan

The main difference in these dolls were their hairstyles and swimsuit styles and colors. The 1967

Twist 'N Turn had long straight hair and wore an orange two piece swimsuit. A white net coverup with orange trim around the arms and legs was worn over the suit. This uniquely styled suit was designed for Mattel by fashion designer Dorothy Schue. Straight long hair was also on the 1968 Twist 'N Turn and she wore a rose pink shorts set with a rose pink patterned top. The top had a vinyl belt at the waistline. By 1969 Twist 'N Turn Barbie doll had long hair which had been curled into a flip all around. Those long straight bangs were combed to the right side of her head. To replace the bangs, Barbie had a spit curl which hung down on her forehead. The suit this year was a yellow, green, and red checked one piece suit. Another one piece suit was worn by the Twist 'N Turn in 1970. This suit was red and white knit. Barbie retained the flip style hair, but the long straight bangs were combed to the left side of her face this year. In 1971, the swimsuit was a one piece knit in yellow and red. She also had the flip style hair, but the bangs were again combed to the right side of the dolls face.

Talking Barbie doll was issued in 1968, and she too, had the rooted eyelashes. This doll featured the new Twist 'N Turn doll face with a long side ponytail. The ponytail was tied with ribbon at three

A 1969 Twist 'N Turn Barbie doll shows the new hair style designed for the doll. Each year Twist 'N Turn Barbie wore newly designed swimwear.

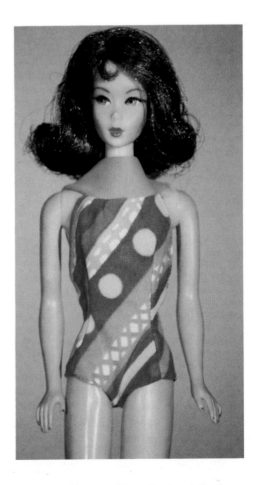

The 1972 Twist 'N Turn Barbie doll shows the auburn hair color.

103

places down the hair. She wore a rose knit top over rose shorts. Talking Barbie was marked:

©1967
Mattel, Inc.
U.S. & Foreign
Pats. Pend.
Mexico

Talking Barbie was designed to say eleven phrases. She was a follow up to an earlier design success, called Chatty Cathy. The Chatty Cathy mechanism, a pull string voice box, was downsized to Barbie measurements and inserted into the body cavity of the doll. It was designed for Mattel by Bill Robb, who began with the company in 1960 as an inventor. Working in the small interior of the Barbie doll body with this talking mechanism was very difficult. The space within the doll was filled with the talking mechanism which made if difficult to keep on the pin and socket connections of the arms and legs.

The Dramatic New Living Barbie doll from 1970 was a doll designed with so many posable innovations she almost came alive. She came with three hair colors and flat feet. Her hair was long, straight, and loose with bangs. She came with a gold and silver swimsuit. An orange net jacket completed the ensemble.

Eyelashes of incredible length were sold on Live Action Barbie doll from 1971.

Although most dolls came with one new innovation at a time, Dramatic New Living Barbie is noted for having another innovation upon her release. She was sold with flat feet. This unusual foot was designed for a one click bendable ankle which was designed for Mattel by Dick May. This ankle was a direct offshoot of the bendable knee which he also designed. Unlike the knee, many foot mechanisms are found frozen because of lack of use. Unless the doll is purchased mint in box where the posable foot is mentioned or a person is enlightened about the possibility by a good friend like Carol Spencer, the click in the foot is often overlooked.

During these formative years Barbie developed a new neck. Designed for better positioning, this neck was on a rotating ball that enabled Barbie's head to be posed in many directions. All earlier neck designs were on a level plane axis and could only be turned from side to side. The new neck, designed for Mattel by the late Jack Ryan, made her head much more posable. The new rotating neck duplicated the function of the atlas and axis vertebrae of the human spine and first appeared on the 1970 issued Dramatic New Living Barbie. This made three new inventions on one doll.

A Sears exclusive that incorporated many of the new innovations was Living Barbie in 1971. She wore a pink and white dotted one shoulder blouse and long matching skirt. Both this special issue and the regular issued Living Barbies came marked:

©1968 Mattel, Inc.
U.S. & For. Pat'd
Other Pats. Pend.
Taiwan

The Living Barbie doll was also the first of the line to be offered with the articulated wrists. With these wrists even the hands were posable.

Further developments in the realm of movement progressed in 1971 with Live Action Barbie. The doll was a real flower child wearing a brightly colored bellbottom jumpsuit with a wide brown belt. Fringed brown wristlets and a matching headband made this Action Barbie a fun toy. Live Action Barbie was sold separately or as Live Action Barbie on Stage. The latter doll came with her own stage and microphone. Live Action Barbie was marked:

©1968 Mattel, Inc.
U.S. & Foreign Patented
Patented in Canada 1967
Other Patents Pending
Taiwan

To compliment those wonderful lashes, Mattel released Growin' Pretty Hair Barbie in 1971. She was wearing a short pink satin party dress with a pentagon inset front panel that created a unique geometric hemline. Growin' Pretty Hair Barbie also came with her own hair pieces. The unique design to the dress was by Carol Spencer for Mattel. If Ruth Handler could have breathed life into the doll she would have tried, because with Growin' Pretty Hair Barbie, she even tried to simulate hair growth. It is difficult today to find this doll and its three hair pieces. A feature of this doll was the new centered eyes along with eyelashes. Along with rooted blonde hair, the doll was sold with a long fall of hair that fit into a hole in the center of her head. The hair could be pushed in or pulled out to simulate growth. The two additional hair pieces were a braided fall of blonde hair and a small group of Shirley Temple ringlets. Growin' Pretty Hair Barbie was marked:

©1967 Mattel, Inc.
U.S. Patented
Other Patents Pending
Patented in Canada 1967
Taiwan

Another Barbie with the eyelashes was the Hair Happenin's Barbie from 1971. She was a department store special from Sears and never appeared in the Mattel catalog. With ear length red hair, this doll had centered eyes and three hair pieces to accompany her. She wore a rose color tricot skirt and white blouse. This doll was marked the same as the Twist 'N Turn Barbie dolls. Hair Happenin's Barbie is now considered extremely rare and hard to find by collectors.

In 1972 Mattel introduced the Busy line of dolls. This innovation introduced a hand on the doll that could be opened and closed and hold items. Both Busy Barbie and Talking Busy Barbie doll of that year came with the new hands. Busy Barbie came with long straight blonde hair and wore a granny dress. However, the Talking Busy Barbie came with a collar length blonde hairstyle with bangs. She wore a bibbed shorts and shirt outfit. Busy Barbie was marked:

©1966
Mattel, Inc.
U.S. & Foreign
Patented
Other Pat's
Pending
Made in
U.S.A.

The Talking Busy Barbie came marked:

©1967
Mattel, Inc.
U.S. & For.
Pat'd Pat'd
In Canada
1967 Other
Pat's. Pend.
Hong Kong

Yet another eyelashed Barbie doll was the Walk Lively Barbie doll of 1972. With long blonde hair parted in the middle, she had the same face mold as the Twist 'N Turn dolls in the late 60's and early 70's. Walk Lively Barbie was marked:

©1967 Mattel, Inc.
U.S. Pat. Pend.
Taiwan

Seeing the world through lashed eyes did not totally disappear with the 1972 line of dolls for Mattel. A bridal Barbie called Beautiful Bride Barbie sold in 1976 was issued with rooted eyelashes. A prized collectible today, this doll was a department store special. The doll came packaged wearing an elegant wedding gown with tulle veil.

Those eyelashed eyes did not last at Mattel. Rooted eyelashes did give the dolls a lovely appearance but as Jean Ann Burger says, "it became too tedious, time consuming, and costly to continue." Mattel returned to painted lashes but with a flair distinctly different from those earlier versions. The lashes were gone at least until Carol Spencer dusted off an old copy of the eyelash rooting procedures manual — sorry Jean and Mellie, they're back!

"They're back!" Rooted eyelashes came back in 1992 on Benefit Ball Barbie doll.

105

Chapter 17

Sensations of the 70's

An extremely rare doll was sold in 1971 called Hair Happenin's Barbie. She was sold as a Sears Roebuck department store special. She came with rooted eyelashes and short titian hair and hair pieces.

As Mattel entered the politically turbulent decade of the 1970's, Barbie's sales rapidly approached the eighty millionth doll. Yet this time is the most confusing for the Barbie collector. Barbies of the early to mid 70's are fraught with puzzling anomalies. Dolls on bubble packs, missing fashion booklets, and baggies to replace the slipcase and cello window boxes.

The history of Mattel during this time can best be described by the three R's; Restructuring, Reflection, and Re-examination. All of which directly affected the marketing of the doll.

The mid 70's found Mattel in management restructuring which was resolved with the Handlers relinquishing control of the corporation resulting in changes in the executive administration of the corporation. The perspectives and insights expressed by the new management caused some changes in the marketing profile of Barbie to conform to the new financial and philosophical objectives. One of the first noticeable changes was that the informative fashion booklets were left out for a few years as a cost saving measure. Secondly, Barbie started appearing not only in department stores but also in drug stores and supermarkets.

Re-examination of the path that Mattel had taken with this all American doll in the past decade displayed a level of diversity, ingenuity, and a full measure of risk taking to break new ground in the development of Barbie. They had created a doll who could move, bend, and pose in any direction; grasp with a posable hand; tilt her head; and change her hair with a myriad of styles. Engineering feats accomplished with the Barbie doll line were known worldwide and copied irregardless of the copyright owned by Mattel. Into the second decade Mattel was searching for new directions to take this doll in order to attain continued success. To build a framework of success on the 60's foundations, Mattel began a search for new ideas. Sometimes new ideas are as close as your own backyard. At least this is the way executives at Mattel found it when they began planning for the 1970 line of Barbie dolls. Inspiration was to come from the California beaches with bathing beauties and surfer boys. Sun, sand, and surf became the theme of the 70's with a line of Malibu dolls clad in bathing suits and sporting suntan skin tones. The first dolls to be considered as a series, not only Barbie but her family and friends were a part of the Malibu line. For Barbie, this was the first of a continuing line of theme linked family dolls. Malibu dolls were issued first in 1971 but the series continued into 1984 with the last line of Malibu dolls called Sun Gold Malibu Barbie, P.J., black Barbie, Skipper, Ken, and black Ken. Clad in bathing suits, some of the early 1971 Malibus were in the bubblepack packaging. Later the Malibus were returned to the box with the clear plastic front format. These dolls came with brush and comb, and did not include shoes. No girl ever wears shoes at the beach and neither did our Barbie.

One of the Malibu series called Sun Lovin' Malibu was produced with the innovation of suntan skin with bathing suit marks. It appeared Barbie and her friends were out sunbathing and had suit marks to show off their tan lines. Ralph Dunn, a chemical engineer for Mattel Toys during those years says this effect was produced with a mercury compound. The first problem with the color change was that it did not last very long and had a tendency to fade. Mr. Dunn says they had to find an anti-ultraviolet inhibitor so that the tantone skin would hold longer. Imagine, this is suntan lotion for a Barbie doll! Placing this in the vinyl was not possible so a spray over the doll was used. This suntan effect was patented by Mattel as an exclusive invention by their staff. The Sun Lovin' Malibu series was marketed in 1979.

Another of Mr. Dunn's innovations released in 1973 was the Quick Curl Barbie and friends. Dunn designed the hair with wire to make styling and curling the hair easily accomplished by children. Along with Barbie in this series were Quick Curl Kelley, Quick Curl Miss America, Quick Curl Skipper, and Quick Curl Francie. By 1976 Quick Curl P.J. was on the market along with a Deluxe Quick Curl Barbie doll and Deluxe Quick Curl Cara.

The baggy dolls were an unusual assortment of items which causes much confusion for the collector. These dolls were a mix and match affair for which Mattel used various body parts. Many of these parts were generated by Mattel's consumer guarantee on all talking and walking products. Packed with each Mattel Talking Barbie or friend came a registration card "guaranteeing within 90 days of purchase replacement or repair of any faulty talking or walking mechanism." Claims by consumers were forwarded directly to Mattel — no handling by retailer or wholesaler was required. To use a phrase coined many years later in the fast food chicken business, "parts are parts" and Mattel was going to make use of this newly created inventory along with present stock in a new and aggressively growing marketing niche.

The bubblepack and cellopack dolls which appeared in the early 70's have always been a mystery for collectors, but no more. Cliff Jacobs was in charge of this marketing approach and says the supermarkets were eagerly establishing toy aisles in their expanded one stop shopping format. Mattel saw a new and imaginative way to present their product. As a new packaging for this market Mattel put the dolls in packages which had a hole that could be hung on the J hooks and the pin and peg board format of supermarket display aisles. The cellophane baggy with a cardboard top came with a Mattel logo in the upper left corner and simply bore the name of the doll enclosed. Even today, other toy companies still use this packaging technique.

Reflecting on the past successes placed "innovation and imagination" as the credo by which preimminence could maintain the Barbie era.

The Talking Barbie continued into the 70's. It was the reduced version of Mattel's successful Chatty Cathy voice box implanted into the body of Barbie that caused so many problems for Mattel. Unfortunately, these talking dolls now are found mute. An essential mechanical part that allowed them to talk was rubber and over time that part has crumbled and broken. It was also this part through repeative use that malfunc-

tioned. Collectors who have ponytail dolls from the early sixties will recognize the crumbling problem of natural rubber as the original rubber bands have broken leaving small pieces clinging to the strands of hair. To repair the talking mechanism, a new synthetic band which will not breakdown over time can be refitted by many doll hospitals.

During the 1960's and early 70's doll hospitals received Mattel hospital order catalogs. Many parts of dolls made since 1964 and 1971 came to the repair hospitals in little cello bags. Heads arrived in boxes sectioned off resembling a carton of eggs. Most replacement heads sold for $1.50 each with some as low as .75¢ each.

Talking Barbie heads have shown up on many other body forms. As the result of efforts by these doll hospitals some have been found on Twist 'N Turn bodies, others on straight leg bodies, yet others on bendable leg bodies. The story is told by one doll dealer in central Ohio this way, "the talking dolls broke very easily. They even broke while never

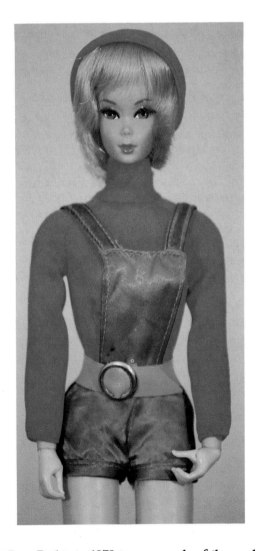

Talking Busy Barbie in 1972 is an example of the mechanical inventions still being made at Mattel in the 70's. Note the closed hand. With a turn of the wrist the workable thumb could open to a Busy Hand. Mattel marketed the Busy Hand on this doll as well as the Busy Barbie sold in 1972.

being removed from their boxes." The leg, neck, and arm joints are very brittle. After only a few days many children found that the doll came apart. Most children taped the arms or legs back on. Many parents have drilled holes into the torso and screwed the arms back to the body. The ways that parents repaired these dolls are endless. Most children popped off an old doll head and substituted the new Talking head to the old body. The Talking Barbie doll had a lovely painted face with rooted eyelashes which was a favorite head mold despite the many shortcomings of the body. This provides the collector with some insights into the tumultuous and sometimes tortured life of Barbie in the seventies. The turbulent times were destined to tarnish a very special event in the coming of age of Barbie.

The candles of Barbie's Sweet 16 birthday party dimmed as in that same year Ruth and Elliot Handler stepped out of the glow of Barbie's fame. It would now be up to Mattel to carry on the tradition of excellence that was the cornerstone of its founder's vision. The creativity displayed in the products marketed from 1975 through the close of the decade were to hold true to the high standards. The new management was also able to avoid the complacency that past success brings with a series of new innovations and molds.

Mechanical engineers were busy at work in Mattel laboratories and in 1975 they introduced another of their moving innovations called Free Moving Barbie. The Free Moving doll was designed with a tab in her back which when pulled allowed the doll's waist to become completely movable. She could swing a golf club or tennis racket or even throw a bowling ball. When the tab was flat against her back she was fully posable like a regular bendable leg Barbie. Other dolls in the Free Moving series with this same design were Ken, P.J., Cara, and Curtis.

Change has been what has kept Barbie doll marketable. In 1976 Mattel entered into a new change for the doll with Ballerina Barbie. A special new mold was created for this innovation which featured legs, arms, and head that had swivel joints. Barbie could move her arms into any position and hold her head in many elegant poses. The legs could pirouette, do splits, and kicks. This Barbie was marked:

©Mattel, Inc. 1966
U.S. Patent Pending
Taiwan

The image of Barbie would be forever changed with the first semblance of a smile. Gone was the expressionless face of the 60's, as the Gold Medal Barbie series was released. The doll was a standard Malibu Barbie doll dressed in Olympic attire to notify the public of Mattel's ties to the U.S. Olympic Committee and a two year multi-million dollar advertising campaign. Gold Medal Barbie wore a red, white, and blue one piece swimsuit and was quickly followed on the market by Gold Medal Bar-

bie Skater, Gold Medal Barbie Skier, Gold Medal Barbie Winter Sports set (a Sears catalogue exclusive), Gold Medal Ken Skier, and Gold Medal P.J. Gymnast. These dolls all featured U.S. Olympic style sports outfits and gear with doll size medals.

The smiles at Mattel broadened further as in 1976 Barbie was voted "favorite doll of the century" and given a place in the "America's Time Capsule" at our nation's bicentennial celebration. All these accolades and praise had a strange affect on Barbie, instead of swelling with pride, Barbie grew to Supersize. And sure enough, in 1977 Mattel marketed a Supersize Barbie doll that stood eighteen inches tall. Several outfits of clothing were designed and sold for this doll which was an attempt to test the pool of the buying public for a change in size. A Supersize Christie was also sold in 1977. By 1978 Mattel marketed a Supersize Bridal Barbie doll and again in 1979 Supersize Barbie with Super Hair appeared in stores.

Now larger than life, or as big as Hollywood can

Ballerina Barbie sold in 1976 featured arms and legs socketed on a rotating ball. With the new joints, arms and legs were more movable to allow the doll to move in ballerina positions.

make an 11½" fem fatale, Barbie was destined to become a Superstar in 1977. Coupling what was to become one of the most successful face molds with a wardrobe that would make the fashions of the silver screen pale, Superstar Barbie was released. As Hollywood's stars shunned the attention of the news media paparazzi, Barbie made it easier to capture her beauty on film. The innovations of Fashion Photo Barbie, animated Barbie in such a way that the child took an interactive part with the design mechanism. Sold with a stand which turned Barbie for poses where she could be photographed from every angle, a child size camera was also included in the box with the doll. Also with the same innovations in this Fashion Photo series were Fashion Photo Christie and Fashion Photo P.J.

To close the 70's with one last innovation Mattel was able to complete what Aldo Favilli describes as "a beautiful concept for a doll but a little nightmare." Kissing Barbie was designed. When the but-

A side view of Kissing Barbie shows the pucker to the face.

Kissing Barbie marketed in 1979 had unique facial expressions with kissing ability. A square button in the doll's back allowed the kissing mechanism to work. Work on this project was described by Aldo Favilli, Mattel sculptor, as "a little nightmare."

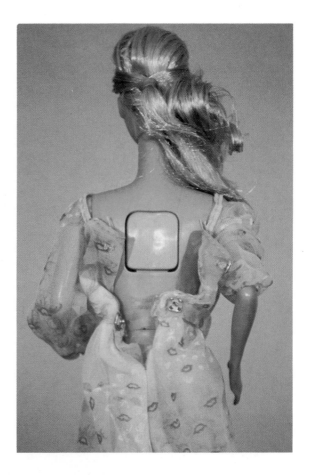

The button in the back of Kissing Barbie allowed the kissing mechanism to work.

ton panel on her back was pushed to tilt her head back, the face would draw up to a kiss. Also featured with the doll was the kissing sound which seemed to be the "nightmare" part of the innovation. As Steve Lewis, manager of the research and development department during those years says, "getting the doll kiss to not sound like a cricket took long hours of work for the engineers involved."

During the 70's and into the 80's many veteran employees at Mattel began to reach retirement age. Mattel, in wanting to show appreciation for years of continued service, attempted to make bronze statues of Barbie. "The first were actual Barbies," says Ralph Dunn, "bronzed like baby shoes. These did not look good and broke easily." One of these attempts was presented to Charlotte Johnson in 1974 when she retired. Carol Spencer tells, "the metal the doll was dipped in would bubble and crack on the doll's surface."

Later, a solid bronze statue was made for Ray Wagner at his retirement in 1983. Dunn took a Barbie doll and coated the body with wax to seal the joints of the doll. Movable parts would cause cracking in the metal later if not sealed. Mellie Phillips was then asked to put glue in the doll hair and comb it into a style. The glue would hold the hair in place and insure against feathering or muss. A mold was formed over the Barbie and a wax mold cast in it. This wax figure was cleaned and joints were filed, then another mold was made. Bronze was then poured into this mold, polished, and gold plated. A dark green marble base was made with a gold plaque attached. Another employee in the model shop made a solid oak case for the statue. Dunn called on the assistance of Fashion Designer Carol Spencer who helped with the fabric designs to line the oak box. After lining the box with a foam pad, emerald green velvet was used to decorate the interior. An emerald green satin ribbon was wrapped across the doll statue to assist in removing the doll from her box. Only one statue was made.

Later in 1988, Bank of America had twenty statues made to give to certain Mattel employees. "Cast differently, these were wearing a molded dress. The type of casting was a 'cold cast' method, they were fashioned of polymer casting resin and heavily filled with bronze powder," says Dunn. "These were not plated and had a standard plastic trophy case," says Ralph Dunn.

The 70's was a decade of surprising developments and a sensational time for Barbie.

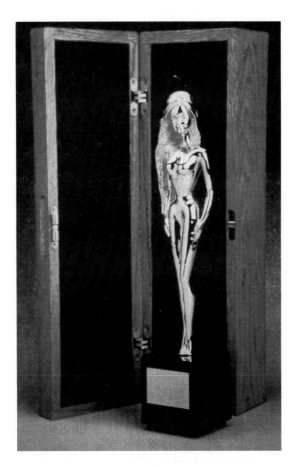

A solid bronze statue of Barbie given to Ray Wagner in 1983 when he retired from Mattel. Work on this statue was done by Ralph Dunn. The interior of the box was designed by Carol Spencer. Photo courtesy of Ralph Dunn.

This is a 1988 version of a Barbie statue made by request from Bank of America for presentation to Mattel executives. Notice the molded dress on this statue. Photo courtesy of Ralph Dunn.

Chapter 18

Elegance of the 80's

A button panel in the back of the Western Barbie from 1980 made the doll's eye wink. The winking eye was designed for Mattel by Bill Kelly.

The decade of the 80's epitomizes Mattel's desire to continually rework the marketing profile of Barbie to maintain a viable and fresh image. Of all the successful engineering feats of the 1970's that accomplished many innovations and inventions, only a few survived in refined forms in the 80's. In the marketing area of the theme linked Barbie and friends, only one category continued. The Malibu series went on until 1984 with Sun Gold Malibu. The success of the boxed dressed dolls, which had its roots in the pink box display dolls and the boxed dressed dolls of the Little Theatre line of the 60's, showed great promise with Superstar Barbie. The expansion of the dressed boxed doll was to be the most challenging stretch of creativity for the design staff at Mattel. As shown in the Ethnic designs in Chapter 20 and the International, Chapter 19, the cultural outreach for Barbie herself was to commence with the 1980 marketing year. Her appeal to the

diverse world community would carry the doll throughout the decade. The focus of designs on the distinctive detailing of the cultural lines and the need for elegant fashions for the dressed boxed dolls would create more pressure on the fashion design department to fulfill the demands of the many divergent theme lines that were to emerge in the 80's.

Mattel regularly marketed concurrently contrasting lines to broaden the appeal of Barbie. The outdoor/rodeo theme was used with Western Barbie sold in 1980. The doll wore a white knit western outfit with black fringe. With a design by Bill Kelly, Barbie had a mechanical eye that when a button in her back was pressed, winked. Along the same theme was Fashion Jeans Barbie sold in 1981 clad in a pink sweater, blue denim jeans, and western boots. In 1982, Horse Lovin' Barbie was sold based on the expanded accessorizing of the outdoor theme. Horse Lovin' Barbie wore red vinyl pants, a red and tan checked shirt, and a leather and fur trimmed vest. With a western hat and saddlebag, she was ready for the rodeo. To compliment the rodeo doll, Mattel marketed horses for Barbie and Ken sold separately. Barbie's horse was named Dallas. Ken could ride the black stallion named Midnight and Honey was a pony for Skipper. Dallas had a colt named Dixie which was also sold separately. A travel trailer for the horses and a jeep for Barbie were sold.

Beauty, glamour, and romantic evening attire were to be the new watchwords in fashion designs. Before donning these beautiful fashions for a night on the town, Barbie shared with her many admirers her secrets. Beauty Secrets Barbie and Twirly Curls Barbie presented similar fashion difficulties.

Testing and more testing was involved as Carol Spencer tells of her designing the outfit which Mattel sold on Twirly Curls Barbie in 1983. The doll was being marketed with long flowing hair which was to be styled by children. No girl styles her hair standing, so Carol found it necessary to design the outfit to look good while sitting down. Hair play was also the theme for Beauty Secrets Barbie sold in 1979 and through the early 80's. Beauty Secrets Barbie wore a bright pink two piece gown with matching jacket. A side split that extended to the knee allowed the doll to sit without disrupting the lines of the garment. As with Beauty Secrets Barbie, Twirly Curls Barbie wore a bright pink halter gown also designed in two pieces. The skirt was a wrap effect with matching ruffle up the side. Again the doll could sit without causing difficulties with the lines of the gown. Each of these dolls were sold with hair arranging accessories.

Disproving that Barbie is preoccupied with pink, Golden Dreams Barbie was marketed by Mattel in 1981. The golden color was both a part of the doll's hair which was blonde streaked with gold and her fashionable outfit. Golden pants, halter top, and long gloves glistened from toy shelves everywhere. Even a silky white overskirt was trimmed with gold. The doll was sold with two distinct styles of hair. One was the basic Farrah Fawcett style but a small number came with what collectors call the "Monster Hairstyle." The monster style was swept away from the face and brought up above the head. Holding to Mattel's policy of consumer satisfaction for those not liking the Monster hairstyle replacement heads were made available.

With hair properly coiffed and armed with Barbie's beauty insights, a dream date was in the wings. In 1982, Dream Date Barbie, a glamorously gowned doll was the key to Mattel's marketing approach. She was wearing a rose pink two pieced gown with blue trim. The halter top of the gown was seeded with sequins which added glitter and a blue satin rose decorated her tiny waist. A ruffled rose and blue overwrap graced one delicate shoulder. Along with, but sold separately, was Ken doll in a tuxedo and Dream Date P.J. in a blue on blue satin gown styled identical to Barbie's.

The image of Barbie attired in a beautiful ballroom gown was continued with Crystal Barbie in 1983. A stiff white fabric that captured and reflected the light like mother of pearl was chosen. A spaghetti strap top to her gown descended into a straight skirt with a wide ruffle at the ankles. A shiny white boa wrap draped around the doll's

A 1982 Magic Curl Barbie doll had tight curly hair which could be wet and restyled. The hair yarn felt like wire to the touch.

Western flavor was carried through into 1982 with Horse Lovin' Barbie and Ken. Horses for the dolls were sold separately.

shoulders. The dress was sold both in black and white. Ken wore a white tuxedo to match.

Having been swept off their feet with Dream Date and Crystal Barbies, collectors fell in love with the Loving You Barbie in 1983. Hearts were the motif and Barbie's gown was filled with them. A red bodice to the gown had a heart shaped front, the skirt was white with tiny red hearts as was a ruffle at the shoulders.

Dressed boxed dolls were not Mattel's only focus to glamorous fashions, because thoughts began to turn to designer wear. The fashionable women in New York and Paris strolled down busy streets in designer clothing. Mattel began a collector series of outfits in the 80's which rivaled those of the top fashion houses of Europe. Beginning in 1982 with a Christmas theme, Heavenly Holidays was introduced to the market. Few of these were available. This was a test market and would be continued only if they sold well. Sold in a large decorative box, the garment came accompanied with a present for the lucky little girl or collector. The picture on the back of the box was a photograph of

Boxed designer fashions were introduced in the 80's. Oscar de la Renta designed a series of glamorous and colorful fashions for America's favorite doll.

Carol Spencer designed many garments for Barbie over the years. Sold in 1985, Astronaut Barbie also had five boxed outfits sold separately. The fashions for the Astronaut Barbie were designed by Carol Spencer for Mattel.

Beauty and hair play were continually popular designs for Barbie. Twirly Curl Barbie sold in 1983. She came with a uniquely designed chair that had a suction cup base to hold it firm to a table top. Carol Spencer designed a gown to look good while the doll sat.

Barbie wearing the costume and was designed so the child could cut out the picture and frame it. Second in the Collectors Series was Springtime Magic, a colorful floor length gown with large picture hat. A basket of flowers came with this outfit. Springtime Magic was sold in Europe as a boxed dressed doll. Silver Sensation was Collectors Series III and as numbered outfits these were more widely produced and marketed. By this point, Mattel began to re-examine the route being taken with these designer fashions and their popularity. Descriptive names no longer appeared on the outfits. Oscar de la Renta, famous fashion designer of Paris, France, began using his name on the remainder of the series. Elegant evening wear came from the Oscar de la Renta imagination which ended with costume number twelve in 1985. Mattel found the buying public receptive to the most attractive and vibrant garments imagination could create for Barbie.

Although Oscar de la Renta was not designing after 1985 for Barbie, Mattel continues with the designer garments each year as boxed assortments in the Designer Fashion Series.

In 1985 Barbie took to the skies to become an astronaut. The garments sold on the doll and the five outfits sold separately were pure fantasy. Carol Spencer designed these costumes for Mattel and in doing the designs she let imagination soar to new heights. Capes, metallic fabric, high shouldered suits, mid thigh boots, and an abundance of glitter were sold in these boxed outfits, bearing names such as Welcome To Venus, Space Racer, Dazzling Dancer, Galaxy A Go Go, and Starlight Slumbers. Naming outfits had not occurred since the 70's. Another new marketing idea was to make its debut in 1983 with Happy Holiday Barbie. Sold in a rectangular windowed box, she wore a party dress and came carrying a present for the lucky birthday child. Each year the doll came differently clad but with the same basic accessories. However, as the years have gone by the Happy Birthday line has evolved into something much more sophisticated. By the late 80's, Happy Birthday Barbie began to appear with elegant gowns and packaged in large clear plastic boxes. These dolls were more for display than for

The Astro Fashions, made for Barbie in 1985, were designed by Ms. Spencer as pure fantasy. High boots, shiny fabric, and glitter were combined to be a spaceage pretend world.

Fabric to reflect light was designed into the dress of Dream Glow Barbie in 1985. Additional boxed fashions with the same light reflecting ability were sold separately for this doll.

play. Still carrying her present, the general use of the doll had taken a new approach.

After consuming all the birthday cake and ice cream, Barbie had to preserve her shapely figure. A physical fitness regimen for Barbie introduced an active exercise doll. Sold in 1983, Great Shape Barbie wore a blue bodysuit with pink sash. Multicolored leg warmers kept her legs from developing muscle cramps. As a theme series, the Great Shape dolls were sold as black Barbie, white Barbie, Skipper, and Ken. Exercise equipment came packaged separately. As a top selling doll series, Mattel made slight changes to the accessories and marketed the Great Shape line again in 1984.

Being returned to top physical form, Barbie was ready for anything day or night. The advertising jingle for the doll was "you can do anything like Barbie." A girl could have any career that she aspired to as Mattel presented their doll in the theme of businesswoman. Called Day To Night Barbie, she wore a pink business suit which could quickly turn into a party dress for evening fun.

Beginning in 1985 a new concept came on the market, My First Barbie. A wealth of information is gathered by the Marketing Research Department at Mattel. Their analysis has served the company well over many years. In the late 70's, marketing research focused on groups who played with Barbie and at what age. Barbie was being designed for children between four and six years old. Marketing research found many received their first Barbie by the age of two. Mothers in these groups said that when their children started playing with the doll they had difficulty dressing Barbie. With this in mind, Carol Spencer became a part of a team to design a doll for much younger children. More simply designed clothing that would be easier to put on and off the dolls were made. Another innovation was used on the doll to make clothing easier to slide on and off the doll. This finish was an invention designed for Mattel by Bill Robb. When put on the doll body it left a slick finish to the body and made cloth glide over the arms and legs.

The friends of Barbie were reflecting a diverse society. Mattel has throughout its history displayed a sensitivity to the varying cultural differences in the U.S.

Perfume Pretty Barbie, sold in 1987, was a scented doll. Additional boxed outfits were sold separately for her also. The outfits were scented with the same perfume as the doll.

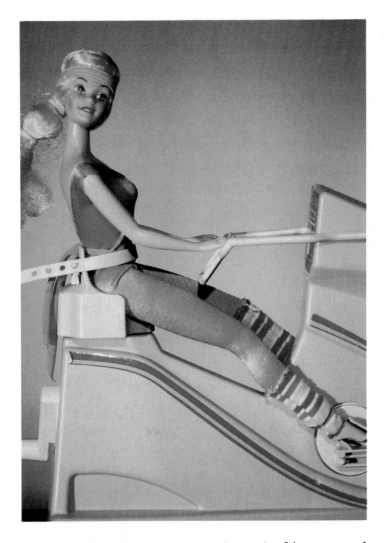

Physical health and exercise were on the minds of Americans and they also were a part of the Barbie world. Great Shape Barbie sold in 1983 came with a gymnasium set sold separately.

society. They dealt with this in the theme dolls making one Oriental, another black and Hispanic and a white European in design. Never straying from the course Ruth Handler had charted, Mattel still continued the path of appealing to all children regardless of race.

Although the Malibu line had been discontinued in 1984 with the Sun Gold Malibu series, the bathing suit dolls were introduced as Tropical in 1985. Tropical Barbie was marketed wearing a Hawaiian print one piece swimsuit. Long flowing hair tied into a ponytail was decorated with a yellow fabric flower. Ken wore matching swim trunks and a yellow lei. Also in the series were Tropical Skipper, black Tropical Barbie, black Tropical Ken, and Tropical Miko. The Tropical theme was a success. In 1986 Mattel presented the Island Fun series, which was a seven doll set. These dolls were an extension of the Malibu idea which presented a doll and swimsuit packaged at an economical price. Island Fun was followed in 1987 by the California Dream Barbie sold as a five doll set. The Island Fun series included Barbie, Ken, Skipper, Miko, Christie,

Teresa, and Steven. The California set featured Barbie, Ken, Christie, Midge, and Teresa. All dolls were sold separately.

Magic Moves was a doll sold in 1985. Mattel had not attempted the mechanical innovations for a few years and once again presented a doll with switch in her back. When the switch was pushed Barbie's arms would raise up and push back her long flowing hair. The mechanical invention was designed for Mattel by Bill Kelly. Sold on the doll was a gown of powder blue knit with a high neckline, open back, and narrow floor length skirt. An overwrap cape of powder blue floor length fabric was trimmed with white faux fur.

A growing market of consumers that wish to display not play with the doll became the newest focus. In 1988, a Christmas holiday series began with a special box design for the doll. She wore an elegant gown with a holiday accent. Happy Holidays Barbie was sold in a red tulle gown with silver accent the first year. The box was designed as a permanent display case. Hair and gown were sewn to the base of the box. As a test market, very few of these Barbies

Mother of pearl was a part of the finish on the gown worn by Crystal Barbie sold in 1983.

Jewel Secrets Barbie was sold in 1986. The gown she wore could also be a purse for the lucky child who owned her.

were made and store managers complained they sold out in a matter of hours. Each holiday following has featured a Happy Holidays Barbie clad in uniquely colorful and glamorous gowns. Other years have featured gowns of white with fur trim in 1989, pink tulle in 1990, green velvet in 1991, and white and silver in 1992. The boxes for these dolls are a testimony to the fine detailing that catered to the collector seeking beautiful NRFB display dolls.

Some series issues are released for only a short time. One of these series was UNICEF Barbie wearing a red, white, and blue gown. She was sold in four cultural versions of Oriental, Hispanic, black, and white and was marketed in 1989. Packaged in a large display box, this doll was also designed to be displayed inside her box. Second in the series was Summit Barbie wearing a white and gold gown in 1990. Here also the doll was offered in Oriental, Hispanic, black, and white. These dolls are also discussed in Chapter 20.

The ever expanding lines of Barbie and friends presented monumental challenges for the Mattel staff to overcome. Their success brought the total to more than 6,000 different fashions for Barbie between 1959 and 1989 with more than twenty million fashions sold yearly. Making Mattel one of the largest fashion design houses in the world and as Bob Mackie attributes, "Mattel is one of the biggest manufacturers of women's clothes in the world, even though they are tiny outfits." From Paris in 1961 to El Segundo, California, elegant fashion is Barbie.

The buying public was in love with Barbie and also Loving You Barbie. She was sold in 1983.

Dream Date Barbie was one the many Barbie's available in 1983. Glamorous gowns were sold on each of the dolls.

Magic Moves Barbie sold in 1985, was a beautiful addition to the mechanical dolls Mattel marketed over the years. A switch in her back caused her arms to come up and the doll's hands smoothed back her hair.

Chapter 19

International Developments

Italian Barbie, from 1980, is noted for being the only doll Mattel marketed with the Italian face mold.

Barbie is a banquet of delights for any collector. Such a large variety of Barbie dolls turns any home into a museum. Sold in 70 countries, she has become an international collectible. With this international experience, Mattel sought to bring the images of the diverse cultural fashion styles to the American collectors with the International Dolls of the World Collection. Seeing these dolls in their costumed finery makes one think of far away places filled with bustling markets and exotic languages. As varied as wild flowers, each doll brings to the collection a vibrant splash of color. The international dolls' hair is styled by Mellie Phillips and Rose Otto for Mattel in El Segundo, California. The series, now into its second decade, has taken on a life of its own. Each year

it becomes a collectors' guessing game as to what countries will be this year's additions.

Those first introductions in 1980 were Italian, Parisian, and Royal Barbies. Sold only in specialty stores, they came modeling costumes of the countries they represented. Also a feature of these dolls were the skin tone and hair color of the nationality represented. Italian Barbie came with a white peasant blouse and a red, white, and green skirt. A blue and white apron and wide brimmed hat also accompanied this dark haired beauty as she carried a basket of flowers from the market place.

Parisian Barbie, sold that same year, was a show girl. Blonde high styled hair and a heavy application of face paint made her ready for French nightlife. A hot pink satin dress with black lace trim was pulled up in front to show white lace ruffles underneath. Black hose were also included with this doll.

England has a Queen and so did Mattel with this Barbie doll who was designed to represent that country. A blonde doll with a golden crown was wearing a white ruffled gown with red sash. She even came carrying a royal scepter. Royal Barbie is the rarest of these first year issues of the doll. Her scarcity commands a high price when found through doll dealers on the secondary market.

Second issue of the International dolls in 1981 were Scottish and Oriental Barbies. The boxes these dolls were packaged in came with information about the countries they represented and examples of the native languages. For many a child the purchase of an international would be his or her first lesson in cultural geography.

Scottish Barbie wore a long red and black kilt, black velour jacket with white lace ruffles at the neck and cuffs, and matching tam. Oriental Barbie was more of a generic representative for all Oriental nations testing the waters for later issues. A yellow silk gown slit up both sides with a red silk jacket accented her long black hair. Her Oriental face mold was a first to be used on a Barbie doll.

Eskimo and India Barbies were the 1982 editions. Although a part of the United States, Mattel included Eskimo in the nationalities category as a recognition of the distinctive cultural heritage of our northern friends. Each of these dolls came with uniquely designed shoes to match their costumes. Only the first three dolls in the series came with booklets depicting the International Dolls of the World Collection.

Eskimo Barbie returned to the successful Oriental face mold with long black silken hair in one long braid down her back. She had a white felt suit with matching bonnet. Gray fur trim was around the bonnet, sleeves, and bottom of the garment. Knee high white felt boots were her footwear to guard against the winter chill of Alaskan nights.

India Barbie too, had long black hair and dark skintone. She wore a red and gold trimmed sari. A gold fabric blouse made a colorful addition to the outfit. This Barbie wore a black painted jewel in the center of her forehead.

A variety of face molds were used in the production of these elegantly designed dolls. The ever popular Steffie, along with Superstar, Italian, and Oriental face molds were used. Parisian was made from the old Steffie mold, while Royal was the Superstar mold, and Italian had a mold known as the Italian mold. This was a new mold seen only on her.

Spanish and Swedish Barbies joined the ranks of International designs in 1983. These dolls were costumed in colorful attire reminiscent of their own countries. Even the boxes are colorful and marked differently from regular Barbie issues.

A brilliant red dress trimmed in black lace was the attire for Spanish Barbie doll. Long black curled hair and bright red lip paint made her a striking addition to the International doll line. Swedish Barbie wore a blue skirt, white blouse, and black vest. She was a blonde doll with white duster cap to protect her hair.

By 1984 Irish and Swiss Barbie dolls came on the market. Very popular additions, Swiss Barbie wore a red skirt, white blouse, and black vest. A wide brimmed straw hat graced her lovely head to shade her from the bright alpine sun. Long blonde tresses were in two braids over her shoulders.

Mattel's representative from the Emerald Isle was Irish Barbie clad in a green satin jumper with a white blouse. Her green Irish eyes were shaded by a white Irish duster cap.

Collectors had become accustomed to having two International dolls issued each year, but in 1985 only one, Japanese Barbie, was issued. The Japanese doll sold out in only a few short weeks. Wearing a Japanese red wedding kimono, she was a beautiful addition. This doll came with the Oriental face mold and a traditional native hairstyle.

Parisian Barbie was sold in 1980 along with Italian in the International and Nationalities series. Notice the lighter tones of facial paint.

A 1992 reissue Parisian Barbie shows more vibrant facial paint. The necklace is plastic instead of fabric as in the 1980 version.

120

Two new additions in 1986, Greek and Peruvian Barbies joined her international sisters. Mattel was still using the Steffie and Superstar face molds. Peruvian wore a Steffie mold and Superstar was seen on Greek Barbie.

Peruvian Barbie was an example of the Indian influence in that hemisphere. She had long dark brunette braids and a rose pink blouse with a multicolored skirt. An aqua cape around her shoulders and purple hat with flower accents completed a costume that links her to the proud history of the Inca dynasty.

Greek Barbie wore a vibrant red satin skirt and white blouse. A black and gold jacket and red turban hat with golden tassel made her the representative of this Mediterranean country. Long brunette hair was caught back in a ponytail for Greek Barbie.

German and Icelandic joined the series in 1987. Long platinum puppytails were Icelandic Barbie's hair design. She came clad in a royal blue velour skirt and vest with white blouse. An apron of pale blue satin trimmed in gold completed her costume.

German Barbie wore the Steffie face mold and had wide bright blue eyes. A skirt of navy floral print,

red velour vest, and white satin apron were her highlights. She had a purple silk flower around her neck. A multicolored bonnet covered long blonde tresses.

With 1988 came Korean and Canadian Barbies. The Oriental face mold graces the face of this Korean doll. Long black hair was tied into a side ponytail. She wore a rose pink and mint green dress with gold braid trim.

Canadian Barbie was one of the Canadian Mounties and rode into the collection in a pair of black riding pants, red velour jacket, and tan felt hat. A brown vinyl belt and pouch completed this selection of the Dolls of the World Collection.

Russian and Mexican Barbie dolls appeared in 1989. A dark skin tone doll with long brunette hair which reached well below the waist, Mexican Barbie wore a Steffie face mold. Aqua blue earrings and an orange plastic necklace accented the orange satin skirt trimmed with white lace. A white and orange floral print blouse and multicolored sash around her waist made this doll unique to the collection.

A rose velvet long sleeved dress trimmed with gold braid and brown fur accented Russian Barbie

Royal Barbie in 1980 was designed as a monarch.

In 1992 the reissue of Royal Barbie was called English Barbie. She was based on a Mary Poppins theme.

doll with the Superstar face. She had platinum blonde hair tucked under a large brown fur hat.

In 1990 the first representative of the black African culture made its debut in the International Dolls of the World Series appearing as Nigerian Barbie. Also that year was Brazilian Barbie.

Nigerian Barbie wore a brown and white dress and underskirt. Her dark brown skin was accented with gold arm bands and trim around the neckline of the dress. A large afro hairstyle was finished with a brown and white turban.

Brazilian Barbie was a pink princess straight off the streets of Carnival in her pink ruffled top and matching skirt. A pink headdress fit atop long brunette curls.

Mattel continued the series in 1991 with two new additions and three reissues to add to doll collectors' wish lists.

The Oriental face mold was used with Malaysian Barbie doll with long luscious black hair pulled into a ponytail. A black, gold, and purple satin skirt was completed with a purple satin long tailed jacket.

Czechoslovakian Barbie wore long blonde hair in a twisted ponytail accented with red ribbon. The Superstar face mold with large green eyes and vibrant face paint made a stunning representative of that country. Her costume was a yellow and black floral print skirt, white blouse, and black vest. Red ribbon sash at the waist and yellow ribbon at the blouse neckline completed her outfit. Also reissued this year was Scottish Barbie with wide green eyes and titian tresses. She had a new plaid skirt and sash this year but the black velour jacket was similar to the first issued Scottish doll. Gold and white lace accented the neckline and wrist and also the front of the jacket.

Parisian Barbie wore a pink satin dress similar to the earlier 1980 issued doll. Ash blonde hair was piled high on her head in large ringlets. A black and

The 1981 Oriental Barbie was the first doll seen with the Oriental face mold. She represented Hong Kong in the series.

Scottish Barbie was issued in 1981 wearing plaid and sporting titian hair.

pink hair decoration was attached to her curls. Different with this doll was the face paint. Bright colors were used in this 1991 reissue. Ruby red lips and bright blue eyes were made more glamorous with lavender eye shadow. A beauty mark beside her left eye added charm to the face. Another difference with this doll was the necklace. The 1980 version had a fabric cameo but the 1991 version was plastic.

The last of the reissued dolls in 1991 was the Eskimo Barbie. She was identical to the doll from 1982.

Dolls of the World continued into 1992 with one new issue, Jamaican Barbie. Another black doll with rich brown skin tone, she had the Superstar face mold. This doll wore a blue floral print cotton dress with ruffled bodice and long sleeves. A red and blue apron and red, yellow, and white shawl hung around her shoulders. Fabric matching the apron was used as a hairband to accent the black curly hair.

Reissues this year were English and Spanish Barbies. Neither of these dolls were like the ones from previous years. All the designs for these were completely changed.

English Barbie was with a "Mary Poppins" theme. She wore a royal blue skirt and a floral print blouse that peeped out from a red and blue felt jacket. A navy blue hat with blue netting fit over her head. Long platinum blonde hair was tied back in a side ponytail. High brown boots were the shoes with this outfit.

Spanish Barbie was designed to represent the people from Catalonia in northeastern Spain. She wore a green satin skirt, floral print and black fringed shawl, and floral apron. A black and gold lace mantilla fell over long black waist length hair. Gold earrings graced the face which was a Steffie face mold.

Mattel has continued this doll series from Timeless Treasures, the Collectible Doll Division of Mattel Toys. Still an ongoing series, each year sees more additions to a very popular collection.

A reissued Scottish Barbie in 1992 wears a new plaid.

Eskimo Barbie was a part of the nationalities represented and sold in 1982. A popular design, she was reissued in 1992 as an identical copy.

India Barbie joined the series in 1982. A vibrant and colorful doll, India Barbie was sold only a short time.

Swedish Barbie was designed with the Superstar face mold and vibrant blue eyes.

Spanish Barbie was reissued in 1992 with an all new design but the Steffie face mold remained.

The International series continued to grow in 1983 with the addition of Spanish Barbie. A Steffie face mold and large brown eyes gave Barbie a lovely appearance.

The Steffie face mold was used for Irish Barbie sold in 1984. The doll representing the Emerald Isle, was clad in emerald green.

Swiss Barbie, in 1984, came with a design based on the children's story of Heidi. Note the Superstar face mold.

In 1985 Japanese Barbie was the only entry in the International and Nationalities series. Japanese Barbie sold out early and became very hard to locate.

The Superstar face mold was used for Greek Barbie sold in 1986.

Peruvian Barbie was sold in 1986. She was colorful in native costume and long brunette braids.

Mattel made German Barbie a bright addition to the 1987 line. The Steffie face mold was used on this doll.

The Superstar face mold was used on Icelandic Barbie in 1987. In royal blue with golden braids, she was very glamorous.

Again, the Oriental face mold appeared in 1988 with Korean Barbie.

The Canadian Mounted Police were the models for Canadian Barbie sold in 1988.

Barbie was a Cossack as Russian Barbie in 1989. She wore a fur hat with fur trim on her outfit.

Mexican Barbie was made with the Steffie face mold in 1989.

The first black doll in the International series was Nigerian Barbie in 1990.

Brazilian Barbie joined the growing International series in 1990. She too, was made with the Steffie face mold.

The Oriental face mold was used for Malaysian Barbie in 1991. Silk fabric accented black hair and wide brown eyes.

A 1991 issue of Czechoslovakian Barbie was seen with the Superstar face mold. A unique side ponytail was braided and highlighted with a red ribbon.

Jamaican Barbie was the new 1992 release in the International series. A native gingham dress and apron accented this black doll.

Chapter 20

Ethnic Creations

Free Moving Brad and Free Moving Cara were introduced in 1975 to give black children a toy to fill their needs. Dolls courtesy of the Mid Ohio Historical Museum.

Mattel's first black doll introduced in 1967 was black Francie. With this doll the company began a long line of ethnic creations. Doll courtesy of the Mid Ohio Historical Museum.

A primary precept that Ruth Handler held that has been continued to this day within Mattel's development of Barbie is that the doll was to provide a healthy and helpful extension of the individual child during playtime. Therefore, by the mid 60's when the appeal of the Barbie venture dictated the longevity in the doll's future, Mattel sought to address a void. Ruth coupled her experience with the local children's foundation with a personal sensitivity from which she recognized the need for a blonde, brunette, and redhead child to purchase a doll resembling oneself and interact with others. Mattel turned its attention to the development of an African-American doll that would fulfill the same dreams and provide the same playtime opportunities for young black children. The need for Mattel's efforts for greater outreach to all children was brought into sharper focus as the Watts riots of

1965 engulfed Los Angeles. Elliot Handler felt it important to make a contribution to solve problems in the community after the events of the summer of 1965. As Cliff Jacobs, vice president of marketing at Mattel in those years tells, "Mr. Handler did not want to just give money to any organization. Instead he chose to commit Mattel to teach a group of people, including executives, how to manufacture and market black ethnic dolls." Handler would be willing to have Mattel help with both money and people to train in the different areas such as manufacturing and marketing.

When the community project was presented by Elliot to Cliff Jacobs, a brother of Mr. Jacobs was associated with two men, Louis Smith and Robert Hall, who were organizers of a community rehabilitation program called Operation Bootstrap. "Bootstrap was attempting to teach people in the Watts area everything from computer programming to how to set up their own business, and rebuilding the business infrastructure from the ground floor," says Jacobs. "These men had several different endeavors going," Jacobs said. Through his brother, Cliff Jacobs met with Smith and Hall and attended a few of their meetings. When Elliot Handler was ready to move ahead with his commitment, Mattel approached Louis Smith and Robert Hall and asked if they were interested in learning how to manufacture and market dolls that would reflect an African-American genre.

"At that time," says Jacobs, "there were only a handful of dolls being made for black children by only a few companies. Very few opportunities existed for a black child to purchase a black doll and those that did were merely a company's white doll line with a dark pigment tone added to the vinyl. The African-American dolls were not abundant nor in good likenesses in the marketplace."

The project began with Smith and Hall as Mattel advanced money, tools, and manufacturing facilities, showing them how to set up the lines of dolls. "The most important part was that the people on the line, in the office, and factory must come from the community. That way we would be making a specific contribution to helping people work," says Jacobs. Although Mattel did not own this factory and had no financial part of it, they did give money advances, over a period of time. "Mattel's assistance amounted to over one million dollars in money and equipment," says Jacobs. When organized, the company was called Shindana Corporation and became a subdivision of Operation Bootstrap. Shindana was set up as a profit organization whose goal was to market the dolls.

Cliff Jacobs had the task of training one of the men, who would serve as the marketing manager of Shindana. Other persons at Mattel were selected to train persons who were to be head of manufacturing and other positions within the new company. Cliff Jacobs and Art Spear, vice president at Mattel were primarily responsible for this whole operation. Other Mattel manufacturing personnel went to the site on Central Avenue and taught the Shindana personnel how to plan and program the manufacture of the dolls. "Mattel donated old doll body molds so that they could start out and get into the marketplace," says Jacobs. For the first few years of operation Shindana was allowed to show their product in the Mattel showroom in New York City at the toy fair. Jacobs tells, "Mattel did everything possible to enable the Shindana Corporation to grow. Mattel worked with them for five or six years, assisting wherever needed." Gradually over time, at the

By 1975 many ethnic additions came in the Barbie line including Hawaiian Barbie. The Steffie face mold was used to make the Hawaiian doll.

Mattel was in full swing with the ethnic line and by 1979 marketed a black Barbie doll. Glamour was the name of the design for this Barbie. Black Barbies met an immediate success.

mutual agreement of both Mattel and Shindana, Mattel pulled away to allow the fledgling company to fly. Shindana remained in business until 1980 when they made not only toys but also games.

Although they had a quality product, they met with many difficulties. Jacobs says, "it was a slow process getting distribution and the market was such that they could not grow rapidly enough." Another problem which faced them was that both Louis Smith and Robert Hall, who were Shindana's founders, had died. With the loss of both men, one from a heart attack and the other from a fatal automobile accident, this removed the original enthusiasm which started the corporation. An obstacle facing Shindana also in the 1980's was the toy industry had found making black ethnic dolls marketable and were working them into their lines. This left tiny Shindana to compete with all the larger toy manufacturers. Shelf space in the retail stores was a major difficulty for Shindana who had little for

The first Ken sold with painted mustache was black Perfume Giving Ken in 1987. Hiroe Okubo-Wolf says, "the painted mustache was added at the suggestion of Mattel's marketing department."

advertising funds. Buyers were reluctant to carry their products when they could carry the larger toy corporation's products which they had established relations with for many years. The losses of corporate leadership and the inability to put forth a strong marketing profile for their products resulted in Shindana ceasing production in 1980. For Mattel's part, the company brought aid amidst the ashes and instead of a blind eye monetary hand out, they provided a purpose and pride in a product produced in the community. Those years of administrative association with Shindana enriched Mattel with a first hand understanding of the black community that would yield dividends in the years to come in the quality of their own doll lines.

The urgency expressed by Elliot to unite the community in the healing process was linked with an effort by Mattel to market alongside the Barbie doll, a black friend. To typify the African-American features in a doll required new sculpting, castings, and refinements in all aspects of the doll's production. For Mattel, Elliot's challenge to accomplish the task of producing a black doll was up against the deadline of the New York City Toy Fair of 1967. Time restraints would deny Mattel the marketing of a doll with uniquely African-American qualities by the close of 1966. The doll chosen to fill the void until further refinements could be made to the black ethnic doll mold was the Francie doll. The first wave of Francie dolls had a warm brown skin tone, large light brown eyes, and long black hair. Soon it was apparent there was a problem with hair as Wanda Clearwater, a member of the chemical engineering department at Mattel in those years, tells, "they had some of the midnight Color Magic Barbie doll hair left over at the manufacturer because when they made black Francie, Julia, and Christie dolls their hair turned red." Wanda says she experimented with Julia doll's hair and found it turned back to black when a base chemical was applied. "The overseas manufacturer was using up left over doll hair and rooted early Julia, Christie, and black Francie dolls with this hair," says Clearwater. By the second production all the coloration was corrected and this doll hair holds its black shade even today.

A new venue was opening and its success would add to the diversity of Barbie's appeal but it was only a first step. The research and design department was able to refine the features reflective of an African-American role model. Hiroe Okubo-Wolf tells of each new design, "sculptors and face painters work together in developing new heads. As the sculptor finalizes the wax model, we paint directly on it to see how the look is progressing." Sculpting these new ethnic models must be accurate.

The first fruits of their efforts were to be released in 1968 with the talking doll Christie, which was sold between 1968 and 1971. In 1969 Mattel again showed work on the ethnic issues with the doll called Julia based on a popular television show of that era. The show, also called "Julia," starred Diahann Carroll who was a character design likeness for the doll. Julia came with rich brown skin tone and brown eyes. She was sold that year both as a Twist 'N Turn Julia and Talking Julia.

In 1970, Mattel issued a black friend for Ken called Brad. With brown skin and eyes, this doll developed the African-American features for the male doll line.

A 1975 issued doll called Cara was yet another black friend for Barbie doll. With a deeper brown skin tone, Cara was made as Free Moving Cara in 1975, Quick Curl Cara in 1975, Deluxe Quick Curl Cara in 1976, and Ballerina Cara in 1976. As Brad was created for Christie as a boyfriend, a doll named Curtis was introduced in 1975 as a boyfriend for Cara. He was made from the same body and head mold as the Brad doll.

Still as Mattel continued to move forward with innovations in 1980, the first black Barbie doll was seen on store shelves. With an assortment of hair styles available for her that year she was made from the Barbie body mold and the old Steffie face mold. She was dressed in a crimson fitted gown with a slit up the side and a gold trimmed neckline. Red plastic earrings dangled from under black curly Afro style hair. Large round brown eyes gave charming appeal to this doll which has continued to sell in many variations over the years.

In the 70's, throughout the southwestern parts of the United States and in the larger metropolitan areas the fastest growing ethnic group was the Hispanic population. To a new emerging ethnic market, the Hispanic Barbie doll was sold. Again the Steffie face mold was used with tan skin and large brown eyes. Dressed in a red skirt and peasant blouse, she was wearing a black shawl which made her reflect Spanish charm. Unfortunately for collectors, Hispanic Barbie was sold only in limited areas of the country where large populations of Spanish speaking persons lived. Even the boxes were printed in Spanish and English. Now found in toy stores in all large cities, Hispanic designed Barbies are no longer in boxes printed in two languages. The only language now printed on the packaging is English.

Further expansion of Mattel's ethnic lines in 1982 was to include changes for Barbie and Ken. The Ken doll was released in 1982 as a black doll with curly rooted black hair. A new head mold for the black doll gave him a closed mouth expression. Large brown eyes and dark brown skin tone made this a welcome addition to the ethnic line. The same body mold as the white Ken doll was used for this doll.

The change for Barbie was of a Polynesian flavor with the release of Hawaiian Barbie. She was made with the Steffie face mold and tan skin tone. A tropical costume accented long straight black hair. She had a ukulele, sailboard, and grass skirt. These dolls

were sold in special department stores which sold only collectible dolls. As a tribute to our fiftieth state, she was a striking addition to the ethnic market.

By the close of the 80's, as Barbie's thirtieth anniversary was approaching, Barbie's outreach to the children of the world was exemplified by UNICEF Barbie in 1989. The UN Ambassador doll represented the black, Hispanic, Oriental, and white races dressed in a patriotic red, white, and blue gown and proclaimed to be worldwide emissary of love and caring. The peace that was taking place between the United States and the Soviet Union brought a new hope of joy for the future generations. To commemorate this new peace, Mattel released the Summit Barbie line. Summit dolls were also issued in white, black, Oriental, and Hispanic. Attired in white and gold gowns, they too made a statement to political reproachment and recognition of a new world accord.

Skipper doll was presented as a black version in 1989 and was marketed as Homecoming Skipper.

Hispanic dolls were marketed in selected areas of the country where the population was largely Hispanic. In 1979 Hispanic Barbie was sold.

Clad in a white gown, she was sold both as black and white this year. Along with the round impish face, the black Skipper had large round brown eyes. Pink lip paint made a striking accent to her features. Long black hair was an invitation to children to style the tresses to their liking.

Black and Hispanic were not the only ethnic issues manufactured by Mattel. In 1981, included in the International Dolls of the World Series, was an Oriental Barbie. Her head mold was all new and face paint with bright tones accented long black hair. Oriental Barbie is discussed in more detail in Chapter 19. With the introduction of this new face mold the Oriental dolls have appeared many times to the delight of collectors.

Especially popular are the Hispanic dolls. They often disappear from store shelves soon after ship-ment is received. The ever popular Hispanic line has continued since 1980 providing the collector with a brunette hair style that adds variety to any collection. Selling for the same price as first intro-duced, the collectible value of the brunette beauties increase at a much faster rate than other dolls.

As an ethnic first, the black Perfume Giving Ken from 1987 was the first Ken doll sold with painted mustache. His white counterpart Ken did not have the mustache. Upon the request of Mattel's market-ing department, they sought to enhance the features of the black Ken by adding the likeness of a Billy Dee Williams' mustache.

With the quality of the ethnic dolls, Mattel has created a successful market of variety with Barbie that represents the racially diverse world in which we live.

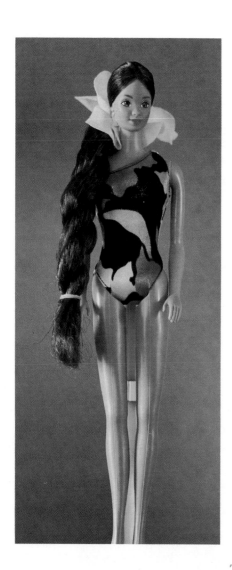

As the years have gone by Hispanic ver-sions of many popular Barbies have been marketed and now can be found in all large cities. Tropical Barbie was sold in 1985.

Flight Time Barbie, sold in 1989, was sold in white, black, and Hispanic.

Not only has Barbie been designed with the Oriental face mold but many of her friends were also, as this Miko doll sold in the early 90's.

Chapter 21

Porcelain Splendor

As a replica of the first wedding gown, Wedding Day Set Porcelain Barbie was marketed in 1988.

There is something about dolls made from porcelain which makes them more art than toy. The word porcelain brings forth images of old world craftsmanship. The beauty of antique dolls pays homage to the skill and dexterity that is embodied in the warm facial tones and diverse textures that only the porcelain process can deliver. The fragile nature of the work only enhances the endearment the collector has for this everlasting treasure. All of the adjectives used to describe Mattel's efforts in the production of Barbie to date can be circumscribed in the development of the timeless creation that became the first porcelain Barbie.

In 1985, Mattel made their first porcelain Barbie doll, Blue Rhapsody. The effort of opening the package foretold the collector that a precious gem awaited them. Packaged inside a heavy cardboard box with only the dolls name and Mattel's logo on the outside, Blue Rhapsody was opened to find yet another lighter weight decorative royal blue box. Looking inside this box the collector found a styrofoam box. Open the styrofoam box and inside was found the elegant doll nestled into an interior built just for her protection during shipment to any collector. Earrings were installed in the doll's ears but came wrapped in a clear plastic tube to create a cushion. The hair and head were wrapped with a clear plastic and the hair was in a white hairnet which was pulled down over the face to insure no strand of her coiffure would be out of place on arrival. The delicate framework inside the styrofoam container insured Blue Rhapsody would be well cushioned against any jostle or jolt.

Mattel had taken a different approach to porcelain than many other doll manufacturers. Many dolls came with cloth bodies but Barbie doll is all porcelain from head to her high heeled feet.

Overseeing the sculpting of these porcelain Barbie dolls is done by senior director and chief sculptor, Aldo Favilli, who has been with Mattel since 1970. Bodies to the porcelain dolls were sculpted by freelance sculptor and former Mattel employee, John Gardner. Heads for the dolls are sculpted by Joyce Clark.

Hiroe Okubo-Wolf designs all the facial features for the porcelain Barbies. "It is much harder to paint on porcelain," says Hiroe. "The porous surface is not as smooth and you can not erase your mistakes. Porcelain dolls create unique problems in production since they must all be hand-painted using brushes and glaze. They are then fired like ceramics," tells Hiroe. The extra detail requires much more hands-on work with each individual doll. Arms, legs, and torso are molded separately then fastened together. They create an arm and leg which can be moveable at the shoulder and hip joints, but bendable knees and wrists are not possible.

Initially only sold in fine stores which only carried collectible dolls, these porcelains are numbered and come with certificates of authenticity. The first of the Barbie porcelain collection was not widely announced. Many collectors happened onto this doll by accident while shopping.

Porcelain, a new medium, was introduced in 1985. Blue Rhapsody Barbie was a lovely beginning of the porcelain line.

In 1986 Enchanted Evening Porcelain Barbie was designed as a replica of the early 60's fashion sold by Mattel.

Blue Rhapsody Barbie came with long blonde curls which instead of being rooted to the doll's head was a wig glued to the scalp. Face paint was applied with fine detail by Japanese artistry. Mattel had found Japanese craftsmen expert in making this new Barbie a beauty. Her gown was a royal blue taffeta with silver glitter similar to the glitz of many of the gowns found on Barbie dolls during that year. Also with the doll were undergarments and hose which Mattel's regular line did not have. Although done in the porcelain medium, this is truly a Barbie doll.

Porcelain Barbies are manufactured and sold by Timeless Creations, the collectible doll division of Mattel toys. At this point, a new area of collectible doll required a division all its own to handle the new products. Most collectors smile at this collectible idea, little did Mattel know all Barbies have been collectible since 1959.

Second in the series was Enchanted Evening Barbie in 1986. She was designed as a replica of a blonde ponytail Barbie from the early 60's. She wore a duplicate of the old number 983 Enchanted Evening outfit that appeared in the 1960 booklet.

Sculpting for Enchanted Evening Barbie required recreation of the old face from the early 60's. With this doll John Gardner sculpted the head and body entirely.

Mattel had chosen to make their new porcelain line copies of past outfits and Barbies which had been very popular. Those gowns designed by Charlotte Johnson were coveted prizes that collectors desired to own. The Enchanted Evening gown was one of the most popular outfits sold of that day and was available from 1960 through 1963. Enchanted Evening was a long straight strapless pink satin gown that was never meant to be walked in. Although the original Enchanted Evening stole was real rabbit fur, this porcelain reproduction is imitation fur, in response to the social awareness to avoid killing animals when a suitable substitute can be found. The 1988 Animal Lovin' Barbie always protects her furry friends.

Many of the porcelain dolls were wearing reproductions of outfits sold for Barbie doll back in the 60's. Carol Spencer says, "patterns for these can no longer be found and must be recreated from copies

140

of the old garments." Another difficulty in making these reproductions of outfits is finding the exact or similar fabric for the gowns. It has been years since these fabrics were manufactured and textile companies need to match as closely as possible the texture and quality of the fabric.

The 1987 issue was brunette and modeled a copy of the 1966 – 1967 Benefit Performance outfit. This porcelain, unlike the two previous, had real eyelashes. Eyecatching rhinestone jewelry accented a beautiful reproduction of the gown. A white gown with full flowing skirt was covered with small red ribbon bows. A coat worn over the gown was of red velvet. The coat was short and revealed much of the white filmy skirt covered with red bows. Benefit Performance Barbie not only had the traditional clear plastic wrap around her head but this doll's wrap was sewn to the hair for added protection. Here also, rhinestone earrings were wrapped in a plastic to insure they not damage the doll, although they had already been implanted in the porcelain ears.

The most popular outfit sold each year by Mattel for Barbie is the wedding gown. Little girls and collectors alike love the endless array of wedding gowns.

That first gown that made Barbie become a bride doll was sold in 1959 and was called Wedding Day Set. The 1988 porcelain was a vision of loveliness in an incredibly accurate recreation of this same outfit. Made in China, she was late being released due to the Tiananmen Square massacre and internal turmoil in China. But when released, the result was worth the anguish. A smaller number of the porcelains were made and in response the collectible price skyrocketed. Although made like the 1959 version of Wedding Day Set, this new doll and dress was different. The lace that the gown was made from had a glittering fiber woven through it giving the dress a sparkle effect. Here too, the doll wore undergarments designed by Mattel's fashion designers.

Mattel chose Solo In The Spotlight for a blonde ponytail porcelain doll in 1989. F. Glen Offield loaned Mattel designers a second copy of his Solo outfit for them to use as a pattern for this dress. Unable to find the same style fabric for this fashion, they used a black velvet material with a glitter finish for the sparkling effect. Here too, Solo In The Spotlight came with the familiar pink scarf, tight fitting tulip gown, and microphone.

Benefit Performance Barbie was a 1987 porcelain designed as a replica of the Twist 'N Turn era. She even featured rooted eyelashes.

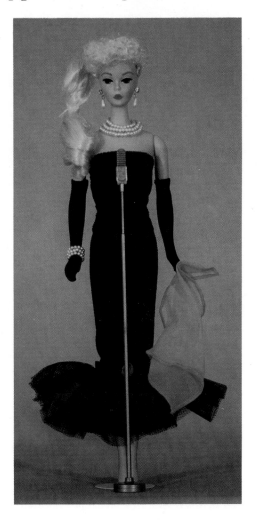

Solo In The Spotlight was a popular outfit in the early 60's. Porcelain Solo In The Spotlight was sold in 1989.

Sophisticated Lady was the outfit chosen in 1990 because of its highly collectible status. Also, much publicity had come to light in 1989 of the rare sidepart American Girl Barbie dolls made in 1965. The dolls are also known as the sidepart Bendable Leg Barbie dolls. Mattel made this combined design in the 1990 porcelain as a brunette sidepart and designed a perfect likeness of the Sophisticated Lady gown and coat. Barbie looked like Cinderella at the ball in her tiara and dainty pink shoes.

The 90's were rolling with yet another brunette reproduction of the number one Barbie wearing an extremely rare Gay Parisienne outfit. With this doll, Mattel began their new porcelain series called Barbie Porcelain Treasures Collection. Mattel had perfected their recreation talents with this doll and clothing. The dress was a close copy of the original and the fabric came very near to the same type material. The gold velvet purse was made to match the 1959 version and was so exactly the same that seeing the two together the older version shows only the aged fabric as a difference. With age, the velvet has faded somewhat, and no longer has the luster of the newer velvet fabric. This same year Walt Disney World in Florida held a doll show and one of the features of the show was the sale of 300 (specifically made just for Disney World) redhead Gay Parisienne Porcelain Barbie dolls. Along with the outfit which was the same as the porcelain sold in doll shops, Disney World included a pin commemorating this doll as a Disney exclusive and also a ribbon sash worn on the doll proclaiming her made for Disney World.

Porcelain Treasures continued with the addition of Plantation Belle Porcelain Barbie doll in 1992. A luscious head of red hair hung beyond the shoulders. Reminiscent of the swirl ponytail Barbie designed by Jean Ann Burger, the Plantation Belle porcelain has hair combed in a swirl around the front of her face and back to a ponytail. True to form, this outfit looked exactly like the Plantation Belle in

Gay Parisienne Porcelain Barbie was released in 1991 with a perfect reproduction of the old outfit.

To celebrate 30 years of Ken doll Mattel issued Porcelain Ken in 1991. The doll came wearing a copy of Tuxedo, which was a 1961 marketed outfit.

In 1992 Mattel introduced a mail order offer for Crystal Rhapsody Barbie doll. Photo courtesy of Mattel.

1959 with full skirted pink sundress and wide brimmed picture hat. A dainty straw purse over her arm makes her look like she is out for a stroll.

Although not officially a part of the porcelain collection, a new experimental series was introduced in 1992 by Mattel called The Presidential Porcelain Collection. Sold only by mail order, Lisa McKendall, of the the corporate communications department at Mattel says, "the continuity of this series is hinged on the public response to the doll." Called Crystal Rhapsody Barbie, the doll and garment contains 75 Austrian Swarovski crystals. The crystals are manu-factured by Swarovski & Co. in a small village in Austria, which has been known for its exquisite crystal for nearly a century. Being such an elegant doll, Crystal Rhapsody Barbie has received the endorsement of Mattel's president Jill Barad. Wearing a silver and black gown, the garment is accented with white fortuny pleated satin giving a butterfly effect. Crystal Rhapsody is the first Barbie doll with contemporary handcrafted porcelain sculpting by Mattel.

The warm reception that the porcelain Barbies have gotten from the collectors dictates continuance of the project well into the 90's.

In 1990 Mattel recreated porcelain Sophisticated Lady Barbie. Even a sidepart hair style was attempted on this doll.

Mattel, aware of the redheaded dolls previously made, designed the 1992 edition porcelain as Plantation Belle with titian hair. She was a copy of the swirl ponytail which was originally designed for Mattel by Jean Ann Burger.

Chapter 22

Special Issues

The first Happy Birthday Barbie was sold in 1983 with party accessories.

nationally, these dolls are dressed in outfits exclusive to the regional store chains they are marketed in. This practice began in the mid 60's when Montgomery Ward and Sears Roebuck carried unique Barbie dolls designed exclusively for them.

Department store specials began in 1964 with Sears Roebuck in their catalog department. A genuine mink stole was sold for Barbie doll for the price of $9.99. Other unique clothing continued through the Sears Roebuck catalog in 1966 with the sale of an exclusive called Pink Formal. A baby pink satin gown trimmed with a silver glitter design on the skirt was accented with a small pink feather boa. Sears also carried specials exclusively in their stores for the Tutti and Todd line during the mid 60's. The Tutti Playhouse came packaged in Sears catalogs with a titian haired Tutti and Todd.

The magic of these dolls is the scarcity of each. They are made in limited numbers and stores who carry them are not always located nationwide. For this reason, the Barbie collector has the opportunity to make penpals in the various marketing areas. Often the hunt for the doll can be as special as the doll itself. With Sears and J.C. Penney stores located throughout the country and catalog availability, these dolls are not so difficult to find. Sears has even sold doll clothing outfits as department store specials, known to collectors as "DSS."

In 1972, to celebrate the 100th anniversary of Montgomery Ward & Company, Mattel issued a remake of an original Barbie doll. Although not a solid body, she was designed similar to the 1964 Barbie dolls, with brunette hair and tan tone skin, she was marked:

Midge T.M.
1962
Barbie ®
1958
by
Mattel, Inc.
Patented

Are you looking for something different? Something that is not found just anywhere. Try shopping for the department store specials. The department store specials dolls are Barbie dolls made by Mattel which are designed to be sold only in selected stores. Packaging varies depending on the nature of the market. Some dolls are packaged in the pink rectangular box with cellophane fronts and others came with an elegantly designed box which can also serve as a display case. Although the package is sometimes similar to other Barbie dolls marketed

As a hollow bodied doll, she had the heavier saran hair of the later issued dolls.

Special issues that began in the mid 60's continued into the 70's and the 80's. Limited edition Barbie dolls were a successful marketing venture such as the 1971 Hair Happenin's Barbie sold only in the Sears Roebuck catalog. Other specials were the 1973 Quick Curl Barbie Christmas Gift Set with an extra dress and the 1976 Beautiful Bride Barbie where the first issue was a different gown than the later mass issued versions. The first issue was sold only in selected stores. In 1977 Superstar Barbie and Ken were sold with both dolls packaged in one box. Mass marketed versions sold separately.

Many of the department store specials were sold as extensions on the mass marketed doll but with added accessories. As examples of this the 1980 Beauty Secrets Barbie Pretty Reflections Gift Set was sold with a three way mirror and in 1983 Twirly Curls Barbie Gift Set was sold with an extra outfit packaged in the box. Rare sets such as the 1983 Ballerina Barbie was sold only at Mervyn's Department Store. Sold only in Western states was the 1983 Barbie and Ken Campin' Out Set. A 1984 Loving You Barbie Gift Set was marketed with a purse for the doll's owner. Dance Sensation Barbie Gift Set was sold in 1985 packaged with dance garments. Another 1985 special was the Happy Birthday Barbie Gift Set sold with party supplies. More recent specials have increased in numbers and marketing areas.

Since 1989, there has been an avalanche of stores taking advantage of the possibilities with specials created just for them. Many of these dolls are never marked on the box which store carried this particular doll. The only identifiable marking on many of these boxes is "Limited Edition" on the front of the box. DSS dolls have a wide range of appeal and can be generally divided into two categories called Glamour 'N Glitz and Mainstream Marketing, capturing the more price conscious shopper.

Toys 'R Us carries a multitude of Barbie and Skipper special editions in both categories such as the 1989 Show 'N Ride, which featured the doll in a red riding suit; Barbie Cool City Blues, (a Barbie, Ken, and Skipper set); Pepsi Barbie, Pepsi Skipper; and Sweet Roses Barbie. Toys 'R Us continued in 1990 with Winter Fun Barbie, wearing a ski costume; Dream Date Skipper, wearing a formal gown; School Fun Barbie; Ski Fun Midge, wearing a ski costume; Sweet Romance Barbie, in ballgown; Barbie and Friends Disney Gift Set; Spring Parade Barbie, wear-

The 1992 Happy Birthday Barbie had blossomed to be a party in every box. A frillier dress and larger boxes proved the success of the Birthday series.

Service Merchandise offered Blue Rhapsody Barbie in 1991 as a department store special. Specials such as this doll are offered during the Christmas season.

Gift sets are another type of Barbie dolls offered as department store specials. The Disney Barbie and Friends Gift Set was a 1991 Toys 'R Us Special Edition.

ing a frilly gown and picture hat; Beauty Pageant Skipper; and Barbie and Ken Tennis Stars all for the 1990 marketing year. Dolls found on the toy shelves in Toys 'R Us for 1991 were Radiant In Red Barbie, featuring red gown, red jewelry, red shoes, and red hair; Totally Hair Skipper and Totally Hair Courtney; and Barbie For President. With Barbie for President, the doll came with an extra outfit and wore a gown of red, white, and blue set for the political convention.

J.C. Penney department stores handle specials by mail order catalog. Some of the more recent dolls were Evening Elegance Barbie in 1990 and Enchanted Evening Barbie in 1991. Also each year special clothing packages are sold exclusively for the doll through the J.C. Penney's catalog. The J.C. Penney department store upscales their specials and are always in the Glamour 'N Glitz category with very eyecatching designs.

Pepsi Barbie was a 1989 Toys 'R Us department store special. Special issues serve two purposes with features for the toy store and advertisement for companies such as Pepsi Cola Bottling Co.

LEFT: Spring Parade Barbie was a 1991 department store special from Toys 'R Us.

Walmart stores sold Dream Fantasy Barbie in 1990. Sales of the doll were incredible. Store employees reported selling out of the doll within a few hours after they placed dolls on the store shelves. Ballroom Beauty Barbie was also a Walmart edition in 1991.

Party In Pink Barbie was found in Ames Stores during 1991. Jewel Jubilee Barbie was sold in Sames Wholesale Stores during that same year. Both dolls were boxed similar to standard Mattel dolls marketed in those areas.

Service Merchandise stores joined the list with a special edition in 1991 called Blue Rhapsody Barbie doll. Their Glamour 'N Glitz trend continued into 1992 with Satin Nights Barbie doll.

Mail order dolls are popular with collectors and Spiegel catalog sold Sterling Wish Barbie as a beautiful addition to their Christmas collectibles catalog in 1991. The doll was all decked out in a black and silver gown as a first Barbie doll for the Spiegel catalog. As a followup in 1992 they offered Regal Reflections Barbie.

Sears department store specials in recent years have been Star Dream Barbie in 1987, Lilac 'N Lovely Barbie in 1988, Evening Enchantment Barbie in 1989, and Southern Belle Barbie doll in 1991. These dolls are available in time for Christmas shopping each year from the catalog section of Sears stores packaged with the usual comb, brush, shoes, and glamorous gown.

F.A.O. Schwarz, the New York City toy store which serves as a fantasyland for children, began to sell special Barbie dolls in 1989. The first doll was Golden Greetings Barbie. She was a vision of loveliness in a gold and white gown. The public response was well received at F.A.O. Schwarz and they have continued each year to sell a new doll. Dolls at F.A.O. Schwarz that followed were Winter Fantasy Barbie in 1990, Night Sensation Barbie in 1991, and Madison Avenue Barbie in 1992.

Applause has issued two Barbies as Christmas time specials. Known only as the Applause Barbies, only limited amounts of these are available each year. The first in 1990 was in a pink monogram fabric

To compliment her famous sister a Pepsi Skipper was also a department store special in 1989 at Toys 'R Us.

Applause joined the special issues in 1990 with Barbie style.

dress with a vibrant pink bow. The packaging was a slip case design with no cellophane to the box. Face paint for these Applause dolls were in bright colors. Green eye shadow accented blue eyes with pink lipstick matching the bow on her satin dress. The 1991 issue was a silver gown with pink accents. Here too, the lavender eye shadow accented lavender eyes. Long flowing tresses curled to the dolls waist.

Hills department stores came in 1989 with the advent of the 30th anniversary and sold Party Lace Barbie. Soon to follow were Evening Sparkles Barbie in 1990 and Moonlight and Roses Barbie in 1991. For 1992 Blue Elegance Barbie doll was the DSS for the Hills department stores.

Some of these stores have recently begun imprinting their names on the front of each limited edition box sold in their stores. Companies such as Childrens Palace also did business in other parts of the country as Childworld. Therefore, as exclusive dolls, they did not bear the name of the store on the packaging, only "Limited Edition."

Childrens Palace, also known as Childworld, issued Disney Barbie in 1990. Because of financial difficulty, the doll planned for 1991 was dropped. Since that time Childworld, Inc. has closed their doors permanently.

Also listed under the mainstream marketing are dolls from Target Stores. They came forth with Party Pink Barbie in 1990 and followed with Cute 'N Curl and Golden Evening Barbies in 1991.

Reminiscent of the 70's when Barbie more commonly adorned grocery shelves, Winn-Dixie, a grocery store chain in the southern states carried Pink Sensation Barbie in 1990.

Mail in refunds are another often overlooked Barbie. In the 70's various companies offered dolls for box tops. In 1989 a doll called Lady Lovely Locks was sold by Mattel. This doll was listed in Sunday newspaper sections. With a coupon and proof of purchase from any of the dolls in this series, Mattel would send the lucky girl a Barbie doll as pictured in the advertisement. The doll offered was mailed in a plain brown box wearing a blue dress, with matching closed toe shoes. The same doll was sold in Germany as Modespaß Barbie that same year.

F.A.O. Schwarz issued Golden Greetings in 1989. Many department stores joined the special issues list in 1989 to celebrate 30 years of Barbie.

A 1992 F.A.O. Schwarz special issue was Madison Avenue Barbie. Styled to resemble Ivana Trump, Madison Avenue Barbie came with many accessories to compliment the doll.

Mattel has had its own examples of special issues. The dolls cover a wide range of costuming and all are beautiful and distinctive. The American Beauties Collection began in 1987 with Mardi Gras Barbie as the first edition. This party girl was wearing a lavender satin, lace, and velvet gown. A tiny black velvet hat was perched on top a head filled with blonde curls. The second in American Beauties was Army Barbie in 1989. In full military uniform, this blonde beauty sported a shorter hair style more customary of an officer serving our country. Air Force Barbie in 1990 wore a pilot's uniform complete with leatherette flight jacket. Navy Barbie followed with the appropriate attire befitting a sailor. Here Barbie doll came with an extra pair of shoes for those tiny feet. Air Force and Navy Barbie boxes no longer mentioned the American Beauties Series but all assume they are a part of the line. In 1992 the Marine Barbie and Ken came both as a set and individually. Both Marine Barbie and Ken were dressed to represent the rank of sergeant and sported the Achievement Medal, Desert Storm Medal, and Good Conduct Medal.

Although the above dolls are special, Mattel created one doll who stands out far above all the others as a special issue. To celebrate 30 years of Barbie, Mattel gave a party at Lincoln Center in New York City. They invited 1200 people to the celebration and as a party favor for all who attended Pink Jubilee Thirty Magical Years Barbie was given. She was packaged in a white slip case box with her name on the outside and dates 1959 – 1989. No cellophane front revealed the beauty inside. A satin ribbon was tied around the box, however. Inside a pink lined box was a Barbie doll with the Superstar face mold. She wore a silver gown accented with rhinestones. A card was enclosed in the box declaring her a Special Limited Edition Barbie.

LEFT: To celebrate Thirty Magical Years of the doll Barbie, Mattel gave a party at Lincoln Center in New York. A favor to the guests was Pink Jubilee Barbie. Packaging was a white box with pink ribbon.

RIGHT: Guests opened the box to find Pink Jubilee Barbie. She was a hand numbered doll with card of authenticity inside.

As the 1992 Presidential election heated up Barbie was offered as candidate for President. Barbie For President was a department store special from Toys 'R Us.

Toys 'R Us sold Radiant in Red in 1992 in two ethnic variations. A brunette Hispanic at the left was offered, as was a redheaded white at the right.

Bride dolls are still popular and in 1991 Mattel issued Dream Bride Barbie in a gown designed by Carol Spencer. The box for the bride was designed so the doll could be displayed without having to be removed. The gown and the doll were sewn into the box.

Hills department store presented Blue Elegance Barbie in 1992 as a department store special.

Ballroom Beauty in 1991 was sold only at Wal-Mart stores.

Party Sensation Barbie in 1990 was an offering from Walgreens drug stores. A group in the fashion design department at Mattel worked long hours creating these special designs for the stores.

Mattel began the American Beauty series in 1988. To celebrate the Mardi Gras in New Orleans, the doll was dressed for a party and called Mardi Gras Barbie.

The American Beauty series continued in 1989 with Army Barbie.

No longer carrying the American Beauties name, Air Force Barbie was issued in 1990. The series is now known as Stars 'N Stripes.

Navy Barbie was a part of the Stars 'N Stripes series in 1991.

Marine Barbie and Ken were sold as a set and separately in 1992. This completed all four branches of the American military.

J.C. Penney department stores issued Enchanted Evening Barbie in 1991 as an elegant Christmas special issue through their catalog.

Holidays were a reason for specials and in 1988 Mattel began the Happy Holidays series.

As a mail order offer in 1988 with proof of purchase from Lady Lovely Locks, Mattel sent this Barbie in blue dress. Sold in Europe, the same doll was called Modespaß Barbie and appeared in stores.

A white Happy Holidays was sold in 1989. With fur trim and snowflakes, the doll was very popular.

Fuschia was the 1990 Happy Holidays color. These dolls were packaged in a way so they could be displayed without removing them from the box.

A vision of green velvet and bright sparkling sequins gave a festive touch to Happy Holidays Barbie in 1991.

Jewels and sparkling rhinestones were a part of the 1992 Happy Holidays Barbie.

CAROL SPENCER

Designer dolls are now being expanded in the Timeless Creations Division of Mattel to include the works of Carol Spencer, fashion designer for Mattel. As the first of a new series, Mattel introduced the Carol Spencer doll called Benefit Ball Barbie doll in 1992. With a luscious head of red curls, Carol chose an iridescent blue and gold jacquard gown. As a reminder of the days in the 60's, this dress featured detailing which included working zippers. Assisting Carol with this project were hairstylist Mellie Phillips and face painter Hiroe Okubo-Wolf. Carol's samplemaker for this project was Benedicto Buenas.

Other Carol Spencer specials for 1992 were two outfits boxed and sold separately by Mattel called Fifth Avenue Style and Hollywood Premiere.

Inspiration for the dolls comes from many areas. Ballerina dolls have been a mainstay since 1959. In 1991 a special issue Barbie doll called Swan Lake Barbie in a special display box was featured by Mattel. The base of the box is musical and plays the Swan Lake music. The doll outfit was designed by Carol Spencer who is responsible for many of the garments sold on the dolls. For 1992 the ballerina beauty added to the series is a doll called Nutcracker Barbie. In a pink and silver flower petal tutu, Barbie again comes in an elegant display box which looks like etched glass. Her pedestal was also a music box and played "The Dance of the Sugar Plum Fairy."

Carol Spencer began a series of designer Barbies in 1992 with her Benefit Ball Barbie. The costume, doll hair, and face paint were all designed by Carol Spencer for Mattel.

The designer of not only women's clothing but now Barbie clothing also, is Bob Mackie. Also known by his adoring press as the "Guru of Glitz" he has created collectible Barbies that boggle the imagination. Photograph courtesy of Bob Mackie

BOB MACKIE

For the Barbie doll collector who is looking for the ultimate in glamour examine a Bob Mackie designed Barbie doll. Mackie, fashion designer for the stars of Hollywood, was asked by Mattel to design a line of special edition clothes for this doll in 1989. "It wasn't the level we're on now," says Mackie. "In the meantime, they changed executives who were then not sure what to do with me. They decided to do just one special edition doll," says Mackie. After sending Mattel sketches of the doll, they created a prototype with which he was not happy. To solve the problem of interpreting sketches Mackie began doing the prototypes in his studio and sending to Mattel the finished doll along with beads and a dress not cut out but beaded so Mattel could see how it went together. The system works much better and is reminiscent of the same system Charlotte Johnson used when the Barbie clothing was being manufactured in Japan.

Mackie starts with a sketch of the garment. He says, "I try not to think of her as this tiny doll. I try to think of what I would like to see on Barbie." After the sketch, Mackie finds the fabric. Renowned for his sequins and bead designs, he glamorizes Barbie with that same flair. Cost is not a factor. There are no ceilings or keeping within a budget. He can give Barbie the look he wants without a cost problem.

Hair style is also a Mackie insight. Stephen Tarmichael, from Mattel's hairstyling department, meets with Mackie at his studio and is shown what will be needed. Mackie says, "what makes my dolls different is that they don't have enormous amounts of hair. The hair is usually pulled back away from the face — very controlled. Because of this it makes my version of Barbie different."

When face painting is ready, Bob Mackie creates a drawing of what the face should look like and sends it to Mattel. Hiroe Okubo-Wolf paints the face of the Mackie Barbie from this drawing.

The first year a "traditional Mackie" was chosen by Mattel. This design was an all golden gown with peep hole front. A high rise ponytail with golden decorations made Barbie a star of collectible dolls. In the second Bob Mackie issued in 1991 two dolls were featured. One black doll called Midnight Barbie wore a glitter sequin hat with hair pulled up the top. The gown was of hand sewn sequins in black and white. The Platinum Barbie was a white ver-

sion. A white satin gown with hand sewn sequins was her attire. The high piled hairdo was a platinum white to match the gown. In 1992, the Mackie releases were Empress Bride Barbie and Neptune's Fantasy Barbie. The bride came in a white and golden gown that was so full and flowing it required an oversize box. Pearl drop earrings and necklace matched the pearls on the gown. A crown of white and gold with rhinestone insets held the floor length veil. Neptune's Fantasy Barbie was different than any doll Mattel has ever released in the Barbie doll line. A shapely gown of green velvet accented with teal and silver beads makes this doll something to see. A standup collar of teal beads and sequins frame the face. Platinum blonde hair streaked with green makes a unique hair style. A jeweled hairpiece which matches the earrings complete her elegant style. Mackie uses an abundance of sequins and jewels to accent the dolls and their

Bob Mackie made his entrance into the doll scene with a Barbie in 1990. The doll gown, hair style, and face paint were designed by Mackie for Mattel.

Bob Mackie begins his creation with a drawing of the doll clad in his gown. Pictured here is the first Bob Mackie Barbie called Golden Mackie Barbie. Drawing courtesy of Bob Mackie.

attire. Mattel is incorporating the use of these adornments into their other lines like the Happy Holiday series to compliment clothing designed from the finest fabrics in the world.

If Bob Mackie's methods of creative design sound like echoes from past work at Mattel, it is because he attended Chouinard Art School in Los Angeles where Charlotte Johnson taught. Mackie says he was at Chouinard in 1960 and Charlotte's work was discussed at length. "They were very proud of Charlotte Johnson and what she was designing," says Mackie. "Those original Charlotte Johnson garments were beautiful with all those little zippers and buttons. So beautifully made!" That

first special edition doll has led to more and yet another is planned for 1993. Collectors can plan to see a regular yearly contribution to their favorite doll from Bob Mackie. In the years to come, it is anyone's guess what magnificent Mackie design Barbie will masquerade in for collectors.

Special editions abound in Barbieland. Doll collectors see even more stores each year join the ranks of the Department Store Specials. For the doll collector that is just beginning or one that is overwhelmed by the prospects of trying to collect every Barbie, the DSS Barbies would be an excellent starting point.

The second doll designed by Bob Mackie for Mattel in 1991 was Platinum Barbie. Here too, an abundance of sequins decorated the gown and hair.

Second issue Mackie Barbie was equally as vibrant and was one of two produced that year. Featured here is the Mackie drawing of Platinum Barbie. Drawing by Bob Mackie.

Another Bob Mackie doll called Starlight Barbie was released in 1991. A traditional Mackie with sequins and feathers spelled glamour for Mattel.

Sold along with Platinum Barbie was a black ethnic doll called Starlight Splendor Barbie. Drawing by Bob Mackie.

Empress Bride Barbie joined the 1992 dolls sold by Mattel. Bob Mackie designed the bride for a fantasy wedding for an Empress.

For the ultimate in bridal dolls Bob Mackie designed Empress Bride Barbie. Drawing by Bob Mackie.

Ablaze with sequins and jewels, Neptune's Fantasy Barbie is direct from the sea. She was a 1992 design for Mattel by Bob Mackie. All Mackie designed dolls were sold through Timeless Treasures, a division of Mattel.

Neptune never dreamed of having a daughter like Barbie, but here she is in all her green splendor. This is the Mackie drawing of Neptune's Fantasy Barbie. Drawing by Bob Mackie.

Chapter 23

Barbie Around the Globe

Ma Ba sold dolls from the old molds wearing both western and Japanese style garments. Here Barbie appears wearing a red kimono.

Vacation travel is a bonanza of new sights, sounds, and ideas. A reason for travel is to get away from it all. Yet for collectors traveling to the ends of the earth, they are never far from the realm of Barbie. Vacationers are avid shoppers and for doll collectors who travel to far away places, they can reward themselves with a treasure trove of new delights. Several foreign countries have legal arrangements with Mattel to manufacture Barbie dolls for sale only in their own countries. Some of these gems are never seen in the United States unless a traveler finds one and comes home with this precious find in hand. Unable, by legal restrictions, to ship these dolls to the United States, they are for the people who live in these nations. Mattel's Barbie molds are used for these dolls and in some cases the clothing is styled like our own. There are other styles which used the usual mold but dress in eyecatching fashions.

Barbie was first introduced to the European market in 1961. Cliff Jacobs, vice president of marketing with Mattel, took Barbie doll to a United States government sponsored exhibit in London, England. This exhibit was held at James Park for American manufacturers. This was an effort for American manufacturers to offer their goods to the British market. Chatty Cathy and Barbie were presented to several doll distributors during this exhibit. Jacobs was accompanied on this adventure by Paul Guggenheim, a Swiss born businessman who assisted Mattel with this expansion. Their efforts met with great success.

One difficulty, though, that arose in England was that Mattel was unable to sell Barbie costumes there in the early years of European expansion. England had trade restrictions against textile imports from the Orient. Dolls sold well in England, and when the restrictions were changed Barbie costumes were also marketed which further enhanced the doll's popularity.

Leaving England, Jacobs and Guggenheim proceeded to Paris, France, where a fashion show was planned. The exhibit showcased the works of Charlotte Johnson. Her elegant designs for Barbie were translated into adult size outfits and worn by models on the runways of Paris fashion houses. In the mecca of fashion design, Barbie and Chouinard shone brightly in the "City of Lights."

Jacobs and Guggenheim moved on to Italy where they again found distributors interested in promoting their products. The European tour was finalized in Germany at the Nuremberg Toy Fair. Europe was in love with this new American product. Mattel continued its expansion into various other countries in Europe and throughout the world. "As each country began selling Barbie in their own country, Mattel designed special costumes for these areas," says Jacobs. "Boxes were printed in the particular language of the area to satisfy the market." With the opening fanfare that announced Barbie's emergence on the Euro-markets the American success story was repeated on an international scale.

The oversight of the worldwide production is handled through Mattel International in Southern

California. The specific outfit designs may be the same or vary greatly from U.S. market depending on the marketability in the country.

For example, the 1988 Happy Holidays Barbie was released in 1989 in Europe. The German variation came packaged and dressed the same as our own U.S. version. The doll had one big difference, the box was written in five languages. Print was in the German, French, English, Spanish, and Italian languages. The doll was prepared for a multi-lingual world. In France the Golden Dreams Reve Dore Barbie was sold in 1980 in the United States as Golden Dreams Barbie. A 1985 Dream Glow Barbie from the U.S. sold in Venezuela as Sueno De Estrellas Barbie and a 1988 Garden Party Barbie sold in 1989 in Spain as Barbie Romantica. However, along with dolls much like those we find on our own toy shelves the Spanish will find those created for their own market. In 1988 Manuel Pertegaz, a Spanish clothing designer, fashioned a stunning red gown with red rose accent for the Barbie Tenth Aniver-

sario en Espana doll. This gown was a luscious red satin with a full flowing skirt. A new hairdo was designed for the doll with red hair ribbon to match this elegant gown. Packaging for the anniversary doll was an extra large size box to accommodate the gown. This doll and others are made by Mattel Espana in Barcelona, Spain.

Paris, France, has been known as the fashion center of our world for many years. One of America's best known jewelry designers is now a resident of this country. He has made his home in Paris for a long time. In 1985 at the request of Mattel, BillyBoy designed a Barbie doll he called Barbie Le Nouveau Theatre de la Mode. A blonde beauty, she had pale blue eyes and pink lips. Large gold link jewelry was an accent on her black knit dress. On the box the doll was pictured with black nail polish but the doll in the box did not have painted fingernails. This doll was introduced at a gala Paris event to celebrate 26 years of the Barbie doll. My own copy of the doll came from a friend who was visiting Paris and

Le Nouveau Theatre De La Mode Barbie, sold only in France in 1985, was designed by BillyBoy for Mattel.

French Golden Dreams Barbie Reve Dore was sold without Quick Curl Hair. The American Golden Dreams was designed with Quick Curl Hair.

happened on to the event taking place near the Eiffel Tower. A non Barbie collector, she still purchased several of the dolls at a table near the sight to bring home.

In 1986 BillyBoy designed another doll for Mattel, Feelin' Groovy Barbie. The doll was billed as glamour-a-go-go. With jet black hair and lavender eyes, her face paint was more colorful with full red lips and pink cheeks. The gown was deep rosy satin and a multicolor coat trimmed in black fur accented the garment. As the last of the BillyBoy Barbies, she was sold as a very limited edition.

As the barriers fall and more people are finding Barbie available to them, Russia too, is swept with Barbiemania. In Moscow's most famous toy store, Detsky Mir, a sparkling pink window display of Barbie doll is viewed. Pink cars and carriages, even a van, are there for the doll enthusiast. Blonde

tressed dolls make an eyecatching sight for Moscow's many children. Unfortunately, Barbie is not yet the doll for everyone in Russia. Their economy continues to struggle and prices for Barbie dolls amount to almost a month's wages for most working mothers. A doll which costs $7.00 in the United States will be twice that price in Moscow. The price for a Barbie van could cost a working mother approximately three times her monthly salary or $75.00.

Even in Russia, the local toy manufacturers try to compete with Mattel by making a fashionable doll of their own. Two of these dolls are called Natasha and Veronika. Not even near copies of Barbie doll, they are sturdy creatures with blonde hair and wearing drab dresses with aprons. But Barbie has arrived in Russia and as their economy improves so will the chances for children to have this icon called Barbie to play with and collect.

In honor of the destruction of the Berlin Wall Mattel issued a doll called Freundschafts Barbie in 1990. Translated, this means Friendship Barbie. For the first time ever these dolls would appear on toy shelves in what was once East Germany, Czechoslovakia, Hungary, and Poland. As a celebration of the removal of mortar and barbwire, which had long separated the East from West, Mattel was able to issue this first Barbie for the people from behind the iron curtain.

To celebrate the removal of the Berlin Wall Mattel issued Freundschafts (Friendship) Barbie in 1990. She was sold in East Germany, Hungary, Poland, and Czechoslovakia.

In 1991 a series of dolls called Benetton were sold in the U.S. and Europe. Teresa and Ken were only available in Europe but the remainder were sold on both continents.

Travel to South America can be an exciting doll hunt. Here, too, the Barbies are made differently for the people who live in our southern hemisphere. One spot to visit for unique dolls is the country of Venezuela. In this region, a company called Rotoplast Industries received a license from Mattel to manufacture Barbies for the Venezuelan market. Dolls in this country come with undated boxes which greatly complicates the chronological history. Hair on these dolls is thick and very long. For example, a Dream Glow Barbie appeared in Caracus with ash blonde locks which hung below her waist. The Dream Glow Barbie doll sold in our own United States had honey blonde hair that was nowhere near the length of this variation. Both the Venezuelan version and our own were dressed identical in pink gowns designed to glow in the dark. Another example of dolls found on Caracus toy shelves is a Tropical Barbie doll. Packages are written in both English and Spanish. Barbie was wearing the same floral pattern swimwear as those sold in the United States. However, face paint on those southern hemisphere dolls is much more vibrant. Brighter colors are used to accent eyes and lips. Tropical Barbie, for Venezuelan children, was made with hair which reached her knees and was ash blonde color.

A doll which has become famous in Venezuela is Llanera Barbie. The word Llanera translated means Plainswoman. Made for several years, she is a brunette with fluffy curls. This long hair is combed to a side part. Coloring on the doll is more tan tone with red lips and bright blue eyes. Clad in an off the shoulder white peasant blouse, she also wears a full flowered skirt. This costume could be thought of as a national design with local flavor. A more recent release was a colorful Barbie called Esmeralda. This doll has painted green eyes, ruby red lips, and perfect pink blush. The jewelry was green. An emerald green off shoulder gown with ruffles and a flower petal skirt is worn by the year's most gorgeous Barbie for Mattel. Esmeralda Barbie was the first of a series of colorful dolls from this nation. Next in the series was Agua Marina Barbie with ash blonde hair in a Cinderella upsweep hair style. She also had bright blue eyes. Her gown was a sheer blue material with a rose design on the front. Jewelry for this doll was blue to match her dress. Fashion booklets included with the Venezuelan dolls are much smaller. Designed as a foldout sheet, the fashions are still elegant and rich and are designed by the fashion staff in El Segundo, California.

Dolls from the Brazilian market are unbelievable. Made by the Estrella Corporation in Brazil, Mattel gives them license to make these beauties only for the Brazilian market. A whole line of dolls are made for Brazil's doll buyers. Yearly releases of a bride doll exhibits the popularity of the wedding day design enjoyed worldwide. All children love the same things, just the languages are different. Here too, dates do not appear on boxes although each year different style dolls are sold. The varying of hair colors extends to the overseas markets, as in the 1990 Passeio Barbie sold in both blonde and brunette. Each hair color accompanied completely different outfits. The blonde was in white blouse and flowered skirt, while the brunette came in a tan coat with red collar and ruby red hat. Here again, the face paint is much brighter colors.

A Feliz Aniversario came in three styles in 1990. The Estrella Corporation was celebrating the tenth anniversary of Barbie in Brazil. Popular in that country is streaked hair and the anniversary dolls come with light streaks through the long luscious brunette hair. When our own country had Rocker Barbie, Brazil also was in the swing with Rock Star Barbie who came with a microphone and guitar. New Wave Barbie came with her own microphone also but she had green and blonde hair. Not only is

The 1992 newly designed Benetton Barbie was sold in Europe. The remainder of the Benetton dolls from the 1992 series were available in the United States, but sold as Limited Editions.

makeup on the dolls bright and imaginative, but clothing also is original. Unique hair colors are not unusual to the dolls from this hemisphere. In past years, a Rock Star Barbie was produced with purple hair. Barbie doll has many doll friends in Brazil. Among these is Viky who Estrella produced and billed as "amiga da Barbie." Translated this means friend of Barbie. Passeio Viky resembles Midge of old with titian hair and freckles. She too has gray-white streaks through her thick head of hair. The face mold for Viky is the ever popular Steffie. Passeio Viky came wearing a white long sleeve blouse and black and white dotted skirt. Two red roses at the waist of her skirt make a lovely accent for the doll. Another Viky creation was in the Animal Lovin' Viky which was made as part of the set with Barbie and Ken. Animal Lovin' Barbie appeared in our own country in 1988 and had an Hispanic friend named Nikki. In this design Viky had brown hair with no streaks. The same Steffie face mold was used and several well placed freckles graced her cheeks and nose. She came with her own tiger cub toy.

Travel to India and you are not leaving Barbie behind. This faraway place too, has dolls on toy shelves to appeal to the local populace. Selections from the Indian market are manufactured by Leo Mattel. One doll is a honey blonde wearing a golden yellow silk sari trimmed with raspberry and gold brocade. An underskirt in golden yellow was also on the doll. Unlike the dolls in our own country, the clothing closures are snaps rather than velcro. A platinum blonde Barbie wearing a raspberry silk sari trimmed with gold rick-rack is also available for the Indian children. Another feature in the 1992 line from Leo Mattel was a brunette haired Barbie doll with large brown eyes. She was attired in an emerald green silk sari. The green silk was trimmed with red and gold brocade. All of these dolls came with white rhinestone inset earrings, gold jeweled necklace, and double hoop bracelets on each wrist. One unique feature of these dolls from India is that they each came with a black painted jewel in the center of her forehead.

A striking feature on the international market by Mattel was the set of wedding Barbie dolls designed

Europe has series of dolls designed only for their area. Wintertime Bride Barbie was part of a bridal set designed for Mattel by Carol Spencer. These dolls were marketed in 1991 in England and throughout Europe. Picture courtesy of Carol Spencer.

Another view of Wintertime Bride Barbie shows an elaborate gown with faux fur trim. The doll is sold in a box which was designed to display the doll without removing it. Picture courtesy of Carol Spencer.

by Carol Spencer. Sold as a seasonal theme, they were called Spring Bride Barbie, Summer Bride Barbie, Wintertime Bride Barbie, and Bridesmaid Barbie. Also included was a Groom Ken sold separately. Approximately three or four samples of the Wintertime Bride Barbie were made and one was given to A. Glenn Mandeville by Mattel. The unusual quality of this doll gown is in the skirt, which is removable to reveal a slim gown with a hand painted fleur de lis design. The head cress on the doll features white fur trim with tulle ruffles. Flowers carried by the doll also match the bridesmaid's dress and groom's cummerbund and lapels.

Travel to these countries can give a person all the thrill of Barbie shopping in exotic lands. Here, too, these dolls will add a variety to the collection of any Barbie doll lover. While setting your sights on touring, just remember there are over 70 countries from which to choose.

For the U.S. collector, long miles do not have to be traveled to find foreign Barbies. Canada is the greatest asset for unique finds of not only Canadian exclusives but also some of the United Kingdom and Euro-market dolls which find their way to the toy shelves of our neighbor to the north. As a reflection back to two top selling dolls in the U.S., Mattel marketed Hawaiian Superstar Barbie in Canada in 1977. Both Superstar Barbie and Hawaiian Barbie were popular in the United States. For the cold Canadian nights Mattel released Fabulous Fur Barbie in 1982. The doll was warmly dressed in a royal blue outfit trimmed in white faux fur. A tribute to the 1988 Olympics in Calgary, Canada, Barbie was released as a world class skater attired in white satin and tulle.

The Canadian market also fulfills many family lines that are sometimes left incomplete in the U.S. market. The 1989 release of the Style Magic line in

In honor of the Winter Olympics held in Canada in 1988 Skating Star Barbie was sold only in Canada.

Venezuela has issued many memorable Barbie dolls. Mattel licensed these dolls to be sold only in that area. As an example, Esmeralda Barbie was sold in 1990.

the U.S. market did not include Skipper, yet she was part of the family found in Canada. Another example is the Benetton line. Ken and Teresa were not sold in the U.S., but again the Canadian market completed the set. The minimal restrictions at the Canadian–United States border further aids the collector in returning to the States with a bounty of Barbie and friends.

There are other ways to find these dolls if you are not a world traveler. One of these ways is to give money to a friend's son or daughter as they leave for a far away country in the student exchange program. So they have already left? Not a problem! Parents are always sending their child money and you can fatten the wallet with a written list of what you want

purchased along with the amount needed. If you are not aware of the styles available in these countries, the element of surprise in what can be brought back is also memorable. Other ways are if friends are planning a vacation to one of these areas send money with them to shop for you. Collectors of Barbie dolls are in every part of the globe and even a swap could be arranged if they are seeking an American version of the doll. Many doll collectors magazines including *Barbie Bazaar* carry advertisements from collectors seeking penpals. There are many ways to collect the dolls from far away. Some collectors have made friends with airline personnel. Barbie doll can reach your home from anywhere in the world; she is well traveled.

Agua marina Barbie was sold in 1991 as the second in a series following Esmeralda Barbie. She, too, is from Venezuela.

Tropical Barbie, marketed in Venezuela, was manufactured with longer ash blonde hair and brighter face paint.

Brazil markets their own dolls through the Estrella Company. All doll designs are done in El Segundo, California and manufactured in the Orient. Rock Star Barbie was sold in 1989.

Passeio Barbie sold in 1989 in Brazil came with blonde and brunette hair colors. Dolls in the two styles were dressed differently for the Brazilian market.

LEFT: As in the United States, Brazilian Barbie has friends. Passeio Viky is a friend of Barbie. The Midge head mold is used on this doll including the famous freckles.

RIGHT: In India children have dolls from their own culture to choose. As an elegant Indian lady, Barbie is clad in silk sari with the painted jewel in her forehead. Photography courtesy of Richard Whittick, Cotswold.

Spain is a place where Barbie collectors can locate unusual dolls for their collections. Here Barbie 10 Anniversario en Espana was issued in Spain in honor of ten years of Barbie doll sales in 1989. The gown and doll were designed by Pertegaz, a famous Spanish fashion designer.

Ma Ba in Japan were licensed for a brief time to manufacture Barbie and Ken from the old molds. Carol Spencer traveled to Japan to assist in designing costumes for these dolls. Pictured here is a Barbie and Ken doll sold as a set for the Japanese market. Photo courtesy of Irene Davis.

Chapter 24

Cleaning and Revitalizing

You have bought Barbies from yard sales and flea markets and they are dirty. They have had long days with children playing with them or have lain in an attic or basement for many years. The hair is a major disaster. Not a problem! This may come as a surprise but these dolls do still have a life. They are still collectible and make excellent fashion display dolls. They can be restored to look almost like new again.

Remember, it is amazing what soap and water can do for a doll. My best work area is the kitchen. I prefer to work at a counter/sink area with a ready source of water. Assemble all the things you will need before you begin. Never use a soap with coloring. The vinyl doll will absorb the coloring in soaps. This will permanently stain the doll. A good clear or white dish detergent is needed for starting the process. Other items needed are cotton balls, Q-tips®, Soft Scrub® with bleach, paper towels, a clean cloth towel, comb, hair pick, Oxy 5®, Clearasil®, shampoo, and cream rinse.

Remove all clothing from the doll. Place the doll under warm running water to dampen. Use a wet paper towel and dish detergent to wash the doll body thoroughly. Be very gentle around the area of the face paint. Keep in mind this paint is old and could easily flake. Use Q-tips® to clean around eyes and ears. This will remove surface dirt. Next pour Soft Scrub® with bleach on a wet cotton ball. This is good for cleaning heavily soiled arms and legs. If the doll is pitted with dirt embedded in the vinyl, prolonged soaking is required followed by a cotton ball scrub with Soft Scrub®. Rinse the doll with clean water. The worked in dirt is usually found in the mid torso or thigh region where the children held the doll during play. The next step is to clean the hair. Break out the shampoo. Suds the hair thoroughly followed by a rinse of clean water. The hair may be very tangled. Saran doll hair tends to tangle with long hours of play. The hair may be so tangled that it stands up like matted shocks but do not be discouraged and maintain your patience. Those tangles can be calmed and subdued. Put several beads of creme rinse in the doll hair. Do not rinse this out. Use a comb or hair pick and *gently* work the tangles down. Be careful not to pull hair out of the doll's head by tugging too hard, too fast. The danger is you may end up with a bald doll. This will be a slow process but the rinse will keep hair slippery enough to work the tangles free. When all the tangles are removed then rinse the hair with clean water and dry with a towel.

Now that the hair is clean the curl and styling needs to be restored. First let the hair air dry before styling. When the hair is dry use a comb or doll brush and brush the hair into a ponytail. You will notice a small section of hair that is longer than the remainder on the right side of the doll's head. This is no accident! Use a small dental rubber band and fasten the ponytail into place about ½" from the back of the doll head. The longer section of the hair is the top wrap which is to curve around the rubber band. Wrap the longer strands of hair around the ponytail counter-clockwise and use a seam ripper to poke the ends into and under the rubber band. If the doll is a swirl ponytail this is set into place slightly differently. The rooting pattern of the swirl ponytail doll is sewn around the hair line and the center of the head is bald. This was designed to make styling the swirl easier. Using a doll hairbrush, curve the front hair across the forehead then brush the sides and back up into a ponytail. Fasten this together with a dental rubber band. This ponytail too should have a section of hair longer than the rest at the right side of the doll head. Again take this section of hair and wrap it around the ponytail counter-clockwise putting the end pieces into the rubber band with a seam ripper.

After all this cleaning and restyling there is no longer a Barbie curl at the end of the ponytail, but this is not a problem. Even Barbie can have a perm put in her hair but by using different techniques than the over the counter permanent wave solutions. Small hair rollers just the right size for Barbie doll can be purchased at Toys 'R Us. Also good to use would be the small blue perm rollers with papers used by beauticians. Put these in the base of the doll's ponytail. Heat water in a pan to a rolling boil. Pour this water over the rollers and rolled doll hair with the doll head laid so that the hair lays in a pan. *Do not allow* the whole doll head to become wet. The boiling water will damage face paint. Leave the rollers and hair to remain in the water until it is room temperature. Remove the hair from the water and leave the rollers in overnight until the hair is dry. The rollers may be removed the next day when hair is dry. Spray the curls with hair styling spritz. This will hold the curl in place.

Another hair cure which will reduce some of the brassy color includes soaking older Barbie's hair in Woolite®. Over time some colors of doll hair oxidize and develop this brassy coloring.

Air and sunlight presents its own measure of

damage to the older dolls. Hair colors can change under the rays of light whether in direct or muted sun. This creates a condition of oxidization that changes colors. The 1966 Color Magic Barbie was designed with changeable hair color. Golden blonde changed to scarlet flame and midnight black changed to ruby red. Most bottles of the changing solution are long gone. Although being household products, they could be mixed again. With our pollution difficulties in most cities and moisture levels these solutions are no longer needed to change the hair colors. As the moisture in the air of our environment has become more acidic, Color Magic Barbie now turns to red without the use of bottled chemicals. There is a good way to return Magic Color Barbie back to her blonde or midnight color with exposure to base chemicals. Over the years the chemicals in the air and in the original solutions have changed and now they no longer work to return a red headed Midnight Color Magic to midnight. There is a solution that does work to return her to midnight again. After numerous attempts I called in an expert, Michael Alexander in Chillicothe, Ohio. He too had tried many chemicals. The one that does work is Comet® cleanser. Dampen the hair with warm water. Sprinkle Comet® directly on the doll's hair. Work the powder through the hair. You will see an immediate change to the midnight color. Rinse the hair, leaving some of the Comet® in the hair will keep the ruby red color from returning. Seal the Color Magic doll inside a large plastic bag with two silica gel packets. The silica gel will remove all moisture from inside the bag and insure the doll hair will retain its original color.

It appears that the midnight Color Magic is much more sensitive to air and moisture than the blonde Color Magic. Many more of those have turned red than the blonde.

The reverse should be considered if a collector has a red Color Magic in a display case and wants her to remain as red. Collectors should be careful to refrain from using window cleaners containing ammonia on the area near the doll. Ammonia is a base chemical and might cause the doll to return to blonde or midnight coloring. Even the mist from a spray may cause the hair to color streak.

Mattel has used pigments in the past which over time changed color. Light bleached the pigments in the first three issues of Barbie. She fades to an ivory or sickly white. Apparently, this was evident early since by number four Barbie the vinyl and pigment for the dolls was much more stable. Some dolls issued in 1961 have arms, legs, and heads made from a type of vinyl which not only oiled but also turned an orange color. Others have been seen to be more yellow or golden in color. Long exposure to light seems to be the main culprit with these. Many dolls sold in 1961 have bodies and heads with oil that leaves spots even on the boxes they are stored inside. Mattel was searching for a new base for the vinyl used in their dolls and purchased an oil to make the

dolls retain their pigment. The oil was purchased from Eastman Kodak Corporation but as Bill Robb, former Mattel inventor tells, "soon complaints from customers telling of dolls oiling out and causing damage brought a quick end to the product's use." Other dolls besides Barbie doll were using this oil product. Larger bodied dolls made by Mattel were being made with this oil base in their vinyl also.

Mattel used yet another type pigment for the Twist 'N Turn dolls. This pigment too seems to be fading to an orange or yellow. Although not to any great numbers, some collectors have found twist dolls with a green tinge to their formerly pink skin tone. Mattel was experimenting with vinyls to achieve a more pliable product and add a new skin tone to their doll. Unfortunately, this has not always remained over the years. Many TNT dolls, however, have remained as pristine as they were when removed from their boxes.

If your doll has a nose nick this can be fixed. An easy remedy for a chipped Barbie nose is to use a diamond dust nail file or common emery board. Rub the nose from top to bottom and from side to side using little or no pressure on the file. Water can also be used with the metal file to avoid scratching the vinyl surface. Use the finer sand side of the emery board. Be patient and with great care even the most distorted nose can be reshaped. This is surgery with no pain and a zero recovery period.

Many of the older Barbie dolls and friends have green ears. This is caused from the metal earrings that the doll came wearing. Some dolls lost their earrings early in life and therefore do not have green ears. Some greening is worse than others depending on the moisture level of where the doll has been. Collectors have learned in recent years to remove the earrings and keep them in a separate bag with the doll. If the doll has green ears there are some products on the market that will remove all or most of this. Soft Scrub® with bleach placed on a Q-tip® can be applied to the green area around the ear holes. Leave this on the doll until it dries and then rinse. Repeat the application of Soft Scrub® to the green area three times a day until it is all gone or greatly reduced. Oxy 5® can also be applied to dolls green ears in the same fashion as Soft Scrub® and left to dry. This will also bleach much of the green away. If the green on the ears is excessive and difficult to remove the doll head can be removed and Soft Scrub® placed on the inside of the doll head at the ear holes. Be careful not to allow Soft Scrub® to come in contact with the doll's hair. The hair will also bleach and the doll will have light spots in the hair.

A similar condition existed in 1990 with an F.A.O. Schwarz limited edition doll called Winter Fantasy Barbie. The doll came wearing royal blue plastic earrings which faded out onto the vinyl ears of the doll. Mattel arranged for a return policy with the doll head. The customer could return the doll head to Mattel and they would by return mail send a new doll head with white earrings. The Soft Scrub® approach removed the blue stain from the doll ears and many collectors did not return their doll heads.

Another problem with the older dolls is neck splits. This happened when children pulled heads of the dolls on and off or turned the heads from side to side frequently during playtime. With the age of some dolls it is recommended that the heads not be removed unless absolutely necessary. However, to repair neck splits removing the head will be required. The best way to accomplish this safely is to heat your hot air popcorn popper and hold the doll's neck area near the air jet. Yes, fingers do get warm too, but keep the doll there only until the vinyl feels very soft. Gently bend the head over to one side and the head will come off easily. Be cautious not to leave the doll head near the air jet too long or the hair will show heat damage. Cup the hair in the palm of your hand to deflect the heat. Neck splits can be best repaired with a strong finger nail bonding glue which is sold in most beauty supply stores. Some lighter weight nail glues that can also be used are sold in most discount store chains or grocery stores but the results are not always as successful. This type glue is much more liquid and only a tiny bead down the split is needed. In the bonding process more glue is not better. This glue is very strong and will even glue together fingers so be careful not to get any on yourself. Clean the area in and around the split with soapy water then rinse with clean water to insure all dirt or other glue attempts are off the work area. This cleaning will also remove all vinyl oils from the area. Put a small bead of glue down the split. Hold the neck split together for 15 minutes with your fingers until the glue is dry. Using a toothpick, scrape all the excess glue from the surface of the neck. This will create a smooth seal to the split. Let the doll head with the glued neck split rest for 24 hours before reattaching the head to the doll body. Reattaching the head is the same principle as removal. The hot air jet on the popcorn popper again needs to heat the doll head around the neck area until soft and ever so gently reattach the head over the neck knob. Use your fingers to support the neck around the area that you have glued. This will aid in discouraging the neck from resplitting.

Another playtime hazard for Barbie is the artistic child. Some of the older Barbies have been found with marker streaks down their legs and arms. Apparently during playtime some children became creative, but these too can be removed with a little effort. Clearasil® is a white cream designed to remove and encourage healing of acne. Little did the manufacturer of this product know one of their best customers would be a doll named Barbie. Place a bead of Clearasil® down the marker stains on the arm or leg of the doll, leaving it to dry. Place the doll in a sunny window and allow the sunshine to dry the Clearasil® on the doll. When the Clearasil® is dry in about three or four hours chip it off with your fingernail. Believe it or not the marker stain will be gone. Sunlight speeds the process of bleaching the stain away. If the doll is laid on a counter and not in sunlight the Clearasil® may have to be applied a second time, but the marker stain will disappear without the sunlight, it will just take more time. Clearasil® also works on ink marks found on some vinyl dolls.

For those who have dolls who are number one, two, or three from 1959 and 1960 and are faded splotchy, there is a cure. That fading can be made overall by removing the clothing of the doll and sunning the doll in a window with plenty of light. This will make a much more even fading and remove the splotchy appearance. Be aware that full sunlight will fade the clothing also, so it is best to remove these before allowing Barbie to sunbathe in the window sill. This will give the doll a milk white color and insure the doll does not develop yellowing.

Some old Barbies have been found with loose arms. Years of play have enlarged the arm socket and it becomes difficult to keep doll arms on. Again the hot air popcorn popper will help. Hold the doll torso so the heat is on the arm socket. When the vinyl becomes soft and pliable use your finger and thumb to work your way around the socket area making the hole smaller. Depending on how stretched the socket has become is how many times this procedure will be repeated. After the socket is the right size then replace the arm.

Another, not as common, problem is bowed legs. This is caused from long months and years on doll stands with feet supporting the body. Changes in temperature also contribute to this warping problem. Keeping dolls on stands is still advisable but raise the stand high enough that the doll feet do not rest on the base. They should be in the air. With the popcorn popper air jet, warm both legs until the vinyl is pliable. This is when saving empty sewing thread spools will be handy. Take several of the spools and fit them between the dolls legs. Fasten the doll legs and spools together with several rubber bands. Leave the spools in place for approximately four weeks. When legs have been straightened, store the doll flat in a box. If you do choose to return her to a stand, raise the stand so the feet do not touch the base. This will take pressure off the legs.

For repair on face paint always use acrylic paints. They go on smoother and leave a matte finish. Oil base or water base paints sometimes soak into the vinyl and create a worse mess. Use the smallest bristle brush and begin work from the center out. This will make a more even effect in the end. Never use permanent felt tip markers on Barbie. This product also soaks into the vinyl over time and creates a stain.

Hairdryers are not good to heat doll bodies. The bonnet requires putting the whole doll inside. This heats everything on the doll including the hair. The saran hair is very heat sensitive and will damage easily. Blow dryers or hot air popcorn poppers are a great source of heat to soften vinyl dolls and can localize the heat in the area you want.

Cleaning and restoring those older outfits of clothing is yet another adventure. Again, remember the age of the fabric with which you are working. Never use bleach on these fabrics. After 30 years many of these fabrics are very fragile and the threads are easily broken. Cold water Woolite® is best used on cotton fabrics that need laundering. Long white nylon gloves worn by the doll can be soaked in Woolite but *never* rub the garment. Over time some of these white fabrics have become dingy and even yellowed. One way to improve some of these would be to soak them in a solution of equal parts water and lemon juice. Rinse the solution out of the garment with clear water and dry in the sun. Some cases require a repeat of this process. Remember to sun dry white fabrics only. The color fabric will fade in sunlight.

The Wedding Day Set wedding outfit from 1959 often yellows also. Soak this in Efferdent® tablets which you have dissolved in a shallow dish. Do not use any colored tablets, only the white. This fabric will absorb the color and create a worse disaster.

Sweaters such as the one in Tennis Anyone should not be washed. The black design on the sweater is a painted design and would run in water. Many of the woolen coats or items could be spot dry cleaned with over the counter products, but I would not recommend major cleaning because of their age. The same applies to satin garments. They are very fragile after these many years. Satin will split with age and lace also splits. Remember that these were the finest fabrics available. Even the furs in those early outfits were real mink and rabbit. Mrs. Handler wanted only the best fabrics for her dream doll and Charlotte Johnson searched out the most elegant possible. Whenever cleaning these fabrics be sure and rinse thoroughly. Never place these outfits in the clothes dryer. Always dry these over the bathroom rod or dry flat on a dry towel. Sunlight drying is not encouraged except on white fabrics. One decision facing a collector with a stained outfit involves the garment still crisp with the original sizing. If cleaned the sizing will wash out and leave the garment limp and no longer pristine. The decision is, does the collector want to sacrifice the pristine crispness or do they want to remove the discoloration.

Many early outfits were sold with sweaters made of woolen yarn. Some of these outfits are called Sweater Girl, Open Road, Sorority Meeting, Mood For Music, and Tennis Anyone. Moths tend to invade these fibers and eat holes in them. Be cautious of where these garments are stored and attempt to insure they are not damaged by insects.

When storing dolls and their clothes always keep them away from direct sunlight and not close to a light bulb. Heat from bulbs does cause damage. Another major "no-no" is setting dolls on a television set. Here too, it is much too hot for dolls. This, too, could cause heat damage. It is always advisable to have shelves with a glass cover for dolls. This keeps the collection dust free but still visible to enjoy. After working to clean those old dolls it would be a shame to have them out gathering dust again.

There is one other area where damage to a doll can occur and few collectors think about this. Those doll collectors who smoke will find their dolls develop a film over the vinyl. This smoke layer is a yellow-brown color which settles on the dolls and stains the vinyl over time. Dolls are best kept in a smoke free area of the home and not near cigar or cigarette smoke, even fireplace smoke could be damaging.

A doll collection of Barbies is meant to be enjoyed. Even those who have spent long hours at playtime can again with some loving care and cleaning have a life as a collectible.

Chapter 25
Buyer Caution

A true sidepart bendable leg Barbie still wearing her aqua blue hair ribbon. Note the way the hair swirls into a part down the side.

With every new collectible there is someone who wants to turn it to their advantage. Deep within human nature is a dark side that is in this case easily explained — greed. Even with doll collecting there are those who find a way to take advantage of the unsuspecting buyers. This is where knowledge of the doll of your choice may be a salvation. Those fine details are as necessary as the more obvious points.

The first trip to a large city doll club show and sale can be overwhelming. One large room with 100 doll dealers, tables laden with old and new dolls and related items turns any collector into a child in a toy store. The urge to buy anything you see must be curbed. Take a shopping list. We all have wish lists and this prioritized list is a necessity to take along to any doll sale. Staying within the list will keep you within a budget. Visit all the tables at the show and then make a decision about which of the things you will buy. More than one dealer may have the same things and by seeing all, you will be able to purchase the item at the lowest price. Feel free to discuss the price with dealers. You could be surprised to find some prices are negotiable, it is never too late to bargain.

Always be cautious when looking at the dolls. Many dealers are very honest but unfortunately, some are not.

While at a show some years past I found a Tutti doll head on a Liddle Kiddle body. This doll was priced at $35.00. Although the dealer was trying to sell the doll this way, it is not of any value unless the proper doll body parts are together.

At another small doll show I found a doll dealer with a German Bild Lilli doll in a plain white box. The face and hair of the doll were in excellent condition. I asked the dealer if I could hold the doll. She was really light — a very bad sign! The doll had a true Bild Lilli head but had been expertly placed on a Hong Kong Lilli body. Someone had put a good head from the O.M. Hausser doll on a Hong Kong company body which made the doll worthless. The price this dealer wanted for the doll was $950.00. She assured me the doll would be worth $2,000.00 in another year. Any Hong Kong Lilli can be bought for $10.00 – 20.00. These Hong Kong versions were made by a "copycat company" during the time that Hausser was manufacturing the real Lilli doll.

I have a friend who found a dealer with a Tutti head on a bendable leg Skipper body. The price tag read "Skooter $50.00." The dealer did not seem thankful when this error was pointed out to her. Any buyer could have bought this doll thinking she was a rare Skooter when really this was just a mismatched set of body parts.

Mix and match pieces are not unusual conditions in which a doll can be found. A California dealer, Joe Blitman, tells of a Midge head found on a Skipper body. When he asked the dealer about the doll she explained, "Oh, it is just a very young Midge." Joe fought back the desire to laugh at the sight of a Midge doll head that was too large for the Skipper doll body.

This subject brings to mind the favorite childhood pastime of switching doll heads. Over the years many women have confessed to me they too switched body and heads with their friends' dolls. Many of these dolls are found in yard sales. The Barbie doll head is fitted over a knob neck which easily popped on and off. This is how many a neck split got its start.

I bought a group of old Barbies at a garage sale with all being bubblecuts except one. When I brought them home I found the unusual doll was none other than a Hair Happenin's Barbie from 1971. The doll, a Sears exclusive, was sold in limited supply in only a few places. The problem: she was wearing a straight leg bubblecut doll body. Some little girl had played the head switch game with her, too. The doll was manufactured with a Twist 'N Turn body also sold on the TNT Barbies that same year. Eighteen months later I was browsing through a doll list and found a TNT body with no head for sale. I bought the doll body and now have Hair Happenin's Barbie head and body back together again.

More recent years have brought new adventures in doll deception with the revelation of the scarcity of the sidepart bendable leg Barbie doll. Creating this doll, Mattel was trying a new hairstyle method and rooted the hair differently. A true sidepart has hair rooted with a part, not a bald line, down the side of her head. The basic pageboy style hair is different in the sidepart. Hair is left longer and styled either straight with a slight curl or flipped out all around the face and back of the head. Hair is long enough on most of these dolls to reach past the collar. Deception on this doll has reached the creative standpoint. Some have been sold with only recombed hair. This results in a bald alley down the side of the doll's head. Other rerooted dolls have appeared. Favorite dolls such as the Color Magic dolls have been found rerooted as a sidepart Barbie. Holes for the hair were placed in the doll head at Mattel's factories many years back so the deception is done using the old holes. Color Magic dolls are rooted differently making the hole placement wrong for the sidepart dolls. The sidepart doll was rooted with hair behind the ear. When a forgery is made using an old Color Magic head the doll hair is rooted in front of the ears. Color Magic hair was rooted with holes placed in front of the ears. Further examination of the interior of the head shows a truly stitched head will have a braided knot inside and without proper machinery this can not be accomplished.

Repainting ponytail Barbies from the early 60's is also popular. Most dolls come with blue eyeshadow on the eyes but some rare numbers were painted with brown liner. If a dealer does not allow you to examine the doll's face with a jeweler's loop or a magnifying glass you should be suspicious. Close examination will show whether a doll has been repainted. Telltale areas at the corners of the eyes are difficult to cover and the blue will show through. As Hiroe Okubo-Wolf told in an earlier chapter, Mattel did not use paint brushes to paint the faces of the factory made dolls. They were airbrushed and tiny metal masks were used to insure the proper colors were painted on the correct area of the faces. Paint brushes were only used within the Mattel office when face painters were creating new designs for the dolls.

A new problem is individuals who are advertising and selling tiny and rare accessories. Many outfits were sold with tiny accessories which may be extremely hard to find today. These items could include

long brown or black gloves, pompoms to Cheerleader, and even a pointer stick for Student Teacher. Other rare items are the hat and compact to Roman Holiday Separates. There are crafty persons who now make reproductions of these items. Earrings and necklaces from outfits of the 60's are being made for sale. Many dealers list these as reproductions and a price appropriate for that is charged. Unfortunately, there are persons who will try to sell these items as the older and rare outfit parts. Joe Blitman, as a dealer for many years, has seen both the authentic and the reproduction items. "Gloves made to look like the older long brown or black gloves fit like oven mitts," says Joe. "Take them off the doll and turn wrong side out and you see that these gloves were cut out with scissors." Mattel had all clothing items, including gloves, machine cut with a template. As Jackie Leighton told, "Mattel would cut large thicknesses of fabric with machines at one time." This left a *clean* cut, smooth all around with no jagged edges. "Gluing on the gloves are also incorrectly applied," says Blitman. "The counterfeit Student Teacher pointer stick has been found with a slightly thicker piece of wood and paint used is glossy not flat black paint," says Blitman. For Cheerleader, the pompoms took a lot of play abuse, therefore, to complete the outfit the copycat pompoms are wider strips of paper than the Mattel versions. Mattel-made earrings were made with pearls strung on small wire. Instead of the usual single loop at the end of the strand, the counterfeit version is wound round and round. A reproduction of the Roman Holiday Separates compact is made from a metal with silver color finish. The original compacts were made with a gold finish.

When buying an NRFB doll, check to see if the box is truly sealed at the bottom of the box. Some boxes have been found to have been opened and reglued leaving the end flap of the box with a rippled effect where the new glue was applied. If paying the NRFB price, it should be an NRFB box.

A top view of both the often seen bendable leg Barbie and sidepart bendable leg Barbie. Notice no bald alley down the scalp. There was rooting with intention to part the hair where rooted.

It is helpful for collectors to arm themselves with the knowledge of each individual accessory to their favorite outfits. With items changing hands at record rates even a dealer could easily resell an item before realizing he or she has a counterfeit accessory.

Yet another deception is a doll called Becky. The doll was never produced and only a prototype exists in a private collection. Recent years have found old Mattel-made doll bodies being reworked by craftsmen and new dolls created. To create a Becky all these craftsmen would need to do is use an old Francie body and Casey head, repaint, and root hair to create a Becky doll. These are being created but at some point the danger lurks that they could be resold to another collector as a true prototype of a Becky doll.

There are other matters that a collector must consider and guard against to insure the safety of their prize collections. The nightmare is theft.

As in the case of the doll heist of F. Glen Offield in San Diego, California, it was a mammoth operation that created great grief. The thief entered Offield's home, bypassing the security system, on October 10, 1992. Offield was away at a doll show and sale in Los Angeles, California. The thief removed some of his 5000 Barbie dolls. Among those dolls were a collection of prototype outfits and prototypes, models, and samples of dolls, some of which are pictured in Chapter 8. Planning on the part of the thief was well done as he came with two semi-trucks expecting a very large haul.

In an attempt to conceal the theft, the house was set ablaze but even with the damage, arson officials discovered the theft.

Police continued investigating the theft and fire of Offield's dolls which were valued at one million dollars. On Monday, October 26, 1992, a break in the case led police to a self-storage locker where the collection of Barbie dolls was found. Glen Offield's good fortune is a storybook ending. It is balanced by thefts which are becoming more brazen that succeed. Like a thief grabbing a number one Barbie from a dealer's table at a crowded California antique show and then making a dash to a waiting manned getaway car.

Security at shows and at home requires sound judgement decisions in alarm systems, insurance, and in the friends we choose. Personal insights from fellow collectors can help one to avoid the pitfalls of the jungle mentality of "eat or be eaten." They care not for your collection, they covet your money. It is better to ask a friend that may be more knowledgeable about a given doll or dealer than to suffer the consequences of a purchase made with an out of state dealer that can not be reached after the error is found.

In essence, remember that doll purchases can be an investment but it is best to buy what you like. You are the person who will be living with the doll. If you buy something that will increase over the short term you could be disappointed. Like the stock market, there are no guarantees whether the values will increase or decrease.

I follow my "gut feeling" about a purchase. If I feel right about this doll, I buy. If there is any feeling of doubt or dissatisfaction in my mind about this, I decline. It is better being safe than sorry.

Those who buy old and new dolls have a certain guideline which they can judge the quality of the dolls. Doll dealers mark dolls and accessories in their sales lists by these grades.

NRFB — Never removed from the original box.
MIB — A mint doll in her original box. This doll should never have been played with.
MOC — Mint on card as some outfits came on a card.
Mint — Unplayed with condition, the doll may have been used for display purposes and looks like she just came out of her box. Clothes that are mint look as though they never were on a doll.
EC — Excellent condition, a doll that is played with but flawless in every way.
VGC — Very good condition, this doll is in played-with condition and may have some minor flaws.
GC — Good condition, this doll has a lot of flaws but could make a good display item. Some of the possible flaws would be cut hair, green by ears, or even fingers or toes missing.
Fair — A fair item could be dirty, buttons missing, could be torn or stained.
C/M — Complete and mint is an outfit which has all the pieces there and appears to never have been on a doll.
NM — Near mint, these items have been greatly played with but in condition good enough to use for display.

Many attempts by other companies to copy the design of Barbie took place in the early 60's. A few of these dolls are pictured here. Dolls courtesy of the Mid Ohio Historical Museum.

Many reputable doll dealers are out there who are honest. As I find, some can find anything and usually do. They are pleasant and fair to deal with. They will state in writing a return policy and many even take layaways for larger purchases. Those of us who buy from these dealers come back time and again to buy from them, adding to our growing collections. This gives both dealer and collector a secure feeling and a profitable relationship is forged for both parties.

Epilogue

After 48 years in the toy industry Mattel has gone from ground zero to $929,775,000.00 in assets in 1992 as reported in the *1992 Directory of Corporate Affiliations.* They also have gone from Elliot and Ruth Handler as the two founders to employing 12,000 people. This company started as a small business but went on to be a major corporation with divisions and interests all over the world.

With their old facilities growing smaller and no room for creative design, Mattel chose to move the offices and design department from Hawthorne, California, to El Segundo, California, in January, 1991. Although only two miles away, this move made sound financial sense. Now in the new building, which is a renovated airplane hanger, the design department is under one roof. This makes an environment more conducive to creating a free flow of information and creative exchange of ideas in the department. In the Hawthorne facility, staffs were housed in separate areas.

Beyond aspiring to maintain Barbie as queen of the toy industry, what does Mattel do with all the profits from Barbie doll and other toys they manufacture? From assistance after the Watts Riots to UNICEF, Mattel has maintained its civic mindedness. According to *Dolls The Collectors Magazine,* November 1992, the Mattel Foundation is an organization that is supported by a percentage of profits from the sale of toys. The organization has allotted one million dollars to establish learning centers for Los Angeles children who live in riot areas. Another way the centers will be supported by Mattel is through its Employee Volunteer Program. During the next three years Mattel plans to fund four Mattel Learning Centers for preschool and daycare educational programs. Also available at the centers will be after school courses for elementary age children and tutoring for high school age students. Adult education will also be available along with workshops. All programs will be offered free. As a reflection back to Ruth Handler's work with the White House Conference On Children and Youth and the Vista Del Mar Child Care Service, Mattel established the Mattel Foundation in 1978 to serve the needs of children. Mattel has chosen to continue the Handler tradition of contributing positively to the children in the Los Angeles community. Mattel also generates business for others with their doll production.

The interest in Barbie has spawned several offshoots in the secondary market. The number of persons selling old and new Barbies has grown with increased space being allotted to classified ads in magazines like *Barbie's Bazaar, Doll Reader,* and *Dolls The Collectors Magazine.* The number of avid collectors span the globe with want ads placed from New Zealand, Australia, Japan, China, throughout Europe, and South America. Canada has its own well-organized clubs and yearly conventions that mirror the enthusiasm for Barbie in the U.S.

Supplying the needs of this ever growing worldwide demand, dealers like Marl Davidson, who has seen the growth of her mailing lists expand from a one or two page format in 1987 to a 20 page compendium that is printed with new items six times a year. To replenish the quickly sold product Marl finds herself traveling the country to doll shows and conventions filling the needs of her faithful clients. Her business, like many others, has expanded to the point that she files her inventory and sales on computer and accepts payment by credit card.

The front of the design department at Mattel headquarters in El Segundo, California. Photo courtesy of Joseph A. Toth, used with permission of Mattel, Inc.

Mail order lists are not the only way to buy the older gems. A new approach is the mail auction. For a small fee, you receive a catalog picturing all the items. Bids can be mailed or telephoned in and after a set amount of days the highest bidder is allowed to purchase the item.

Auctions are held throughout the country with all or part including old and more recent Barbie dolls. These auctions give bidders the opportunity to purchase dolls they wish to add to their ever growing collections. It also serves as a way for people to sell dolls.

Another avenue of doll making has been spawned by the taste for Barbie dolls. A cottage industry has come into existence making fashions and dolls using the Mattel made body forms of Barbie and friends, sending the imaginative designs to new reals of character creativity focusing on themes varying from mythology to contemporary celebrities.

Special outfits created by Pat Zuzinec can turn Barbie into Cleopatra, Queen of Egypt. Fashion artists such as Bruce A. Nygren design glamorous beaded and sequined garments for dolls. Complete makeovers for older dolls are designed by Michael Alexander under the business name MiKelman.

European doll collectors have difficulty finding Barbie dolls sold in the United States during those first years. These collectors have advertised in American doll magazines with a swap aggreement. They offer newer Barbie dolls to American collectors for the older dolls more available in the U.S. Dolls may be purchased from these European collectors but it takes longer. Mailing the doll to American shores takes longer, but also the check takes a journey through banking channels, not arriving in your statement until approximately eight weeks later. I purchased a doll from a German collector and when my cancelled check finally came in the statement, the rubber stamps on its back and front made it appear to have stopped at every bank branch on both continents.

In a nutshell, this doll collecting has become big business for some. Barbie doll collectors are constantly seeking new information about the doll that captured their heart. Every collector has some doll which can not be found. They are on an eternal quest for the

Entering Mattel's design department is like visiting Santa's workshop in Southern California. You are greeted by a pair of six-foot Barbie and Ken mannequins. Mannequins are by Goldsmith, Inc. under license by Mattel. Photo courtesy of Joseph A. Toth, used with permission of Mattel, Inc.

Bustling with activity, the design staff creates Barbies that are sold throughout the world in this facility. Photo courtesy of Joseph A. Toth, used with permission of Mattel, Inc.

missing piece. This continuous cycle is non stop as Mattel continues to create dolls. They are still searching for new approaches to the doll. Hiring Bob Mackie to design for Barbie was one way. Moving into the porcelain market was yet another way. As an up to the minute doll, Barbie, has been a rocker and is now a rapper. She goes to parties which require sophisticated clothes and she is an athlete which requires equipment. Proper clothing for any theme has been created by Mattel's talented designers who are now an entire department. It is no longer possible for one woman like Charlotte Johnson to maintain the clothing designs. Houses, cars, vans, and boats have all been designed by the Mattel design department. Mattel has divided their design department into Barbie doll workers and other designers. Barbie's work force is divided into hair design, engineering, face painting, fashions, and much more. Each department contributes a part toward the doll's production. Much artistic talent is behind the creation of this work of art called Barbie doll.

Keeping track of all the retired and former employees creates another group of people. An organization called the Mattel Alumni Association was founded in 1989 by Sherry Simonek and other former Mattel workers. The organization is made up entirely of retired and former employees of Mattel. A published directory lists five hundred members in 1992. Newsletters and social gatherings keep members in touch with each other. These Alumni still maintain a steadfast loyalty to Mattel even today. Drawing from such an inspirational fountainhead that links Barbie's past to the present, the collector can rest assured that any fleeting glimpse of Barbie's future will be based on the time honored traditions of Mattel.

A peek into the keyhole of the future shows a productive career ahead for America's favorite doll, Barbie.

Bibliography

Barbie's Bazaar various issues.

The Barbie – News Network Volume II No. 1 September/October, 1987.

Bryan, Sandra. *Barbie, The Eyelash Era Fashions, 1967 – 1972.*

DeWein, Sibyl and Jean Ashabraner. *The Collector's Encyclopedia of Barbie Dolls and Collectibles.* Paducah, KY: Schroeder Publishing, 1977.

Directory of Corporate Affiliations Volume I, 1992, 25th edition.

Eames, Sarah Sink. *Barbie Fashion Volume I 1959 – 1967.* Paducah, KY: Schroeder Publishing, 1990.

International Doll World Volume 15 No. 5 October, 1991.

Mandeville, A. Glenn. *Doll Fashion Anthology and Price Guide.*

Manos, Paris and Susan. *The Wonder of Barbie Dolls and Accessories, 1976 – 1986.* Paducah, KY: Schroeder Publishing.

Manos, Paris and Susan. *The World of Barbie Dolls.* Paducah, KY: Schroeder Publishing.

"Mattel Lends a Hand." *Dolls The Collectors Magazine* November, 1992.

Mattel Toy Catalogs: 1965, 1966, 1967, 1968, 1969, 1970, 1971, 1972, 1973, and 1992.

Mesdag, Lisa Miller. "From Barbie Dolls to Real Life." *Fortune Magazine* September, 1980.

Quinn, William G. "Ruth Handler, Intrepid Entrepeneur." *Fortune Magazine* March/April, 1985.

Timeless Treasures catalog: 1992.

Who's Who of American Women 1972 – 1973.

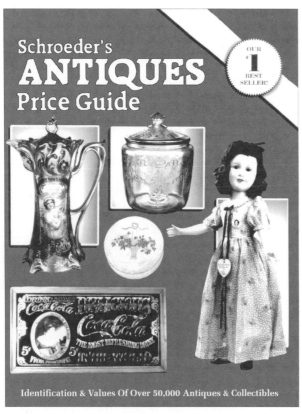